Pro Puppet

James Turnbull
Jeffrey McCune

Pro Puppet

ISBN-13 (pbk): 978-1-4302-3057-1

ISBN-13 (electronic): 978-1-4302-3058-8

President and Publisher: Paul Manning
Lead Editor: Frank Pohlmann
Technical Reviewer: Jessica Fraser
Editorial Board: Steve Anglin, Mark Beckner, Ewan Buckingham, Gary Cornell, Jonathan Gennick, Jonathan Hassell, Michelle Lowman, Matthew Moodie, Jeff Olson, Jeffrey Pepper, Frank Pohlmann, Douglas Pundick, Ben Renow-Clarke, Dominic Shakeshaft, Matt Wade, Tom Welsh
Coordinating Editor: Anita Castro
Copy Editor: Seth Kline
Compositor: Bytheway Publishing Services
Indexer: John Collin
Artist: April Milne
Cover Designer: Anna Ishchenko

Distributed to the book trade worldwide by Springer Science+Business Media, LLC., 233 Spring Street, 6th Floor, New York, NY 10013. Phone 1-800-SPRINGER, fax (201) 348-4505, e-mail orders-ny@springer-sbm.com, or visit www.springeronline.com.

For information on translations, please e-mail rights@apress.com, or visit www.apress.com.

Apress and friends of ED books may be purchased in bulk for academic, corporate, or promotional use. eBook versions and licenses are also available for most titles. For more information, reference our Special Bulk Sales–eBook Licensing web page at www.apress.com/bulk-sales.

The source code for this book is available to readers at www.apress.com. You will need to answer questions pertaining to this book in order to successfully download the code.

Dedicated to my partner and best friend, Ruth Brown, who continues to be wonderful.

James Turnbull

Dedicated to my parents, Pete and Gloria, who year after year accommodate my inability to shut the laptop while on vacation with them, and to Dave Alden for teaching me about configuration management, being a great mentor, and encouraging me to learn.

Jeff McCune

Contents at a Glance

Contents

About the Authors

James is the author of five technical books about open source software and a long-time member of the open source community. James authored the first (and this second!) book about Puppet and works for Puppet Labs running Client Services.

James speaks regularly at conferences including OSCON, Linux.conf.au, FOSDEM, OpenSourceBridge, DevOpsDays and a number of others. He is a past president of Linux Australia and has run Linux.conf.au and serves on the program committee of Linux.conf.au and OSCON.

James is Australian but currently lives in Portland, Oregon. His interests include cooking, wine, political theory, photojournalism, philosophy, and most recently the Portland Timbers association football team.

James Turnbull

Jeff is a long-time Puppet community member and open source software advocate. He started off with computers and Unix at a young age thanks to his parents' company, Summit Computer Services. Before graduating with his BS CSE degree, Jeff managed Mac OS X and Linux systems at the Mathematics Department at Ohio State University where he got started with configuration management and Puppet.

Jeff works for Puppet Labs, hacking on code and working with customers to improve their Puppet deployments. Jeff also speaks regularly at conferences including Apple's World Wide Developer Conference, Macworld, Open Source Bridge, Velocity, and others. He travels the world teaching and consulting on Puppet.

Jeff grew up in Ohio and currently lives in Portland, Oregon. His interests include hacking on microcontrollers, anime, photography, music, hiking, and long walks on the beach.

Jeff McCune

About the Technical Reviewer

 **Jes Fraser** is a solutions consultant from New Zealand specializing in Linux and Puppet in the Enterprise. She enjoys singing, playing the piano, and of course, writing.

Acknowledgments

Thanks are owed to the following people for input and insight into the project:

Dan Bode

Luke Kanies

Nigel Kersten

Dennis Matotek

Hal Newton

R.I. Pienaar

Trevor Vaughan

All of the team at Puppet Labs who continue to make Puppet cool

James Turnbull

Introduction

"ssh in a for loop is not a solution" – Luke Kanies, Puppet developer

The lives of system administrators and operations staff often revolve around a series of repetitive tasks: configuring hosts, creating users, and managing applications, daemons, and services. Often these tasks are repeated many times in the life cycle of one host, from building to decommissioning, and as new configuration is added or corrected for error or entropy.

The usual response to these repetitive tasks is to try to automate them with scripts and tools. This leads to the development of custom-built scripts and applications. In my first role as a systems administrator, I remember creating a collection of Control Language (CL) and Rexx scripts that I subsequently used to manage and operate a variety of infrastructure. The scripts were complex, poorly documented and completely customized to my environment.

My experience is not unique, and this sort of development is a common response to the desire to make life easier, automate boring, manual tasks and give you a few more minutes in the day for the more interesting projects and tasks (or to get to the pub earlier).

Very few of the scripts developed in this ad hoc manner are ever published, documented, or reused. Indeed, copyright for most custom material rests with the operator or system administrator's organization and is usually left behind when they move on. This leads to the same tool being developed over and over again. Sometimes they are even developed over and over again in the same company if previous incarnations don't suit a new incumbent (or occasionally, if they are indecipherable to a new incumbent!).

These custom scripts and applications rarely scale to suit large environments, and they often have issues of stability, flexibility, and functionality. In multi-platform environments, such scripts also tend to suit only one target platform, resulting in situations such as the need to create a user creation script for BSD, another one for Linux, and still another for Solaris. This increases the time and effort required to develop and maintain the very tools you are hoping to use to reduce administrative efforts.

Other approaches include the purchase of operations and configuration management tools like HP's Opsware, BMC's CONTROL-M, IBM's Tivoli suite, and CA's Unicenter products. But commercial tools generally suffer from two key issues: price and flexibility. Price, especially, can quickly become an issue: The more platforms and hosts that you are managing, the greater the price. In large environments, licensing for such tools can run to millions of dollars.

Flexibility is also a key concern. Commercial tools are usually closed source and are limited to the features available to them, meaning that if you want to extend them to do something custom or specific to your environment, you need to request a new feature, potentially with a waiting period and associated cost. Given the huge varieties of deployments, platforms, configurations and applications in organizations, it is rare to discover any tool that provides the ability to completely customize to suit your environment.

There is an alternative to both in-house development and commercial products: Free and Open Source Software (FOSS). Free and open source configuration management tools offer two key benefits for organizations:

- They are open and extensible.
- They are free!

With FOSS products, the tool's source code is at your fingertips, allowing you to develop your own enhancements or adjustments. You don't need to wait for the vendor to implement the required functionality or pay for new features or changes. You are also part of a community of users and developers who share a vision for the development of the tool. You and your organization can in turn contribute to that vision. In combination, you can shape the direction of the tools you are using, giving you a more flexible outcome for your organization.

The price tag is another important consideration for acquisition of any tool. With free and open source software, it isn't an issue. You don't pay anything for the software, and you get the source code with it.

Of course, we all know there is no such thing as a free lunch, so what's the catch? Well unlike commercial software, open source software doesn't come with any guaranteed support. This is not to say there is no support available: Many open source tools have large and active communities where members answer questions and provide assistance via mechanisms like email lists, forums, Wikis and IRC.

▓ **Note** Many open source tools, including Puppet, also have organizations that provide commercial editions or support for these tools. For full disclosure, both the author James Turnbull and co-author Jeff McCune work at Puppet Labs, the organization that supports the development of Puppet.

Puppet (http://www.puppetlabs.com/puppet) is a reaction to these gaps in the tools available to SysAdmins, Operators and Developers. It is designed to make their lives easier by making infrastructure easy, simple and cheap to manage. This book will introduce you to Puppet, an open source configuration management tool, and take you through installation, configuration and integration of Puppet into your environment.

CHAPTER 1

■ ■ ■

Getting Started with Puppet

Puppet is an open source framework and toolset for managing the configuration of computer systems. In this book, we're going to look at how you can use Puppet to manage your configuration. As the book progresses, we'll introduce Puppet's features and then show you how to integrate Puppet into your provisioning and management lifecycle. To do this, we'll take you through configuring a real-world scenario that we'll introduce in Chapter 2.

In this chapter, we start with a quick overview of Puppet, what it is, how it works, and which release to use, and then we show you how to install Puppet and its inventory tool, Facter. We show you how to install it on Red Hat, Debian, Ubuntu, Solaris, Microsoft Windows, and via a Ruby gem. We'll then configure it and show you how create your first configuration items. We'll also introduce you to the concept of "modules," Puppet's way of collecting and managing bundles of configuration data. We'll then show you how to apply one of these modules to a host using the Puppet agent.

What Is Puppet?

Puppet is Ruby-based, licensed as GPLv2 and can run in either client-server or stand-alone modes. Puppet is principally developed by Luke Kanies and his company, Puppet Labs (formerly Reductive Labs). Kanies has been involved with Unix and systems administration since 1997 and developed Puppet from that experience. Unsatisfied with existing configuration management tools, Kanies began working with tool development in 2001 and in 2005 he founded Puppet Labs, an open source development house focused on automation tools. Shortly after this, Puppet Labs released their flagship product, Puppet.

Puppet can be used to manage configuration on UNIX (including OSX) and Linux platforms, and recently Microsoft Windows platforms as well. Puppet is often used to manage a host throughout its lifecycle: from initial build and installation, to upgrades, maintenance, and finally to end-of-life, when you move services elsewhere. Puppet is designed to continuously interact with your hosts, unlike provisioning tools which build your hosts and leave them unmanaged.

Puppet has a simple operating model that is easy to understand and implement. The model is made up of three components:

- Deployment

- Configuration Language and Resource Abstraction Layer

- Transactional Layer

1

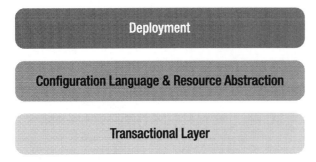

Figure 1-1. The Puppet model

Deployment

Puppet is usually deployed in a simple client-server model (Figure 1-2). The server is called a "Puppet master", the Puppet client software is called an agent and the host itself is defined as a node.

The Puppet master runs as a daemon on a host and contains the configuration required for your environment. The Puppet agents connect to the Puppet master via an encrypted and authenticated connection using standard SSL, and retrieve or "pull" any configuration to be applied.

Importantly, if the Puppet agent has no configuration available or already has the required configuration then Puppet will do nothing. This means that Puppet will only make changes to your environment if they are required. The whole process is called a configuration run.

Each agent can run Puppet as a daemon via a mechanism such as cron, or the connection can be manually triggered. The usual practice is to run Puppet as a daemon and have it periodically check with the master to confirm that its configuration is up-to-date or to retrieve any new configuration. However, many people find being able to trigger Puppet via a mechanism such as cron, or manually, better suits their needs. By default, the Puppet agent will check the master for new or changed configuration once every 30 minutes. You can configure this period to suit your environment.

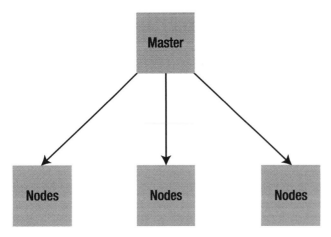

Figure 1-2. Puppet client-server model

Other deployment models also exist. For example, Puppet can also run in a stand-alone mode where no Puppet master is required. Configuration is installed locally on the host and the puppet binary is run to execute and apply that configuration. We discuss this mode later in the book.

Configuration Language and Resource Abstraction Layer

Puppet uses a declarative language to define your configuration items, which Puppet calls "resources." This declarative nature creates an important distinction between Puppet and many other configuration tools. A declarative language makes statements about the state of your configuration - for example, it declares that a package should be installed or a service should be started.

Most configuration tools, such as a shell or Perl script, are imperative or procedural. They describe HOW things should be done rather than the desired end state - for example, most custom scripts used to manage configuration would be considered imperative.

This means Puppet users just declare what the state of their hosts should be: what packages should be installed, what services should be running, etc. With Puppet, the system administrator doesn't care HOW this state is achieved – that's Puppet's problem. Instead, we abstract our host's configuration into resources.

Configuration Language

What does this declarative language mean in real terms? Let's look at a simple example. We have an environment with Red Hat Enterprise Linux, Ubuntu, and Solaris hosts and we want to install the vim application on all our hosts. To do this manually, we'd need to write a script that does the following:

- Connects to the required hosts (including handling passwords or keys)

- Checks to see if vim is installed

- If not, uses the appropriate command for each platform to install vim, for example on Red Hat the yum command and on Ubuntu the apt-get command

- Potentially reports the results of this action to ensure completion and success

---

▓ **Note** This would become even more complicated if you wanted to upgrade vim (if it was already installed) or apply a particular version of vim.

Puppet approaches this process quite differently. In Puppet, we define a configuration resource for the vim package. Each resource is made up of a *type* (what sort of resource is being managed: packages, services, or cron jobs), a *title* (the name of the resource), and a series of *attributes* (values that specify the state of the resource - for example, whether a service is started or stopped).

You can see an example of a resource in Listing 1-1.

Listing 1-1. A Puppet Resource

```
package { "vim":
    ensure => present,
}
```

The resource in Listing 1-1 specifies that a package called **vim** should be installed. It is constructed like:

```
type { title:
    attribute => value,
}
```

In Listing 1-1, the resource type is the **package** type. Puppet comes with a number of resource types by default, including types to manage files, services, packages, and cron jobs, among others.

■ **Note** You can see a full list of the types Puppet can currently manage (and their attributes) at `http://docs.puppetlabs.com/references/stable/type.html`. You can also extend Puppet to support additional resource types, as we'll discuss in Chapter 10.

Next is the title of the resource, here the name of the package we want to install, **vim**. The type and title of the resource can be combined together to allow Puppet to create a reference to the resource. For example, our resource would be called **Package["vim"]**. We'll see this a lot more in later chapters when we build relationships between resources, allowing us to create structure in our configuration, for example installing a package before starting its associated service.

Lastly, we've specified a single attribute, **ensure**, with a value of **present**. Attributes tell Puppet about the required state of our configuration resource. Each type has a series of attributes available to configure it. Here the **ensure** attribute specifies the state of the package: installed, uninstalled, etc. The **present** value tells Puppet we want to install the package. To uninstall the package we would change the value of this attribute to **absent**.

Resource Abstraction Layer

With our resource created, Puppet takes care of the details of how to manage that resource when our agents connect. Puppet handles the "how" by knowing how different platforms and operating systems manage certain types of resources. Each type has a number of "providers." A provider contains the "how" of managing packages using a particular package management tool. For the package type, for example, for there are more than 20 providers covering a variety of tools including **yum**, **aptitude**, **pkgadd**, **ports**, and **emerge**.

When an agent connects, Puppet uses a tool called "Facter" to return information about that agent, including what operating system it is running. Puppet then chooses the appropriate package provider for that operating system and uses that provider to check if the **vim** package is installed. For example, on Red Hat it would execute **yum**, on Ubuntu it would execute **aptitude**, and on Solaris it would use the **pkg** command. If the package is not installed, then Puppet will install it. If the package is already installed, Puppet does nothing.

Puppet will then report its success or failure in applying the resource back to the Puppet master.

INTRODUCING FACTER AND FACTS

Facter is a system inventory tool that we use throughout the book. It returns "facts" about each agent, such as its hostname, IP address, operating system and version, and other configuration items. These facts are gathered when the agent runs. The facts are then sent to the Puppet master, and automatically created as variables available to Puppet.

You can see the facts available on your clients by running the `facter` binary from the command line. Each fact is returned as a key => value pair. For example:

```
operatingsystem => Ubuntu
ipaddress => 10.0.0.10
```

We can then use these values to individually configure each host. For example, knowing the IP address of a host allows us to configure networking on that host.

These facts are made available as variables that can be used in your Puppet configuration. When combined with the configuration you define in Puppet, they allow you to customize that configuration for each host. For example, they allow you to write generic resources, like your network settings, and customize them with data from your agents.

Facter also helps Puppet understand how to manage particular resources on an agent. For example, if Facter tells Puppet that a host runs Ubuntu, then Puppet knows to use aptitude to install packages on that agent. Facter can also be extended to add custom facts for specific information about your hosts. We'll be installing Facter shortly after we install Puppet, and we'll discuss it in more detail in later chapters.

Transactional Layer

Puppet's transactional layer is its engine. A Puppet transaction encompasses the process of configuring each host including:

- Interpret and compile your configuration
- Communicate the compiled configuration to the agent
- Apply the configuration on the agent
- Report the results of that application to the master

The first step Puppet takes is to analyze your configuration and calculate how to apply it to your agent. To do this, Puppet creates a graph showing all resources, their relationships to each other and to each agent. This allows Puppet to work out in what order, based on relationships you create, to apply each resource to your host. This model is one of Puppet's most powerful features.

Puppet then takes the resources and compiles them into a "catalog" for each agent. The catalog is sent to the host and applied by the Puppet agent. The results of this application are then sent back to the master in the form of a report.

The transaction layer allows configurations to be created and applied repeatedly on the host. Puppet calls this *idempotent*, meaning multiple applications of the same operation will yield the same results. Puppet configuration can be safely run multiple times with the same outcome on your host and hence ensuring your configuration stays consistent.

Puppet is not fully transactional though; your transactions aren't logged (other than informative logging) and hence you can't roll back transactions as you can with some databases. You can, however, model transactions in a "noop," or no operation mode, that allows you to test the execution of your changes without making any actual changes.

Selecting the Right Version of Puppet

The best version of Puppet to use is usually the latest release, which at the time of writing is the 2.6.x branch of releases; newer ones are currently in development. The biggest advantage of the 2.6.x branch of releases onward is their replacement of XML-RPC as a transport layer. The 2.6.x releases instead use REST APIs, resulting in greatly improved performance. The 2.6.x releases are also stable, perform well, and contain a wide of variety of new features and functions unavailable in earlier releases.

WHY DID PUPPET CHANGE VERSION NUMBERING?

If you are familiar with Puppet's development, you are aware that Puppet jumped release numbers from 0.25.5 straight to 2.6.0. So why did this happen – is the 2.6.0 release 11 times more powerful and stable than the 0.25.5 release? Well, yes and no. The 2.6.0 release included substantial feature additions and removed the last of the XML-RPC transport layer. Importantly though, the jump in release numbering was also an acknowledgment that the previous release numbering was not an accurate reflection of the growth and change in Puppet. In stability and functionality terms, the 0.24.x and 0.25.x releases should have had the decimal place moved to the right. Additionally, since the 0.25.0 release, Puppet has not really been the "pre-V1.0" product that its version numbering would suggest.

Older releases of Puppet, especially releases before the 0.24.x branch of releases, tend to be very poorly featured and contain a number of bugs and issues. They are largely unsupportable and requests for help for with 0.20.x, 0.22.x, and 0.23.x or earlier releases will be largely met with suggestions that you upgrade. We do not recommend you use any of these releases.

■ **Note** This book assumes you are using either a 2.6.x or later release, although most of the material (except where specifically indicated) is supported back to release 0.24.7. It is important to remember that if you use the 0.24.7 or 0.24.8 releases, you will not get the benefit of the performance improvements in the 0.25.x and later releases.

There are a variety of releases, some older than others, packaged for operating systems. The 0.24.x releases are broadly packaged. The 2.6.x and 0.25.x releases are packaged and distributed in newer versions of operating systems and platforms. If you can't find later Puppet releases packaged for your distribution you have the option of rolling your own packages, backporting, or installing from source (though we don't recommend the latter – see below).

Can I mix releases of Puppet?

The most common deployment model for Puppet is client-server. Many people ask if you can have differing releases of Puppet on the master and as agents. The answer is yes, with some caveats. The first caveat is that the master needs to be a later release than the agents. For example, you can have a version 0.24.8 agent connected to a version 2.6.0 master but not a version 2.6.0 agent connected to a 0.24.8 master.

The second caveat is that the older the agent release, the less likely it will function correctly with a newer release of the master. It is highly unlikely that a version 0.20.0 agent will correctly work with a version 2.6.0 master. Generally, the 0.24.x branch of agents will happily connect to and function with 2.6.x and 0.25.x-based masters. Later versions of masters may not be so forgiving of earlier agents and some functions and features may not behave correctly.

Lastly, mixing 2.6.x and later release masters with 0.24.x and earlier agents will mean you won't get the full performance enhancements available in 2.6.x. The 0.24.x agents will still communicate with the slower XML-RPC transport layer rather than taking advantage of the newer REST interface.

Installing Puppet

Puppet can be installed and used on a variety of different platforms, including the following:

- Red Hat Enterprise Linux, CentOS, Fedora & Oracle Enterprise Linux
- Debian and Ubuntu
- Mandrake and Mandriva
- Gentoo
- Solaris and OpenSolaris
- MacOS X and MacOS X Server
- *BSD
- AIX
- HP UX
- Microsoft Windows hosts (in versions after 2.6.0 and with only limited support for file resources)

On these platforms, Puppet manages a variety of configuration items, including (but not limited to):

- Files
- Services
- Packages
- Users
- Groups
- Cron jobs

- SSH keys

- Nagios configuration

For Puppet, the agent and master server installations are very similar, although most operating systems and distribution packaging systems divide the master and agent functions into separate packages. On some operating systems and distributions, you'll also need to install Ruby and its libraries and potentially some additional packages. Most good packaging systems will have most of the required packages, like Ruby, as prerequisites of the Puppet and Facter packages. For other features (i.e., some types of reporting that I'll demonstrate later in this book), you may also need to install additional packages. When we look at these functions, I'll let you know what additional packages you'll need to install.

We'll also demonstrate how to install Puppet from source, but we don't recommend this approach. It is usually operationally easier and simpler to use your operating system's package management system, especially if you are installing Puppet on a large number of hosts.

Installing on Red Hat Enterprise Linux and Fedora

On Red Hat Enterprise Linux and Red Hat based-derivatives, you need to install some prerequisites (such as the Ruby programming language, the Ruby libraries and the Ruby Shadow library) to allow Puppet to manage users and groups. You can do this with Red Hat's package management tool, Yum.

```
# yum install ruby ruby-libs ruby-shadow
```

Next, to get the latest releases of Puppet, you will need to add the EPEL repository (see sidebar) to your host and then install packages from that repository. You can add the EPEL repository by adding the epel-release RPM (.rpm package manager).

```
# rpm -Uvh http://download.fedora.redhat.com/pub/epel/5/i386/↵
epel-release-5-3.noarch.rpm
```

▪ **Note** The EPEL repository is a volunteer-based community effort from the Fedora project to create a repository of high-quality add-on packages for Red Hat Enterprise (RHEL) and its compatible spinoffs such as CentOS, Oracle Enterprise Linux or Scientific Linux. You can find more details on EPEL including how to add it to your host at http://fedoraproject.org/wiki/EPEL and http://fedoraproject.org/wiki/EPEL/FAQ#howtouse.

On the master, you need to install the puppet, puppet-server, and facter packages from the EPEL repository.

```
# yum install puppet puppet-server facter
```

The puppet package contains the agent, the puppet-server package contains the master, and the facter package contains the system inventory tool Facter. As mentioned earlier, Facter gathers information, or "facts," about your hosts that are used to help customize your Puppet configuration.

On the agent, you only need to install the prerequisites and the puppet and facter packages.

```
# yum install puppet facter
```

INSTALLING VIA RUBY GEMS

Like most Ruby-based applications, you can also install Puppet and Facter via Ruby Gems. To do this you'll need to install Ruby and the appropriate RubyGems package for your operating system. On Red Hat, CentOS, Fedora, SUSE/SLES, Debian and Ubuntu, this package is called `rubygems`. Once this package is installed the `gem` command should be available to use. You can then use this command to install Puppet and Facter like so:

```
# gem install puppet facter
```

Installing on Debian and Ubuntu

On Debian and Ubuntu we also need to install the Ruby packages as a prerequisite:

```
# apt-get install ruby libshadow-ruby1.8
```

Then you can install the required packages for Puppet: `puppet`, `puppetmaster`, and `facter`. The `puppet` package contains the Puppet agent, the `puppetmaster` package contains the master, and the `facter` package contains the Facter system inventory tool.

On the master, you need to install this:

```
# apt-get install puppet puppetmaster facter
```

On the agent, you only need to install the following packages:

```
# apt-get install puppet facter
```

■ **Note** Installing the `puppet`, `puppetmaster`, and `facter` packages will also install some prerequisite packages, such as Ruby itself, if they are not already installed.

Installing on OpenSolaris

Installing Puppet on OpenSolaris requires installing Ruby first. Then install Puppet and Facter via a RubyGem. Start by using the **pkg** command to install Ruby.

```
# pkg install -q SUNWruby18
```

Once Ruby is installed (it can take a little while to download and install), there are two ways to install Puppet. The first is to use the RubyGems packaging system. RubyGems is installed by default when the SUNWruby18 package is installed. You can use the **gem** command to install the required Gems.

```
# gem install puppet facter
```

Alternatively, if you use Blastwave packages, Puppet and Facter are also available from the Blastwave repositories at `http://www.blastwave.org` and can be added using the **pkgutil** command.

Further instructions are available on the Puppet wiki at
`http://projects.puppetlabs.com/projects/puppet/wiki/Puppet_Solaris`.

Installing from Source

You can also install Puppet and Facter from source tarballs. We don't recommend this approach
because it makes upgrading, uninstalling and generally managing Puppet across a lot of hosts difficult.
To do this you'll need to ensure some prerequisites are installed, for example Ruby and its libraries,
using the appropriate packages for your host or via source again. First, download the Facter tarball from
the Puppet Labs site.

```
$ cd /tmp
$ wget http://puppetlabs.com/downloads/facter/facter-1.5.7.tar.gz
```

Unpack the tarball and run the `install.rb` script to install Facter.

```
$ tar -zxf facter-1.5.7.tar.gz
$ cd facter-1.5.7
# ./install.rb
```

This will install Facter into the default path for Ruby libraries on your host, for example
`/usr/lib/ruby/` on many Linux distributions.

Next, we need to download and install Puppet using the same process:

```
$ cd /tmp
$ wget http://puppetlabs.com/downloads/puppet/puppet-2.6.1.tar.gz
$ tar -zxf puppet-2.6.1.tar.gz
$ cd puppet-2.6.1
# ./install.rb
```

Like the Facter steps, this will install Puppet into the default path for Ruby libraries on your host.

▓ **Note** You can find the latest Puppet and Facter releases at
`http://projects.puppetlabs.com/projects/puppet/wiki/Downloading_Puppet`.

Installing on Microsoft Windows

Since version 2.6.0, Puppet has supported running on Microsoft Windows. For the 2.6.0 release Puppet
only manages a limited subset of configuration, primarily managing files, but other configuration types
should be available in later releases.

Installing Puppet on Microsoft Windows can be achieved a couple of different ways, but the first
step of both methods is to install Ruby. The easiest way to do this is with the Ruby One-Click Installer
available at `http://rubyinstaller.rubyforge.org/wiki/wiki.pl?RubyInstaller`. You can also download
binaries at `http://www.ruby-lang.org/en/downloads/` if you wish.

We're going to use the One-Click installer. Download the latest version, which at the time of writing
is at `http://rubyforge.org/frs/download.php/47082/ruby186-27_rc2.exe`. Run the downloaded
executable and install Ruby. During the installation, select the **Use RubyGems** tick box.

Once Ruby is installed, start the RubyGems Package Manager from the start menu:

```
Programs -> Ruby-186-27 -> RubyGems -> RubyGems Package Manager
```

From the command window that opens, you can then install the Facter and Puppet gems.

```
C:\gem install puppet facter
```

Installing on other Platforms

We've just explained how to install Puppet on some popular platforms. Puppet can also be installed on a wide variety of other platforms. Puppet is also available in varying versions on:

- MacOS X via MacPorts and from
  https://sites.google.com/a/explanatorygap.net/puppet/

- Solaris via Blastwave

- SLES/OpenSuSE via http://software.opensuse.org/

- Gentoo via Portage

- Mandrake and Mandriva via the Mandriva contrib repository

- FreeBSD via ports tree

- NetBSD via pkgsrc

- OpenBSD via ports tree

- ArchLinux via ArchLinux AUR

▓ **Note** You can find a full list of additional operating systems and specific instructions at
http://projects.puppetlabs.com/projects/puppet/wiki/Downloading_Puppet.

Puppet's tarball also contains some packaging artifacts in the conf directory, for example an RPM spec file and OS X build scripts, that can allow you to create your own packages for compatible operating systems. Now you've installed Puppet on your chosen platform, we can start configuring it.

Configuring Puppet

Let's start by configuring a Puppet master that will act as our configuration server. We'll look at Puppet's configuration files, how to configure networking and firewall access and how to start the Puppet master. Remember that we're going to be looking at Puppet in its client-server mode. Here, the Puppet master contains our configuration data, and Puppet agents connect via SSL and pull down the required configuration.

On most platforms, Puppet's configuration will be located under the /etc/puppet directory. Puppet's principal configuration file is called puppet.conf and is stored at /etc/puppet/puppet.conf. It is likely that this file has already been created when you installed Puppet, but if it hasn't, then you can create a simple file using the following command:

```
# puppetmasterd --genconfig > puppet.conf
```

▓ **Note** We're assuming your operating system uses the /etc/ directory to store its configuration files, as most Unix/Linux operating systems and distributions do. If you're on a platform that doesn't, for example Microsoft Windows, substitute the location of your puppet.conf configuration file.

The puppet.conf configuration file is constructed much like an INI-style configuration file and divided into sections. Each section configures a particular element of Puppet. For example, the [agent] section configures the Puppet agent, and the [master] section configures the Puppet master binary. There is also a global configuration section called [main]. All components of Puppet will set options specified in the [main] section.

▓ **Note** On releases before 2.6.0, each section was named for the Puppet binary command rather than the function, for example the [master] section was called [puppetmasterd] and the [agent] section was [puppetd]. If you have this older style configuration, then Puppet 2.6.0 and later versions will prompt you to update your configuration file when you start Puppet.

At this stage, we're only going to add one entry, certname, to the puppet.conf file. The certname option specifies the name of the Puppet master. We'll add the certname value to the [master] section (if the section doesn't already exist in your file, then create it).

```
[master]
certname=puppet.example.com
```

Replace puppet.example.com with the fully qualified domain name of your host.

▓ **Note** We'll look at other options in the puppet.conf file in later chapters.

Adding the certname option and specifying our fully qualified domain name does two things: it makes troubleshooting certificate issues easier, and it addresses a bug with the Ruby SSL code present on many Linux-based hosts. This bug requires that we manually specify the name used by your Puppet master's SSL certificates. You can read more about the precise bug at http://projects.puppetlabs.com/projects/puppet/wiki/Ruby_Ssl_2007_006.

We recommend you also create a DNS CNAME for your Puppet host, for example puppet.example.com, and add it to your /etc/hosts file and your DNS configuration:

```
# /etc/hosts
127.0.0.1 localhost
192.168.0.1 puppet.example.com puppet
```

Once we've configured appropriate DNS for Puppet we need to add the site.pp file which holds the basics of the configuration items we want to manage.

The site.pp file

The site.pp file tells Puppet where and what configuration to load for our clients. We're going to store this file in a directory called manifests under the /etc/puppet directory.

▨ **Note** "Manifest" is Puppet's term for files containing configuration information. Manifest files have a suffix of .pp.

This directory and file is often already created when the Puppet packages are installed. If it hasn't already been created, then create this directory and file now:

```
# mkdir /etc/puppet/manifests
# touch /etc/puppet/manifests/site.pp
```

▨ **Tip** Puppet will not start without the site.pp file being present.

We'll add some configuration to this file later in this chapter, but now we just need the file present.

▨ **Note** You can also override the name and location of the manifests directory and site.pp file using the manifestdir and manifest configuration options, respectively. These options are set in the puppet.conf configuration file in the [master] section. See http://docs.puppetlabs.com/references/stable/configuration.html for a full list of configuration options. We'll talk about a variety of other options throughout this book.

Firewall Configuration

The Puppet master runs on TCP port 8140. This port needs to be open on your master's firewall (and any intervening firewalls and network devices), and your client must be able to route and connect to the master. To do this, you need to have an appropriate firewall rule on your master, such as the following rule for the Netfilter firewall:

```
-A INPUT -p tcp -m state --state NEW --dport 8140 -j ACCEPT
```

The preceding line allows access from everywhere to TCP port 8140. If possible, you should lock this down to only networks that require access to your Puppet master. For example:

```
-A INPUT -p tcp -m state --state NEW -s 192.168.0.0/24 --dport 8140 -j ACCEPT
```

Here we've restricted access to port 8140 to the 192.168.0.0/24 subnet.

■ **Note** You can create similar rules for other operating systems' firewalls such as pf or the Windows Firewall.

Starting the Puppet Master

The Puppet master can be started via an `init` script on most Linux distributions. On Red Hat, we would run the init script with the `service` command, like so:

```
# service puppetmaster start
```

On Debian or Ubuntu, we run it using the `invoke-rc.d` command:

```
# invoke-rc.d puppetmaster start
```

Other platforms should use their appropriate service management tools.

■ **Note** Output from the daemon can be seen in `/var/log/messages` on Red Hat-based hosts and `/var/log/daemon.log` on Debian and Ubuntu hosts. Puppet will log via the daemon facility to Syslog by default on most operating systems. You will find output from the daemons in the appropriate location and files for your operating system.

Starting the daemon will initiate your Puppet environment, create a local Certificate Authority, certificates and keys for the master, and open the appropriate network socket to await client connections. You can see Puppet's SSL information and certificates in the `/etc/puppet/ssl` directory.

```
# ls -l /etc/puppet/ssl
drwxrwx--- 5 puppet puppet 4096 2009-11-16 22:36 ca
```

```
drwxr-xr-x 2 puppet root   4096 2009-11-16 22:36 certificate_requests
drwxr-xr-x 2 puppet root   4096 2009-11-16 22:36 certs
-rw-r--r-- 1 puppet root    361 2009-11-16 22:36 crl.pem
drwxr-x--- 2 puppet root   4096 2009-11-16 22:36 private
drwxr-x--- 2 puppet root   4096 2009-11-16 22:36 private_keys
drwxr-xr-x 2 puppet root   4096 2009-11-16 22:36 public_keys
```

The directory on the master contains your Certificate Authority, certificate requests from your clients, a certificate for your master and certificates for all your clients.

■ **Note** You can override the location of the SSL files using the ssldir option.

You can also run the Puppet master from the command line to help test and debug issues. I recommend doing this when testing Puppet initially. To do this we start the Puppet master daemon like so:

```
# puppet master --verbose --no-daemonize
```

The --**verbose** option outputs verbose logging and the --**no-daemonize** option keeps the daemon in the foreground and redirects output to standard out. You can also add the --**debug** option to produce more verbose debug output from the daemon.

A SINGLE BINARY

From version 2.6.0 and later, all the functionality of Puppet is available from a single binary, puppet, in the style of tools like git, rather than the individual binaries previously used (the individual binaries are still available for backwards-compatibility at this time). This means you can now start the Puppet master by either running:

```
# puppet master
```

Or,

```
# puppetmasterd
```

The agent functionality is also available in the same way:

```
# puppet agent
```

Or,

```
# puppetd
```

You can see a full list of the available functionality from the puppet binary by running:

```
$ puppet --help
```

We reference both the individual binaries and the single binary commands in this book.

Connecting Our First Agent

Once you have the Puppet master configured and started, we can configure and initiate your first agent. On the agent, as we mentioned earlier, you need to install the appropriate packages, usually **puppet** and **facter**, using your operating system's package management system. We're going to install a client on a host called **node1.example.com** and then connect to our **puppet.example.com** master.

When connecting our first client, we want to run the Puppet agent from the command line rather than as a service. This will allow us to see what is going on as we connect. The Puppet agent daemon is run using **puppet agent** (or in versions previous to 2.6.0, using the **puppetd** binary) and you can see a connection to the master initiated in Listing 1-2.

▦ **Tip** You can also run a Puppet client on the Puppet master, but we're going to start with the more traditional client server. And yes, that means you can use Puppet to manage itself!

Listing 1-2. Puppet Client Connection to the Puppet Master

```
node1# puppet agent --server=puppet.example.com --no-daemonize --verbose
info: Creating a new certificate request for node1.example.com
info: Creating a new SSL key at /var/lib/puppet/ssl/private_keys/node1.example.com↵
.pem
warning: peer certificate won't be verified in this SSL session
notice: Did not receive certificate
```

In Listing 1-2, we executed the Puppet agent with three options. The first option, **--server**, specifies the name or address of the Puppet master to connect to.

▦ **Tip** If we don't specify a server, Puppet will look for a host called "puppet." It's often a good idea to create a CNAME for your Puppet master, for example **puppet.example.com**.

We can also specify this in the **main** section of the **/etc/puppet/puppet.conf** configuration file on the client.

```
[main]
server=puppet.example.com
```

Your client must be able to resolve the hostname of the master to connect to (this is why it is useful to have a Puppet CNAME and to specify your Puppet master in the **/etc/hosts** file on your client). The **--no-daemonize** option runs the Puppet client in the foreground and outputs to standard out. By default, the Puppet client runs as a daemon.

▓ **Tip** The `--verbose` option enables verbose output from the client. Adding the `--debug` option can provide further output that is useful for troubleshooting.

In Listing 1-1, you can see the output from our connection. The agent has created a certificate signing request and a private key to secure our connection. Puppet uses SSL certificates to authenticate connections between the master and the agent. The agent sends the certificate request to the master and waits for the master to sign and return the certificate.

At this point, the agent is still running and awaiting the signed certificate. It will continue to check for a signed certificate every two minutes until it receives one or is canceled (using Ctrl-C, for example).

▓ **Note** You can change the time the Puppet agent will wait by using the `--waitforcert` option. You can specify a time in seconds or o to not wait for a certificate, in which case the agent will exit.

Completing the Connection

To complete the connection and authenticate our agent we now need to sign the certificate the agent has sent to the master. We do this using **puppet cert** (or the **puppetca** binary) on the master.

```
puppet# puppet cert --list
node1.example.com
```

▓ **Tip** You can find a full list of the binaries that come with Puppet at
`http://puppetlabs.com/trac/puppet/wiki/PuppetExecutables`.

The `--list` option displays all the certificates waiting to be signed. We can then sign our certificate using the `--sign` option.

```
puppet# puppet cert --sign node1.example.com
Signed node1.example.com
```

You can sign all waiting certificates with the **puppet cert --sign --all** command.

▓ **Note** Rather than signing each individual certificate, you can also enable "autosign" mode. In this mode, all incoming connections from specified IP addresses or address ranges are automatically signed. This obviously has some security implications and should only be used if you are comfortable with it. You can find more details at `http://puppetlabs.com/trac/puppet/wiki/FrequentlyAskedQuestions#why-shouldn-t-i-use-autosign-for-all-my-clients`.

On the client, two minutes after we've signed our certificate, we should see the following entries (or you can stop and restart the Puppet agent rather than waiting two minutes):

```
notice: Got signed certificate
notice: Starting Puppet client version 2.6.1
```

The agent is now authenticated with the master, but we have another message present:

```
err: Could not retrieve catalog: Could not find default node or by name with ↵
'node1.example.com, node1' on node node1.example.com
```

The agent has connected and our signed certificate has authenticated the session with the master. The master, however, doesn't have any configuration available for our puppet node, node1.example.com, and hence we have received an error message. We now have to add some configuration for this agent on the master.

▓ **Caution** It is important that the time is accurate on your master and agent. SSL connections rely on the clock on hosts being correct. If the clocks are incorrect then your connection may fail with an error indicating that your certificates are not trusted. You should use something like NTP (Network Time Protocol) to ensure your host's clocks are accurate.

Creating Our First Configuration

Let's get some more understanding of Puppet's components, configuration language and capabilities. We learned earlier that Puppet describes the files containing configuration data as manifests. Puppet manifests are made up of a number of major components:

- Resources – Individual configuration items

- Files – Physical files you can serve out to your agents

- Templates – Template files that you can use to populate files

- Nodes – Specifies the configuration of each agent

- Classes – Collections of resources

- Definitions – Composite collections of resources

These components are wrapped in a configuration language that includes variables, conditionals, arrays and other features. Later in this chapter we'll introduce you to the basics of the Puppet language and its elements. In the next chapter, we'll extend your knowledge of the language by taking you through an implementation of a multi-agent site managed with Puppet.

▧ **Note** In addition to these components, Puppet also has the concept of a "module," which is a portable collection of manifests that contain resources, classes, definitions, files, and templates. We'll see our first module shortly.

Extending the site.pp file

Our first step in creating our first agent configuration is defining and extending the `site.pp` file. See an example of this file in Listing 1-3.

Listing 1-3. The `site.pp` File

```
import 'nodes.pp'
$puppetserver = 'puppet.example.com'
```

▧ **Note** Puppet manifest files are traditionally suffixed with `.pp`. If your manifest file has the .pp suffix, you can drop the suffix when importing files.

The `import` directive tells Puppet to load a file called `nodes.pp`. This directive is used to include any Puppet configuration we want to load. For example, if we specify resources in a file called `resources.pp`, we would need to import it this way:

```
import 'resources.pp'
```

When Puppet starts, it will now load the `nodes.pp` file and process the contents. In this case, this file will contain the node definitions we create for each agent we connect. You can also import multiple files like so:

```
import 'nodes/*'
import 'classes/*'
```

The `import` statement will load all files with a suffix of `.pp` in the directories `nodes` and `classes`.

The `$puppetserver` statement sets a variable. In Puppet, configuration statements starting with a dollar sign are variables used to specify values that you can use in Puppet configuration.

In Listing 1-3, we've created a variable that contains the fully qualified domain name of our Puppet master, enclosed in double quotes.

▧ **Note** In Puppet manifests, strings with double-quotes are subject to variable interpolation and strings with single quotes are not. If you want to use a variable in a string, you should enclose it in double-quotes, for example: "This is a $variable string". You can also add braces, { }, to variables in strings to define them more clearly, "This is a ${variable} string". You can find quoting rules for Puppet at
http://docs.puppetlabs.com/guides/more_language.html#quoting.

Agent Configuration

Let's add our first agent definition to the **nodes.pp** file we've just asked Puppet to import. In Puppet manifests, agents are defined using **node** statements.

```
# touch /etc/puppet/manifests/nodes.pp.
```

You can see the node definition we're going to add in Listing 1-4.

Listing 1-4. *Our Node Configuration*

```
node 'node1.example.com' {
    include sudo
}
```

For a node definition we specify the node name, enclosed in single quotes, and then specify the configuration that applies to it inside curly braces { }. The client name can be the hostname or the fully qualified domain name of the client. At this stage, you can't specify nodes with wildcards (e.g., ***.example.com**) but you can use regular expressions, such as:

```
node /^www\d+\.example\.com/ {
    include sudo
}
```

This example will match all nodes from the domain **example.com** with the hostname **www1**, **www12**, **www123**, etc.

▩ **Note** We'll see more of node regular expressions in Chapter 3.

Next, we specify an **include** directive in our node definition. The **include** directive specifies a collection of configuration that we want to apply to our host. There are two types of collections we can include in a node:

- Classes – a basic collection of resources

- Modules – an advanced, portable collection of resources that can include classes, definitions, and other supporting configuration

You can include multiple collections by using multiple **include** directives or separating each collection with commas.

```
include sudo
include sshd
include vim, syslog-ng
```

In addition to including collections of resources, you can also specify individual resources to a node, like so:

```
node 'node1.example.com' {
```

```
    include sudo
    package { 'vim': ensure => present }
}
```

In this case however, as we've seen in Listing 1-4, we're just going to add a single collection of resources: the **sudo** module.

■ **Note** Puppet also has an inheritance model in which you can have one node inherit values from another node. You can read about node inheritance at

http://docs.puppetlabs.com/guides/language_tutorial.html#nodes; we'll talk more about it in Chapter 3.

Creating our first module

The next step is to create the **sudo** module. A module is a collection of manifests, resources, files, templates, classes, and definitions. A single module would contain everything required to configure a particular application. For example, it could contain all the resources (specified in manifest files), files and associated configuration to configure Apache or the **sudo** command on a host.

Each module needs a specific directory structure and a file called **init.pp**. This structure allows Puppet to automatically load modules. To perform this automatic loading, Puppet checks a series of directories called the module path. The module path is configured with the **modulepath** configuration option in the **[main]** section of the **puppet.conf** file. By default, Puppet looks for modules in the **/etc/puppet/modules** and **/var/lib/puppet/modules** directories, but you can add additional locations if required:

```
[main]
moduledir = /etc/puppet/modules:/var/lib/puppet/modules:/opt/modules
```

The automatic loading of modules means, unlike our **nodes.pp** file, modules don't need to be loaded into Puppet using the **import** directive.

Module Structure

Let's start by creating a module directory and file structure in Listing 1-5. We're going to create this structure under the directory **/etc/puppet/modules**. We will name the module **sudo**. Modules (and classes) must be normal words containing only letters, numbers, underscores and dashes.

Listing 1-5. Module Structure

```
# mkdir -p /etc/puppet/modules/sudo/{files,templates,manifests}
# touch /etc/puppet/modules/sudo/manifests/init.pp
```

The **manifests** directory will hold our **init.pp** file and any other configuration. The **init.pp** file is the core of your module and every module must have one. The **files** directory will hold any files we wish to serve as part of our module. The **templates** directory will contain any templates that our module might use.

The init.pp file

Now let's look inside our sudo module, starting with the init.pp file, which we can see in Listing 1-6.

Listing 1-6. The sudo module's init.pp file

```
class sudo {
    package { sudo:
        ensure => present,
    }

    if $operatingsystem == "Ubuntu" {
        package { "sudo-ldap":
            ensure => present,
            require => Package["sudo"],
        }
    }

    file { "/etc/sudoers":
        owner => "root",
        group => "root",
        mode => 0440,
        source => "puppet://$puppetserver/modules/sudo/etc/sudoers",
        require => Package["sudo"],
    }
}
```

Our sudo module's init.pp file contains a single class, also called sudo. There are three resources in the class, two packages and a file resource.

The first package resource ensures that the sudo package is installed, ensure => present. The second package resource uses Puppet's if/else syntax to set a condition on the installation of the sudo-ldap package.

▧ **Note** Puppet also has two other conditional statements, a case statement and a selector syntax. You can see more details of Puppet's conditional syntaxes at

http://docs.puppetlabs.com/guides/more_language.html#conditionals.

Puppet will check the value of the operatingsystem fact for each connecting client. If the value of the $operatingsystem fact is Ubuntu, then Puppet should install the sudo-ldap package.

▧ **Note** We discovered Facter and its values earlier in this chapter. Each fact is available as a variable, the fact name prefixed with a $ sign, in your Puppet manifests.

Lastly, in this resource we've also specified a new attribute, `require`. The `require` attribute is a metaparameter. Metaparameters are resource attributes that are part of Puppet's framework rather than belonging to a specific type. They perform actions on resources and can be specified for any type of resource.

The `require` metaparameter creates a dependency relationship between the `Package["sudo-ldap"]` resource and the `Package["sudo"]` resource. In this case, adding the `require` metaparameter to the resource tells Puppet that the `Package["sudo"]` is required by the `Package["sudo-ldap"]` resource. Hence, the `Package["sudo"]` resource must and will be installed first.

Relationships are an important part of Puppet. They allow you to instantiate real world relationships between configuration components on your hosts. A good example of this is networking. A number of resources on your hosts, for example a Web server or an MTA (Mail Transfer Agent), would rely on your network being configured and active before they can be activated. Relationships allow you to specify that certain resources, for example those configuring your network, are processed before those resources that configure your Web server or MTA.

The usefulness of relationships does not end there. Puppet can also build triggering relationships between resources. For example, if a file resource changes, then you can tell Puppet to restart a service resource. This means you can change a service's configuration file and have that change trigger a restart of that service to ensure it is running with the updated configuration. We'll see a lot more of these relationships and other metaparameters in Chapter 3.

▓ **Note** You can see a full list of the available metaparameters at

`http://docs.puppetlabs.com/references/stable/metaparameter.html`.

The last resource in the `sudo` class is a file resource, `File["/etc/sudoers"]`, which manages the `/etc/sudoers` file. Its first three attributes allow us to specify the owner, group and permissions of the file. In this case, the file is owned by the `root` user and group and has its mode set to 0440 (currently the mode can only be set using octal notation).

The next attribute, `source`, allows Puppet to retrieve a file from the Puppet file server and deliver it to the client. The value of this attribute is the name of the Puppet file server and the location and name of the file to retrieve.

`puppet://$puppetserver/modules/sudo/etc/sudoers`

Let's break down this value. The `puppet://` part specifies that Puppet will use the Puppet file server protocol to retrieve the file.

▓ **Note** Currently, the Puppet file server protocol is the only protocol available. In future versions of Puppet, the file server will support other protocols, such as HTTP or rsync.

The `$puppetserver` variable contains the hostname of our Puppet server. Remember that we created this variable and placed it in our `site.pp` file earlier? Instead of the variable, you could also specify the host name of the file server here.

`puppet://puppet.example.com/modules/sudo/etc/sudoers`

■ **Tip** One handy shortcut is to just remove the server name. Then Puppet will use whatever server the client is currently connected to, for example our source line would look like: puppet:///modules/sudo/etc/sudoers.

The next portion of our source value tells Puppet where to look for the file. This is the equivalent of the path to a network file share. The first portion of this share is modules, which tells us that the file is stored in a module. Next we specify the name of the module the file is contained in, in this case sudo. Finally, we specify the path inside that module to find the file.

All files in modules are stored under the files directory; this is considered the "root" of the module's file "share." In our case, we would create the directory etc under the files directory and create the sudoers file in this directory.

```
puppet$ mkdir -p /etc/puppet/modules/sudo/files/etc
puppet$ cp /etc/sudoers /etc/puppet/manifests/files/etc/sudoers
```

VERSION CONTROL

As your configuration gets more complicated, you should consider adding it to a version-control system such as Subversion or Git. A version-control system allows you to record and track changes to files, and is commonly used by software developers. For configuration management, version control allows you to track changes to your configuration. This is highly useful if you need to revert to a previously known state or make changes without impacting your running configuration.

You can find information about how to use Subversion at http://svnbook.red-bean.com/ and some specific ideas about how to use it with Puppet at http://projects.puppetlabs.com/projects/puppet/wiki/Puppet_Version_Control. We'll also show you how a version control system might work with Puppet in Chapter 3.

Applying Our First Configuration

We've created our first Puppet module! Let's step through what will happen when we connect an agent that includes this module.

1. It will install the sudo package.

2. If it's an Ubuntu host, then it will also install the sudo-ldap package

3. Lastly, it will download the sudoers file and install it into /etc/sudoers.

Now let's see this in action and include our new module on the agent we've created, node1.example.com. Remember we created a node statement for our host in Listing 1.4:

```
node 'node1.example.com' {
    include sudo
}
```

When the agent connects it will now include the **sudo** module. To do this we run the Puppet agent again, as shown in Listing 1-7.

Listing 1-7. *Applying Our First Configuration*

```
puppet# puppet agent --server=puppet.example.com --no-daemonize --verbose --onetime
```

■ **Note** Puppet has a handy mode called "noop." The "noop" mode runs Puppet but doesn't make any changes on your host. It allows you to see what Puppet would do, as a dry run. To run in "noop" mode, specify --noop on the command line.

In Listing 1-7, we've run the Puppet agent and connected to the master. We've run the agent in the foreground, in verbose mode and with the --onetime option that tells the Puppet agent to only run once and then stop. We can see a configuration run commence on our host:

■ **Tip** In Puppet, the combined configuration to be applied to a host is called a "catalog" and the process of applying it is called a "run." You can find a glossary of Puppet terminology at http://projects.puppetlabs.com/projects/puppet/wiki/Glossary_Of_Terms.

```
notice: Starting Puppet client version 2.6.1
info: Caching catalog for node1.example.com
info: Applying configuration version '1272631279'
notice: //sudo/Package[sudo]/ensure: created
notice: //sudo/File[/etc/sudoers]/checksum: checksum changed↵
 '{md5}9f95a522f5265b7e7945ff65369acdd2' to '{md5}d657d8d55ecdf88a2d11da73ac5662a4'
info: Filebucket[/var/lib/puppet/clientbucket]: Adding↵
 /etc/sudoers(d657d8d55ecdf88a2d11da73ac5662a4)
info: //sudo/File[/etc/sudoers]: Filebucketed /etc/sudoers to puppet with sum↵
 d657d8d55ecdf88a2d11da73ac5662a4
notice: //sudo/File[/etc/sudoers]/content: content changed↵
 '{md5}d657d8d55ecdf88a2d11da73ac5662a4' to '{md5}9f95a522f5265b7e7945ff65369acdd2'
notice: Finished catalog run in 10.54 seconds
```

Let's look at what has happened during our run. First we see that the agent has cached the configuration for the host. By default, Puppet uses this cache if it fails to connect to the master during a future run.

Next, we can see our resources being applied. First the **sudo** package is installed and then the /etc/sudoers file is copied across. We can see that during the copy process Puppet has backed up the old file, a process Puppet calls file bucketing. This means that if we've made a mistake and overwritten the file incorrectly we can always recover it.

▓ **Tip** Puppet can back up files remotely to our master using the `filebucket` type. See
`http://docs.puppetlabs.com/references/stable/type.html#filebucket`. We'll show you how to do this in
Chapter 3.

The last line of the catalog run tells us this process took 10.54 seconds to complete.
If we look on the Puppet master, we can see the results of the run logged there too.

```
notice: Starting Puppet server version 2.6.1
info: Autoloaded module sudo
info: Expiring the node cache of node1.example.com
info: Not using expired node for node1.example.com from cache; expired at Fri Apr 30↵
 08:44:46 -0400 2010
info: Caching node for node1.example.com
notice: Compiled catalog for node1.example.com in 0.02 seconds
```

Here we can see that Puppet has loaded our sudo module and compiled the catalog for
node1.example.com. This catalog is then sent down to the agent and applied on the target host.

If the Puppet agent is running as a daemon, it would then wait 30 minutes and then connect to the
master again to check if the configuration has changed on our host or if a new configuration is available
from the master. We can adjust this run interval using the `runinterval` option in the
`/etc/puppet/puppet.conf` configuration file on the agent host.

```
[agent]
runinterval=3600
```

Here we've adjusted the run interval to 3600 seconds, or 60 minutes.

Summary

So that's it - we've used Puppet to configure our first agent. You've also been introduced to the
theoretical underpinnings of Puppet and how to:

- Install Puppet

- Configure Puppet

- Use Puppet to manage some simple configuration on a single host

In the next chapter, we'll extend our Puppet configuration to multiple agents, learn more about
Puppet's configuration language and learn how to build more complex configurations.

Resources

- Introduction to Puppet http://docs.puppetlabs.com/guides/introduction.html

- Installation - http://docs.puppetlabs.com/guides/installation.html

- Configuration Guide - http://docs.puppetlabs.com/guides/configuring.html

- Configuration Reference - http://docs.puppetlabs.com/references/stable/configuration.html

CHAPTER 2

■ ■ ■

Building Hosts with Puppet

In Chapter 1 we installed and configured Puppet, created our first module, and applied that module and its configuration via the Puppet agent to a host. In this chapter, we're going to extend this process to build some more complete modules and hosts with Puppet for a hypothetical company, Example.com Pty Ltd. Each host's functionality we build will introduce new Puppet concepts and ideas.

Example.com Pty Ltd has four hosts we're going to manage with Puppet: a Web server, a database server, a mail server and our Puppet master server located in a flat network. You can see that network in Figure 2-1.

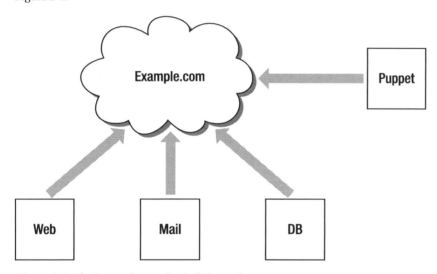

Figure 2-1. The Example.com Pty Ltd Network

Like many organizations, though, Example.com is not a very homogenous environment and each host uses a different operating system, as follows:

- `mail.example.com` – (Red Hat Enterprise Linux 5)

- `db.example.com` – (Solaris 10)

- `web.example.com` – (Ubuntu 10.04)

- `puppet.example.com` – (Ubuntu 10.04)

To solve this problem, we'll begin by working through how we use Puppet in a multiple operating system environment. Be sure you've installed the base operating system on these hosts as described in Chapter 1, because we'll perform some basic configuration on the hosts. We'll start with configuring SSH for each host, then we'll install and configure some role-specific applications for the hosts as follows:

- Postfix (`mail.example.com`)

- MySQL (`db.example.com`)

- Apache and a website (`web.example.com`)

- Manage the Puppet master with Puppet (`puppet.example.com`)

As we configure each host, we'll introduce some of the different features and functions available in Puppet. By the end of the chapter you'll have a firm grasp of the basics. In subsequent chapters, we'll build on this knowledge and introduce some of Puppet's more advanced features.

Getting Started

Before proceeding, we must have the proper setup, so we need to install the Puppet master and agent and then create node definitions for each of our hosts.

■ **Note** As we mentioned in Chapter 1, the Puppet software is called the "agent." Puppet calls the definition of the host itself a "node."

Installing Puppet

First, we need to install the Puppet master and agent. We're going to install the Puppet master on `puppet.example.com` and the Puppet agent on all our hosts, including `puppet.example.com`. We're installing the agent on the Puppet master because we're going to use Puppet to manage itself! We then need to connect, create and sign certificates for each host. To do this, you should follow the installation instructions for the relevant operating system from Chapter 1 on each of the four hosts. For example, for installation on the Red Hat Enterprise Linux host, use the instructions in the **Installing on Red Hat Enterprise Linux and Fedora** section. You can then move on to configuring the nodes (aka hosts).

■ **Tip** If you use a provisioning tool like Kickstart or Preseed, you can also include Puppet installation and signing as part of your build process. You can see an example of how to do that at
`http://projects.puppetlabs.com/projects/1/wiki/Bootstrapping_With_Puppet`.

Configuring Nodes

After installing the Puppet master and associated agents, we need to create node definitions for each of our hosts in the node.pp file. We created this file in the /etc/puppet/manifests/ directory in Chapter 1. As you can see in Listing 2-1, we've created empty node definitions for each of the nodes in our network.

Listing 2-1. Node defintions in nodes.pp

```
node 'puppet.example.com' {
}

node 'web.example.com' {
}

node 'db.example.com' {
}

node 'mail.example.com' {
}
```

We haven't included any configuration on our node definitions – Puppet will just recognize the node as it connects and do nothing.

As you might imagine, if you've got a lot of nodes, the nodes.pp file could become quite large and complex. Puppet has some simple ways of dealing with this issue, described next.

Working With Similar Hosts

The first method works best for large number of similar hosts, such as Web servers, where the configuration of the host is largely identical. For example, if our environment had multiple hosts called web1, web2, web3, etc., we could specify:

```
node 'web1.example.com', 'web2.example.com', 'web3.example.com' { }
```

In version 0.25.0 and later, we can also specify these nodes in the form of a regular expression:

```
node /^web\d+\.example\.com$/ { }
```

This would match any host starting with webx where x is a digit or digits, such as web1 or web20.

Using External Sources

Puppet also has the ability to use external sources for your node data. These sources can include LDAP directories, databases or other external repositories. This allows you to leverage existing sources of information about your environment, such as asset management systems or identity stores. This functionality is called External Node Classification, or ENC, and we'll discuss it in more detail in Chapter 3.

Specifying a Default Node

You can also specify a special node called default. This is, as you'd imagine, a default node. If no other node definition exists, then the contents of this node are applied to the host.

```
node default {
    include defaultclass
}
```

Node Inheritance Structure

Lastly, Puppet has a simple node inheritance structure. You can use this to have one node inherit the contents of another node. Only one node can be inherited at a time. So, for example, we might want the node web host to inherit the contents of a node called base.

```
node base {
    include  sudo, mailx
}

node 'web.example.com' inherits base {
    …
}
```

Here we've defined the base node to include the modules sudo and mailx and then specified that the web node inherits the contents of this node. This means the web node would include sudo and mailx in addition to any classes included in its own node definition. Inheritance is cumulative and you can specify an inheritance structure like so:

```
node base {
    …
}

node webserver  inherits base {
    …
}

node 'web.example.com' inherits webserver {
    …
}
```

Here the webserver node inherits the contents of the base node, and then in turn the web.example.com node cumulatively inherits the contents of both nodes.

▓ **Caution** When starting out with Puppet it is common to structure the assignment of classes to nodes using inheritance and a base node. This structure allows classes common to every node to be placed in the base node. This organization structure may pose a problem in the future as the number of nodes and the scale of puppet increases and base classes need to be added or removed from only a subset of all nodes. In order to avoid future refactoring, avoid using node inheritance in preference of a flat node classification tree. A good alternative to the base node and class inheritance is to employ conditional statements, which we'll introduce later in this chapter, to determine which classes a node should and should not receive instead of relying on node inheritance.

Variable Scoping

The concept of node inheritance is a good place to talk about an important and sometimes tricky concept in Puppet: variable scoping. Let's imagine we've decided to configure some variables in our nodes, for example:

```
node base {
  $location = "dc1"
  ...
  $location = "dc2"
}
```

In most programming languages, the $location variable would start out with a value of "dc1" and then, when it was next assigned, it would change to a value of "dc2". In Puppet, these same two statements cause an error:

```
err: Cannot reassign variable location at /etc/puppet/manifests/node.pp:4
```

Why is this? Puppet is declarative and hence dynamically scoped. Allowing variable reassignment would have to rely on order in the file to determine the value of the variable and order does not matter in a declarative language. The principal outcome of this is that you cannot redefine a variable inside the same scope it was defined in, like our node. Let's take another example, of a class this time instead of a node:

```
class ssh_sudo {
    $package = "openssh"
    package { $package: ensure => installed }

    $package = "sudo"
    package { $package: ensure => installed }
}
```

You can see that we've tried to define the $package variable twice. If we were to try to compile and apply this configuration, the Puppet agent would return the following error:

```
err: Cannot reassign variable package at /etc/puppet/modules/ssh/manifests/init.pp:5
```

■ **Note** The error helpfully also tells us the file, and line number in the file, where we've tried to redefine the variable.

So what's a scope? Each class, definition, or node introduces a new scope, and there is also a top scope for everything defined outside of those structures. Scopes are created hierarchically and the important thing you need to remember about scope hierarchy is that it is created when Puppet code is evaluated, rather than when it is defined, for example:

```
$package = "openssh"

class ssh {
  package { $package:
    ensure => installed,
  }
}

class ssh_server
  include ssh
  $package = "openssh-server"
}

include ssh_server
```

Here a top level scope, in which $package is defined, is present. Then there's a scope for the ssh_server class and a scope below that for the ssh class. When Puppet runs the $package variable will have a value of "openssh-server" because this is what the variable was when evaluation occurred.

Naturally, in these different scopes, you can reassign the value of a variable:

```
class apache {
    $apache = 1
}

class passenger {
    $apache = 2
}
```

The same variable can be used and defined in both the apache and passenger classes without generating an error because they represent different scopes.

Going back to node inheritance, you can probably see how this dynamic scoping is going to be potentially confusing, for example:

```
class apache {
  $apacheversion = "2.0.33"
  package { "apache2":
    ensure => $apacheversion,
  }
}
```

```
node 'web.example.com' {
  include  apache
}

node 'web2.example.com' inherits 'web.example.com' {
  $apacheversion = "2.0.42"
}
```

Here we've created a class called apache and a package resource for the apache2 package. We've also created a variable called $apacheversion and used that as the value of the ensure attribute of the package resource. This tells Puppet that we want to install version 2.0.33 of Apache. We've then included our apache class in a node, web.example.com.

But we've also decided to create another node, web2.example.com, which inherits the contents of the web.example.com node. In this case, however, we've decided to install a different Apache version and therefore we specified a new value for the $apacheversion variable. But instead of using this new value, Puppet will continue to install the 2.0.33 version of Apache because the $apacheversion variable is maintained in its original scope of the web.example.com node and the new variable value is ignored.

There is a work-around for this issue that you can see here:

```
class apache {
  $apacheversion = "2.0.33"
  package { "apache2":
    ensure => $apacheversion,
  }
}

class base {
  include  apache
}

node 'web.example.com' {
  $apacheversion = "2.0.42"
  include base
}
```

Instead of defining a base node we've defined a base class that includes the apache class. When we created our node, we specified the $apacheversion we want and then included the base class, ensuring we're in the right scope. We could put other like items in our base class and specify any required variables.

▧ **Note** You can learn more about variable scoping, workarounds and related issues at
http://projects.puppetlabs.com/projects/puppet/wiki/Frequently_Asked_Questions#Common+Misconce ptions.

With Puppet installed and node definitions in place, we can now move on to creating our modules for the various hosts. But first, let's do a quick refresher on modules in general.

Making (More) Magic With Modules

In Chapter 1, we learned about modules: self-contained collections of resources, classes, files that can be served, and templates for configuration files. We're going to use several modules to define the various facets of each host's configuration. For example, we will have a module for managing Apache on our Web server and another for managing Postfix on our mail server.

Recall that modules are structured collections of Puppet manifests. By default Puppet will search the module path, which is by default /etc/puppet/modules/ and /var/lib/puppet/modules, for modules and load them. These paths are controlled by the modulepath configuration option. This means we don't need to import any of these files into Puppet – it all happens automatically.

It's very important that modules are structured properly. For example, our sudo module contains the following:

```
sudo/
sudo/manifests
sudo/manifests/init.pp
sudo/files
sudo/templates
```

Inside our init.pp we create a class with the name of our module:

```
class sudo {
configuration…
}
```

Lastly, we also discovered we can apply a module, like the sudo module we created in Chapter 1, to a node by using the include function like so:

```
node 'puppet.example.com' {
  include sudo
}
```

The included function adds the resources contained in a class or module, for example adding all the resources contained in the sudo module here to the node puppet.example.com.

Let's now see how to manage the contents of our modules using version control tools as we recommended in Chapter 1.

▓ **Note** You don't have to always create your own modules. The Puppet Forge at http://forge.puppetlabs.com contains a large collection of pre-existing modules that you can either use immediately or modify to suit your environment. This can make getting started with Puppet extremely simple and fast.

Version Controlling Your Modules

Because modules present self-contained collections of configuration, we also want to appropriately manage the contents of these modules, allowing us to perform change control. To manage your content, we recommend that you use a Version Control System or VCS.

Version control is the method most developers use to track changes in their application source code. Version control records the state of a series of files or objects and allows you to periodically capture that state in the form of a revision. This allows you to track the history of changes in files and objects and potentially revert to an earlier revision should you make a mistake. This makes management of our configuration much easier and saves us from issues like undoing inappropriate changes or accidently deleting configuration data.

In this case, we're going to show you an example of managing your Puppet manifests with a tool called Git, which is a distributed version control system (DVCS). Distributed version control allows the tracking of changes across multiple hosts, making it easier to allow multiple people to work on our modules. Git is used by a lot of large development projects, such as the Linux kernel, and was originally developed by Linux Torvalds for that purpose. It's a powerful tool but it'sd easy to learn the basic steps. You can obviously easily use whatever version control system suits your environment, for example many people use Subversion or CVS for the same purpose.

First, we need to install Git. On most platforms we install the git package. For example, on Red Hat and Ubuntu:

```
$ sudo yum install git
```
or,
```
$ sudo apt-get install git
```

Once Git is installed, let's identify ourselves to Git so it can track who we are and associate some details with actions we take.

```
$ git config --global user.name "Your Name"
$ git config --global user.email your@email.address.com
```

Now let's version control the path containing our modules, in our case /etc/puppet/modules. We change to that directory and then execute the git binary to initialize our new Git repository.

```
$ cd /etc/puppet/modules
$ git init
```

This creates a directory called .git in the /etc/puppet/modules directory that will hold all the details and tracking data for our Git repository.

We can now add files to this repository using the git binary with the add option.

```
$ git add *
```

This adds everything currently in our path to Git. You can also use git and the rm option to remove items you don't want to be in the repository.

```
$ git rm filename
```

This doesn't mean, however, that our modules are already fully tracked by our Git repository. Like Subversion and other version control systems, we need to "commit" the objects we'd like to track. The commit process captures the state of the objects we'd like to track and manage, and it creates a revision to mark that state. You can also create a file called .gitignore in the directory. Every file or directory specified in this file will be ignored by Git and never added.

Before we commit though, we can see what Git is about by using the git status command:

```
$ git status
```

This tells us that when we commit that Git will add the contents to the repository and create a revision based on that state.

Now let's commit our revision to the repository.

```
$ git commit -a -m "This is our initial commit"
```

The -m option specifies a commit message that allows us to document the revision we're about to commit. It's useful to be verbose here and explain what you have changed and why, so it's easier to find out what's in each revision and make it easier to find an appropriate point to return to if required. If you need more space for your commit message you can omit the -m option and Git will open your default editor and allow you to type a more comprehensive message.

The changes are now committed to the repository and we can use the git log command to see our recent commit.

```
$ git log
```

We can see some information here about our commit. First, Git uses SHA1 hashes to track revisions; Subversion, for example, uses numeric numbers – 1, 2, 3, etc. Each commit has a unique hash assigned to it. We will also see some details about who created the commit and our commit message telling us what the commit is all about.

Every time you add a new module or file you will need to add it to Git using the git add command and then commit it to store it in the repository. I recommend you add and commit changes regularly to ensure you have sufficiently granular revisions to allow you to easily roll back to an earlier state.

▓ **Tip** If you're interested in Git, we strongly recommend Scott Chacon's excellent book *Pro Git* – also published by Apress. The book is available in both dead tree form and online at `http://progit.org/book/`. Scott is also one of the lead developers of the Git hosting site, GitHub – `http://www.github.com`, where you can find a number of Puppet related modules.

Our simple sudo module is a good introduction to Puppet, but it only showcased a small number of Puppet's capabilities. It's now time to expand our Puppet knowledge and develop some new more advanced modules, starting with one to manage SSH on our hosts. We'll then create a module to manage Postfix on `mail.example.com`, one to manage MySQL on our Solaris host, `db.example.com`, another to manage Apache and web sites, and finally one to manage Puppet with Puppet itself.

We'll also introduce you to some best practices for structuring, writing and managing modules and configuration.

Creating a module to Manage SSH

We know that we first need to create an appropriate module structure. We're going to do this under the /etc/puppet/modules directory on our Puppet master.

```
$ cd /etc/puppet/modules
$ mkdir -p ssh/{manifests,templates,files}
$ touch ssh/manifests/init.pp
```

Next, we create some classes inside the init.pp file and some initial resources, as shown in Listing 2-2.

Listing 2-2. The ssh module

```
class ssh::install {
  package { "openssh":
    ensure => present,
  }
}

class ssh::config {
  file { "/etc/ssh/sshd_config":
    ensure = > present,
    owner => 'root',
    group => 'root',
    mode => 0600,
    source => "puppet:///modules/ssh/sshd_config",
    require => Class["ssh::install"],
    notify => Class["ssh::service"],
  }
}
class ssh::service {
  service { "sshd":
    ensure => running,
    hasstatus => true,
    hasrestart => true,
    enable => true,
    require => Class["ssh::config"],
  }
}

class ssh {
  include ssh::install, ssh::config, ssh::service
}
```

We've created three classes: ssh, ssh::install, ssh::config, and ssh::service. As we mentioned earlier, modules can be made up multiple classes. We use the :: namespace syntax as a way to create structure and organization in our modules. The ssh prefix tells Puppet that each class belongs in the ssh module, and the class name is suffixed.

▓ **Note** We'd also want to create a sshd_config file in the ssh/files/ directory so that our File["/etc/ssh/sshd_config"] resource can serve out that file. The easiest way to do this is to copy an existing functional sshd_config file and use that. Later we'll show you how to create template files that allow you to configure per-host configuration in your files. Without this file Puppet will report an error for this resource.

In Listing 2-2, we created a functional structure by dividing the components of the service we're managing into functional domains: things to be installed, things to be configured and things to be executed or run.

Lastly, we created a class called ssh (which we need to ensure the module is valid) and used the include function to add all the classes to the module.

Managing Our Classes

Lots of classes with lots of resources in our init.pp file means that the file is going to quickly get cluttered and hard to manage. Thankfully, Puppet has an elegant way to manage these classes rather than clutter the init.pp file. Each class, rather than being specified in the init.pp file, can be specified in an individual file in the manifests directory, for example in a ssh/manifests/install.pp file that would contain the ssh::install class:

```
class ssh::install {
  package { "openssh":
    ensure => present,
  }
}
```

When Puppet loads the ssh module, it will search the path for files suffixed with .pp, look inside them for namespaced classes and automatically import them. Let's quickly put our ssh::config and ssh::service classes into separate files:

```
$ touch ssh/manifests/{config.pp,service.pp}
```

This leaves our init.pp file containing just the ssh class:

```
class ssh
  include ssh::install, ssh::config, ssh::service
}
```

Our ssh module directory structure will now look like:

```
ssh
ssh/files/sshd_config
ssh/manifests/init.pp
ssh/manifests/install.pp
ssh/manifests/config.pp
ssh/manifests/service.pp
ssh/templates
```

Neat and simple.

■ **Tip** You can nest classes another layer, like ssh::config::client, and our auto-importing magic will still work by placing this class in the ssh/manifests/config/client.pp file.

The ssh::install Class

Now that we've created our structure, let's look at the classes and resources we've created. Let's start with the ssh::install class containing the Package["openssh"] resource, which installs the OpenSSH package.

It looks simple enough, but we've already hit a stumbling block – we want to manage SSH on all of Example.com's hosts, and across these platforms the OpenSSH package has different names:

- Red Hat: openssh-server

- Ubuntu: openssh-server

- Solaris: openssh

How are we going to ensure Puppet installs the correctly-named package for each platform? The answer lies with Facter, Puppet's system inventory tool. During each Puppet run, Facter queries data about the host and sends it to the Puppet master. This data includes the operating system of the host, which is made available in our Puppet manifests as a variable called $operatingsystem. We can now use this variable to select the appropriate package name for each platform. Let's rewrite our Package["openssh"] resource:

```
package { "ssh":
  name => $operatingsystem ?
    /(Red Hat|CentOS|Fedora|Ubuntu|Debian)/ => "openssh-server",
    Solaris => "openssh",
    },
  ensure => installed,
}
```

You can see we've changed the title of our resource to ssh and specified a new attribute called name. As we explained in Chapter 1, each resource is made up of a type, title and a series of attributes. Each resource's attributes includes its "name variable," or "namevar," and the value of this attribute is used to determine the name of the resource. For example, the Package and Service resources use the name attribute as their namevar while the File type uses the path attribute as its namevar. Most of the time we wouldn't specify the namevar, as it is synonymous with the title, for example in this resource:

```
file { "/etc/passwd":
  ...
}
```

We don't need to specify the namevar because the value will be taken from the title, "/etc/passwd". But often we're referring to resources in many places and we might want a simple alias, so we can give the resource a title and specify its namevar this way:

```
file { "passwd":
  path => "/etc/passwd",
  ...
}
```

We can now refer to this resource as File["passwd"] as an aliased short-hand.

▓ **Note** You should also read about the `alias` metaparameter, which provides a similar capability, at
`http://docs.puppetlabs.com/references/latest/metaparameter.html#alias`.

In our current example, the name of the package we're managing varies on different hosts. Therefore, we want to specify a generic name for the resource and a platform-selected value for the actual package to be installed.

You can see that inside this new `name` attribute we've specified the value of the attribute as `$operatingsystem` followed by a conditional syntax that Puppet calls a "selector." To construct a selector, we specify the a variable containing the value we want to select on as the value of our attribute, here `$operatingsystem`, and follow this with a question mark (?). We then list on new lines a series of selections, for example if the value of `$operatingsystem` is Solaris, then the value of the `name` attribute will be set to `openssh`, and so on. Notice that we can specify multiple values in the form of simple regular expressions, like `/(Solaris|Ubuntu|Debian)/`.

▓ **Note** Selector matching is case-insensitive. You can also see some other examples of regular expressions in
selectors at `http://docs.puppetlabs.com/guides/language_tutorial.html#selectors`.

We can also specify a value called `default`.

```
default => "ssh",
```

This value is used if no other listed selection matches. If we don't specify a `default` value and no selection matches then the `name` attribute would be set to a nil value.

As can you imagine, this requirement to select the appropriate value for a particular platform happens a lot. This means we could end up scattering a lot of very similar conditional statements across our Puppet code. That's pretty messy; a best practice we recommend is to make this look a lot neater and more elegant by moving all your conditional checks to a separate class.

We usually call that class `module::params`, so in our current case it would be named `ssh::params`. Like before, we're going to store that class in a separate file. Let's create that file:

```
$ touch ssh/manifests/params.pp
```

We can see that class in Listing 2-3.

Listing 2-3. The ssh::params class

```
class ssh::params {
  case $operatingsystem {
    Solaris: {
      $ssh_package_name = 'openssh'
    }
    /(Ubuntu|Debian)/: {
      $ssh_package_name = 'openssh-server'
```

```
    }
    /(RedHat|CentOS|Fedora)/: {
      $ssh_package_name = 'openssh-server'
    }
  }
}
```

You can see that inside our ssh::params class we've created another type of conditional, the case statement. Much like a selector, the case statement iterates over the value of a variable, here $operatingsystem. Unlike a selector, case statements allow us to specify a block of things to do if the value of the variable matches one of the cases. In our case we're setting the value of a new variable we've created, called $ssh_package_name. You could do other things here, such as include a class or a resource, or perform some other function.

▪ **Note** You can read more about case statements at http://docs.puppetlabs.com/guides/language_ tutorial.html#case_statement. Also available is an if/else syntax that you can read about at http://docs.puppetlabs.com/guides/language_tutorial.html#ifelse_statement.

And finally, we need to include our new class in the ssh class:\

```
class ssh {
  include ssh::params, ssh::install, ssh::config, ssh::service
}
```

These includes tell Puppet that when you include the ssh module, you're getting all of these classes.

FUNCTIONS

The include directive we use to include our classes and modules is called a function. Functions are commands that run on the Puppet master to perform actions. Puppet has a number of other functions, including the generate function that calls external commands and returns the result, and the notice function that logs messages on the master and is useful for testing a configuration. For example:

```
notice("This is a notice message including the value of the $ssh_package variable")
```

Functions only run on the Puppet master and cannot be run on the client, and thus can only work with the resources available on the master.

You can see a full list of functions at http://docs.puppetlabs.com/references/stable/function.html and we'll introduce you to a variety of other functions in subsequent chapters. You can also find some documentation on how to write your own functions at http://projects.puppetlabs.com/projects/puppet/wiki/Writing_Your_Own_Functions, and we'll talk about developing functions in Chapter 10.

We're going to come back to the ssh::params class and add more variables as we discover other elements of our OpenSSH configuration that are unique to particular platforms, but for the moment how does including this new class change our Package["ssh"] resource?

```
package { $ssh::params::ssh_package_name:
  ensure => installed,
}
```

You can see our namespacing is useful for other things, here using variables from other classes. We can refer to a variable in another class by prefixing the variable name with the class it's contained in, here ssh::params. In this case, rather than our messy conditional, the package name to be installed will use the value of the $ssh::params::ssh_package_name parameter. Our resource is now much neater, simpler and easier to read.

▓ **Tip** So how do we refer to namespaced resources? Just like other resources,

Package[$ssh::params::ssh_package_name].

The ssh::config Class

Now let's move onto our next class, ssh::config, which we can see in Listing 2-4.

Listing 2-4. The ssh::config class

```
class ssh::config {
  file { "/etc/ssh/sshd_config":
    ensure = > present,
    owner => 'root',
    group => 'root',
    mode => 0440,
    source => "puppet:///modules/ssh/sshd_config",
    require => Class["ssh::install"],
    notify => Class["ssh::service"],
  }
}
```

We know that the location of the sshd_config files will vary across different operating systems. Therefore, we're going to have to add another conditional for the name and location of that file. Let's go back to our ssh::params class from Example 2-3 and add a new variable:

```
class ssh::params {
  case $operatingsystem {
    Solaris {
      $ssh_package_name = 'openssh'
      $ssh_service_config = '/etc/ssh/sshd_config'
  }
  …
}
```

We add the $ssh_service_config variable to each of the cases in our conditional and then update our file resource in the ssh::config class:

```
file { $ssh::params::ssh_service_config:
  ensure = > present,
  ...
}
```

Again, we have no need for a messy conditional in the resource, we can simply reference the $ssh::params::ssh_service_config variable.

We can also see that the file resource contains two metaparameters, require and notify. These metaparameters both specify relationships between resources and classes. You'll notice here that both metaparameters reference classes rather than individual resources. They tell Puppet that it should create a relationship between this file resource and every resource in the referenced classes.

▓ **Tip** It is a best practice to establish relationships with an entire class, rather than with a resource contained within another class, because this allows the internal structure of the class to change without refactoring the resource declarations related to the class.

For example, the require metaparameter tells Puppet that all the resources in the specified class must be processed prior to the current resource. In our example, the OpenSSH package must be installed before Puppet tries to manage the service's configuration file.

The notify metaparameter creates a notification relationship. If the current resource (the service's configuration file) is changed, then Puppet should notify all the resources contained in the ssh::service class. In our current case, a "notification" will cause the service resources in the ssh::service class restart, ensuring that if we change a configuration file that the service will be restarted and running with the correct, updated configuration.

▓ **Tip** In Puppet 2.6.0, a shorthand method called "chaining" was introduced for specifying metaparameter relationships, such as require and notify. You can read about chaining at
http://docs.puppetlabs.com/guides/language_tutorial.html#chaining_resources.

So why specify the whole ssh::service class rather than just the Service["sshd"] resource? This is another piece of simple best practice that allows us to simplify maintaining our classes and the relationships between them. Imagine that, instead of a single package, we had twenty packages. If we didn't require the class then we'd need to specify each individual package in our require statement, like this:

```
require => [ Package["package1"], Package["package2"], Package["package3"] ],
```

> ■ **Note** Adding [ ]s around a list creates a Puppet array. You can specify arrays as the values of variables and many attributes; for example, you can specify many items in a single resource: package { ["package1", "package2", "package3"]: ensure => installed }. In addition to arrays, Puppet also supports a hash syntax, which you can see at http://docs.puppetlabs.com/guides/language_tutorial.html#hashes.

We'd need to do that for every resource that required our packages, making our require statements cumbersome, potentially error prone, and most importantly requiring that every resource that requires packages be updated with any new package requirements.

By requiring the whole class, it doesn't matter how many packages we add to the ssh::install class – Puppet knows to install packages before managing configuration files, and we don't have to update a lot of resources every time we make a change.

> ■ **Tip** In our current example we could make use of arrays to extend the variables in the ssh::params class. For example, by changing $ssh_package_name to an array, we could specify multiple packages to be installed without needing to create another Package resource in the ssh::install class. Puppet is smart enough to know that if you specify a variable with a value of an array then it should expand the array, so changing the value of the $ssh_package_name variable to [openssh, package2, package3] would result in the ssh::install class installing all three packages. This greatly simplifies the maintenance of our ssh module, as we only need to change values in one place to manage multiple configuration items.

The ssh::service Class

Let's look at our last class, ssh::service, and update it to reflect our new practice:

```
class ssh::service {
  service { $ssh::params::ssh_service_name:
    ensure => running,
    hasstatus => true,
    hasresstart => true,
    enable => true,
    require => Class["ssh::config"],
  }
}
```

We've added our new variable, $ssh_service_name, to the ssh:params class too:

```
class ssh::params {
  case $operatingsystem {
    Solaris {
      $ssh_package_name = 'openssh'
```

```
    $ssh_service_config = '/etc/ssh/sshd_config'
    $ssh_service_name = 'sshd'
  }
…
}
```

Let's also look at our Service[$ssh::params::ssh_service_name] resource (at the start of this section), as this is the first service we've seen managed. You'll notice two important attributes, ensure and enable, which specify the state and status of the resource respectively. The state of the resource specifies whether the service is running or stopped. The status of the resource specifies whether it is to be started at boot, for example as controlled by the chkconfig or enable-rc.d commands.

Puppet understands how to manage a variety of service frameworks, like SMF and init scripts, and can start, stop and restart services. It does this by attempting to identify the service framework your platform uses and executing the appropriate commands. For example, on Red Hat it might execute:

```
$ service sshd restart
```

If Puppet can't recognize your service framework, it will revert to simple parsing of the process table for processes with the same name as the service it's trying to manage. This obviously isn't ideal, so it helps to tell Puppet a bit more about your services to ensure it manages them appropriately. The hasstatus and hasrestart attributes we specified in the ssh::service class is one of the ways we tell Puppet useful things about our services. If we specify hasstatus as true, then Puppet knows that our service framework supports status commands of some kind. For example, on Red Hat it knows it can execute the following:

```
$ service sshd status
```

This enables it to determine accurately whether the service is started or stopped. The same principle applies to the hasrestart attribute, which specifies that the service has a restart command.

Now we can see Puppet managing a full service, if we include our new ssh module in our Puppet nodes, as shown in Listing 2-5.

Listing 2-5. *Adding the ssh Module*

```
class base {
  include sudo, ssh
}

node 'puppet.example.com' {
  include base
}

node 'web.example.com' {
  include base
}

node 'db.example.com' {
  include base
}
```

```
node 'mail.example.com' {
  include base
}
```

Here we've created a class called base, in which we're going to place the modules that will be base or generic to all our nodes. Thus far, these are our sudo and ssh modules. We then include this class in each node statement.

■ **Note** We talked earlier about node inheritance and some of its scoping issues. As we explained there, using a class instead of node inheritance helps avoids these issues. You can read about it at

http://projects.puppetlabs.com/projects/puppet/wiki/Frequently_Asked_Questions#Common+Misconce ptions.

With a basic SSH module in place, and we can now manage the SSH daemon and its configuration.

Creating a Module to Manage Postfix

Let's now create a module to manage Postfix on mail.example.com. We start with a similar structure to our SSH module. In this case, we know which platform we're going to install our mail server on so we don't need to include any conditional logic. However, if we had multiple mail servers on different platforms, it would be easy to adjust our module using the example we've just shown to cater for disparate operations systems.

```
postfix
postfix/files/master.cf
postifx/manifests/init.pp
postfix/manifests/install.pp
postfix/manifests/config.pp
postfix/manifests/service.pp
postfix/templates/main.cf.erb
```

The postfix::install class

We also have some similar resources present in our Postfix module that we saw in our SSH module, for example in the postfix::install class we install two packages, postfix and mailx:

```
class postfix::install {
  package { [ "postfix", "mailx" ]:
    ensure => present,
  }
}
```

Note that we've used an array to specify both packages in a single resource statement this is a useful shortcut that allows you specify multiple items in a single resource.

The postfix::config class

Next, we have the postfix::config class, which we will use to configure our Postfix server.

```
class postfix::config {
  File {
    owner => "postfix",
    group => "postfix",
    mode => 0644,
  }

  file { "/etc/postfix/master.cf":
    ensure = > present,
    source => "puppet:///modules/postfix/master.cf",
    require => Class["postfix::install"],
    notify => Class["postfix::service"],
  }

  file { "/etc/postfix/main.cf":
    ensure = > present,
    content => template("postfix/main.cf.erb"),
    require => Class["postfix::install"],
    notify => Class["postfix::service"],
  }
}
```

You may have noticed some new syntax: We specified the File resource type capitalized and without a title. This syntax is called a resource default, and it allows us to specify defaults for a particular resource type. In this case, all File resources within the postfix::config class will be owned by the user postfix, the group postfix and with a mode of 0644. Resource defaults only apply to the current scope, but you can apply global defaults by specifying them in your site.pp file.

A common use for global defaults is to define a global "filebucket" for backing up the files Puppet changes. You can see the filebucket type and an example of how to use it globally at http://docs.puppetlabs.com/references/stable/type.html#filebucket.

▓ **Tip** A common use for global defaults is to define a global "filebucket" for backing up the files Puppet changes. You can see the filebucket type and an example of how to use it globally at

http://docs.puppetlabs.com/references/stable/type.html#filebucket.

METAPARAMETER DEFAULTS

Like resource defaults, you can also set defaults for metaparameters, such as `require`, using Puppet variable syntax. For example:

```
class postfix::config {
  $require = Class["postfix::install"]
  ...
}
```

This would set a default for the `require` metaparameter in the `postfix::config` class and means we could remove all the `require => Class["postfix::install"]` statements from our resources in that class.

We've also introduced a new attribute in our File["/etc/postfix/main.cf"] resource – content. We've already seen the source attribute, which allows Puppet to serve out files, and we've used it in one of our File resources, File["/etc/postfix/master.cf"]. The content attribute allows us to specify the content of the file resources as a string. But it also allows us to specify a template for our file. The template is specified using a function called template.

As previously mentioned, functions are commands that run on the Puppet master and return values or results. In this case, the template function allows us to specify a Ruby ERB template (http://ruby-doc.org/stdlib/libdoc/erb/rdoc/), from which we can create the templated content for our configuration file. We specify the template like this:

```
content => template("postfix/main.cf.erb"),
```

We've specified the name of the function, "template," and inside brackets the name of the module that contains the template and the name of the template file. Puppet knows when we specify the name of the module to look inside the postfix/templates directory for the requisite file – here, main.cf.erb.

THE REQUIRE FUNCTION

In addition to the `include` function, Puppet also has a function called `require`. The `require` function works just like the `include` function except that it introduces some order to the inclusion of resources. With the `include` function, resources are not included in any sequence. The only exception is individual resources, which have relationships (using metaparameters, for example) that mandate some ordering. The `require` function tells Puppet that all resources being required must be processed first. For example, if we specified:

```
class ssh {
require ssh::params
include ssh::install, ssh::config, ssh::service
}
```

then the contents of `ssh::params` would be processed before any other includes or resources in the `ssh` class. This is useful as a simple way to specify some less granular ordering to your manifests than metaparameter relationships, but it's not recommended as a regular approach. The reason it is not recommended is that Puppet does this by creating relationships between all the resources in the required class and the current class. This can lead to cyclical dependencies between resources. It's cleaner, more elegant and simpler to debug if you use metaparameters to specify the relationships between resources that need order.

In Listing 2-6 we can see what our template looks like.

Listing 2-6. The Postfix main.cf template

```
soft_bounce = no
command_directory = /usr/sbin
daemon_directory = /usr/libexec/postfix
mail_owner = postfix
myhostname = <%= hostname %>
mydomain = <%= domain %>
myorigin = $mydomain
mydestination = $myhostname, localhost.$mydomain, localhost, $mydomain
unknown_local_recipient_reject_code = 550
relay_domains = $mydestination
smtpd_reject_unlisted_recipient = yes
unverified_recipient_reject_code = 550
smtpd_banner = $myhostname ESMTP
setgid_group = postdrop
```

You can see a fairly typical Postfix main.cf configuration file with the addition of two ERB variables that use Facter facts to correctly populate the file. Each variable is enclosed in <%= %> and will be replaced with the fact values when Puppet runs. You can specify any variable in a template like this.

This is a very simple template and ERB has much of the same capabilities as Ruby, so you can build templates that take advantage of iteration, conditionals and other features. You can learn more about how to use templates further at http://docs.puppetlabs.com/guides/templating.html.

▓ **Tip** You can easily check the syntax of your ERB templates for correctness using the following command: erb -x -T '-' mytemplate.erb | ruby -c. Replace mytemplate.erb with the name of the template you want to check for syntax.

The postfix::service class

Next we have the postfix::service class, which manages our Postfix service:

```
class postfix::service {
  service { "postfix":
    ensure => running,
    hasstatus => true,
    hasrestart => true,
    enable => true,
    require => Class["postfix::config"],
  }
}
```

And finally, we have the core `postfix` class where we include all the other classes from our Postfix module:

```
class postfix {
    include postfix::install, postfix::config, postfix::service
}
```

We can then apply our `postfix` module to the `mail.example.com` node:

```
node "mail.example.com" {
    include base
    include postfix
}
```

Now when the `mail.example.com` node connects, Puppet will apply the configuration in both the base and `postfix` modules.

CLASS INHERITANCE

As with nodes, Puppet classes also have a simple inherit-and-override model. A subclass can inherit the values of a parent class and potentially override one or more of the values contained in the parent. This allows you to specify a generic class and override specific values in subclasses that are designed to suit some nodes, for example:

```
class bind::server {
        service {
                "bind":
                hasstatus => true,
                hasrestart => true,
                enable => true,
        }
}

class bind::server::enabled inherits bind::server {
        Service["bind"] { ensure => running, enable => true }
}
class bind::server::disabled inherits bind::server {
        Service["bind"] { ensure => stopped, enable => false }
}
```

Here, class `bind::server` is the parent class and defines a service that controls the `bind` service. It uses the service resource type to `enable` the `bind` service at boot time and specify the service must be stopped. We then specify two new subclasses, called `bind::server::enabled` and `bind::server::disabled`, which inherit the `bind::server` class. They override the `ensure` and `enable` attributes, and specify that the `bind` service must be running for all nodes with the `bind::server::enabled` subclass included. If we wish to disable `bind` on some nodes, then we need to simply include `bind::server::disabled` rather than `bind::server::enabled`. The use of class inheritance allows us to declare the bind service resource in one location, the bind::server class, and achieve the desired behavior of enabling or disabling the service without completely re-declaring the bind service resource. This organization structure also ensures we avoid duplicate resource declarations, remembering that a resource can only be declared once.

You can also add values to attributes in subclasses, like so:

```
class bind {
        service { "bind": require => Package["bind"] }
}

class bind::server inherits bind {
        Service["bind"] { require +> Package["bind-libs"] }
}
```

Here we have defined the proxy class containing the bind service, which in turn requires the bind package to be installed. We have then created a subclass called bind::server that inherits the bind service but adds an additional package, bind-libs, to the require metaparameter. To do this, we use the +> operator. After this addition, the bind service would now functionally look like this:

```
service { "bind":
        require => [ Package["bind"], Package["bind-libs"] ]
}
```

We can also unset particular values in subclasses using the undef attribute value.

```
class bind {
        service { "bind": require => Package["bind"] }
}

class bind::client inherits bind {
        Service["bind"] { require => undef }
}
```

Here, we again have the bind class with the bind service, which requires the bind package. In the subclass, though, we have removed the require attribute using the undef attribute value.

It is important to remember that class inheritance suffers from the same issues as node inheritance: variables are maintained in the scope they are defined in, and are not overridden. You can learn more at http://projects.puppetlabs.com/projects/1/wiki/Frequently_Asked_Questions#Class+Inheritance+and+Variable+Scope.

Managing MySQL with the mysql Module

Our next challenge is managing MySQL on our Solaris host, db.example.com. To do this we're going to create a third module called mysql. We create our module structure as follows:

```
mysql
mysql/files/my.cnf
mysql/manifests/init.pp
mysql/manifests/install.pp
mysql/manifests/config.pp
```

```
mysql/manifests/service.pp
mysql/templates/
```

The mysql::install class

Let's quickly walk through the classes to create, starting with mysql::install.

```
class mysql::install {
  package { [ "mysql5", "mysql5client", "mysql5rt", "mysql5test", "mysql5devel" ]:
    ensure => present,
    require => User["mysql"],
}

  user { "mysql":
    ensure => present,
    comment => "MySQL user",
    gid => "mysql",
    shell => "/bin/false",
    require => Group["mysql"],
}

  group { "mysql":
    ensure => present,
  }
}
```

You can see that we've used two new resource types in our mysql::install class, User and Group. We also created a mysql group and then a user and added that user, using the gid attribute, to the group we created. We then added the appropriate require metaparameters to ensure they get created in the right order.

The mysql::config class

Next, we add our mysql::config class:

```
class mysql::config {
  file { "/opt/csw/mysql5/my.cnf":
    ensure = > present,
    source => "puppet:///modules/mysql/my.cnf",
    owner => "mysql",
    group => "mysql",
    require => Class["mysql::install"],
    notify => Class["mysql::service"],
  }

  file { "/opt/csw/mysql5/var":
    group => "mysql",
    owner => "mysql",
    recurse => true,
    require => File["/opt/csw/mysql5/my.cnf"],
  }
}
```

You can see we've added a File resource to manage our /opt/csw/mysql5 directory. By specifying the directory as the title of the resource and setting the recurse attribute to true, we are asking Puppet to recurse through this directory and all directories underneath it and change the owner and group of all objects found inside them to mysql.

The mysql::service class

Then we add our mysql::service class:

```
class mysql::service {
  service { "cswmysql5":
    ensure => running,
    hasstatus => true,
    hasrestart => true,
    enabled => true,
    require => Class["mysql::config"],
  }
}
```

Our last class is our mysql class, contained in the init.pp file where we load all the required classes for this module:

```
class mysql {
  include mysql::install, mysql::config, mysql::service
}
```

Lastly, we can apply our mysql module to the db.example.com node.

```
node "db.example.com" {
  include base
  include mysql
}
```

Now, when the db.example.com node connects, Puppet will apply the configuration in both the base and mysql modules.

AUDITING

In addition to the normal mode of changing configuration (and the --noop mode of modelling the proposed configuration), Puppet has a new audit mode that was introduced in version 2.6.0. A normal Puppet resource controls the state you'd like a configuration item to be in, like this for example:

```
file { '/etc/hosts':
    owner => 'root',
    group => 'root',
    mode => 0660,
}
```

This file resource specifies that the /etc/hosts file should be owned by the root user and group and have permissions set to 0660. Every time Puppet runs, it will check that this file's settings are correct and make changes if they are not. In audit mode, however, Puppet merely checks the state of the resource and reports differences back. It is configured using the audit metaparameter.

Using this new metaparameter we can specify our resource like this:

```
file { '/etc/hosts':
  audit => [ owner, group, mode ],
}
```

Now, instead of changing each value (though you can also add and mix attributes to change it, if you wish), Puppet will generate auditing log messages, which are available in Puppet reports (see Chapter 9):

```
audit change: previously recorded value owner root has been changed to owner daemon
```

This allows you to track any changes that occur on resources under management on your hosts. You can specify this audit metaparameter for any resource and all their attributes, and track users, groups, files, services and the myriad of other resources Puppet can manage.

You can specify the special value of all to have Puppet audit every attribute of a resource rather than needing to list all possible attributes, like so:

```
file { '/etc/hosts':
  audit => all,
}
```

You can also combine the audited resources with managed resources, allowing you to manage some configuration items and simply track others. It is important to remember though, unlike many file integrity systems, that your audit state is not protected by a checksum or the like and is stored on the client. Future releases plan to protect and centralise this state data.

Managing Apache and Websites

As you're starting to see a much more complete picture of our Puppet configuration, we come to managing Apache, Apache virtual hosts and their websites. We start with our module layout:

```
apache
apache/files/
apache/manifests/init.pp
apache/manifests/install.pp
apache/manifests/service.pp
apache/manifests/vhost.pp
apache/templates/vhost.conf.erb
```

The apache::install class

Firstly, we install Apache via the apache::install class:

```
class apache::install {
  package { [ "apache2" ]:
```

```
    ensure => present,
  }
}
```

This class currently just installs Apache on an Ubuntu host; we could easily add an apache::params class in the style of our SSH module to support multiple platforms.

The apache::service class

For this module we're going to skip a configuration class, because we can just use the default Apache configuration. Let's move right to an apache::service class to manage the Apache service itself.

```
class apache::service {
  service { "apache2":
    ensure => running,
    hasstatus => true,
    hasrestart => true,
    enable => true,
    require => Class["apache::install"],
  }
}
```

This has allowed us to manage Apache, but how are we going to configure individual websites? To do this we're going to use a new syntax, the definition.

The Apache definition

Definitions are also collections of resources like classes, but unlike classes they can be specified and are evaluated multiple times on a host. They also accept parameters.

▓ **Note** Remember that classes are singletons. They can be included multiple times on a node, but they will only be evaluated ONCE. A definition, because it takes parameters, can be declared multiple times and each new declaration will be evaluated.

We create a definition using the define syntax, as shown in Listing 2-7.

Listing 2-7. The First Definition

```
define apache::vhost( $port, $docroot, $ssl=true, $template='apache/vhost.conf.erb',
$priority, $serveraliases = '' ) {

  include apache

  file {"/etc/apache2/sites-enabled/${priority}-${name}":
    content => template($template),
    owner => 'root',
    group => 'root',
    mode => '777',
    require => Class["apache::install"],
```

```
    notify => Class["apache::service"],
  }
}
```

We gave a definition a title (apache::vhost) and then specified a list of potential variables. Variables can be specified as a list, and any default values specified, for example $ssl=true. Defaults will be overridden if the parameter is specified when the definition is used.

Inside the definition we can specify additional resources or classes, for example here we've included the apache class that ensures all required Apache configuration will be performed prior to our definition being evaluated. This is because it doesn't make sense to create an Apache VirtualHost if we don't have Apache installed and ready to serve content.

In addition to the apache class, we've added a basic file resource which manages Apache site files contained in the /etc/apache2/sites-enabled directory. The title of each file is constructed using the priority parameter, and the title of our definition is specified using the $name variable.

■ **Tip** The $name variable contains the name, also known as the title, of a declared defined resource. This is the value of the string before the colon when declaring the defined resource.

This file resource's content attribute is specified by a template, the specific template being the value of the $template parameter. Let's look at a fairly simple ERB template for an Apache VirtualHost in Listing 2-8.

Listing 2-8. VirtualHost Template

```
NameVirtualHost *:<%= port %>
<VirtualHost *:<%= port %>>
  ServerName <%= name %>
<%if serveraliases.is_a? Array -%>
<% serveraliases.each do |name| -%><%= "  ServerAlias #{name}\n" %><% end -%>
<% elsif serveraliases != '' -%>
<%= "  ServerAlias #{serveraliases}" -%>
<% end -%>
  DocumentRoot <%= docroot %>
  <Directory <%= docroot %>>
    Options Indexes FollowSymLinks MultiViews
    AllowOverride None
    Order allow,deny
    allow from all
  </Directory>
  ErrorLog /var/log/apache2/<%= name %>_error.log
  LogLevel warn
  CustomLog /var/log/apache2/<%= name %>_access.log combined
  ServerSignature On
</VirtualHost>
```

Each parameter specified in the definition is used, including the $name variable to name the virtual host we're creating.

You can also see some embedded Ruby in our ERB template:

```
<%if serveraliases.is_a? Array -%>
<% serveraliases.each do |name| -%><%= "  ServerAlias #{name}\n" %><% end -%>
<% elsif serveraliases != '' -%>
<%= "  ServerAlias #{serveraliases}" -%>
<% end -%>
```

Here we've added some logic to the serveraliases parameter. If that parameter is an array of values, then create each value as a new server alias; if it's a single value, then create only one alias.

Let's now see how we would use this definition and combine our definition and template:

```
apache::vhost { 'www.example.com':
  port => 80,
  docroot => '/var/www/www.example.com',
  ssl => false,
  priority => 10,
  serveraliases => 'home.example.com',
}
```

Here we have used our definition much the same way we would specify a resource by declaring the apache::vhost definition and passing it a name, www.example.com (which is also the value of the $name variable). We've also specified values for the required parameters. Unless a default is already specified for a parameter, you need to specify a value for every parameter of a definition otherwise Puppet will return an error. We could also override parameters, for example by specifying a different template:

```
template => 'apache/another_vhost_template.erb',
```

So in our current example, the template would result in a VirtualHost definition that looks like Listing 2-9.

Listing 2-9. *The VirtualHost Configuration File*

```
NameVirtualHost *:80
<VirtualHost *:80>
  ServerName www.example.com
  ServerAlias home.example.com
  DocumentRoot /var/www/www.example.com
  <Directory /var/www/www.example.com>
    Options Indexes FollowSymLinks MultiViews
    AllowOverride None
    Order allow,deny
    allow from all
  </Directory>
  ErrorLog /var/log/apache2/www.example.com_error.log
  LogLevel warn
  CustomLog /var/log/apache2/www.example.com_access.log combined
  ServerSignature On
</VirtualHost>
```

The final class in our module is the apache class in the init.pp file, which includes our Apache classes:

```
class apache {
  include apache::install, apache::service
}
```

You can see we've included our three classes but not the definition, apache::vhost. This is because of some module magic called "autoloading." You learned how everything in modules is automatically imported into Puppet, so you don't need to use the import directive. Puppet scans your module and loads any .pp file in the manifests directory that is named after the class it contains, for example the install.pp file contains the apache::install class and so is autoloaded.

The same thing happens with definitions: The vhost.pp file contains the definition apache::vhost, and Puppet autoloads it. However, as we declare definitions, for example calling apache::vhost where we need it, we don't need to do an include apache::vhost because calling it implies inclusion.

Next, we include our classes into our www.example.com node and call the apache::vhost definition to create the www.example.com website.

```
node "www.example.com" {
  include base
  include apache

  apache::vhost { 'www.example.com':
    port => 80,
    docroot => '/var/www/www.example.com',
    ssl => false,
    priority => 10,
    serveraliases => 'home.example.com',
  }
}
```

We could now add additional web servers easily and create additional Apache VirtualHosts by calling the apache::vhost definition again, for example:

```
apache::vhost { 'another.example.com':
    port => 80,
    docroot => '/var/www/another.example.com',
    ssl => false,
    priority => 10,
}
```

Managing Puppet with the Puppet Module

In our very last module we're going to show you Puppet being self-referential, so you can manage Puppet with Puppet itself. To do this we create another module, one called puppet, with a structure as follows:

```
puppet
puppet/files/
puppet/manifests/init.pp
puppet/manifests/install.pp
```

```
puppet/manifests/config.pp
puppet/manifests/params.pp
puppet/manifests/service.pp
puppet/templates/puppet.conf.erb
```

Our first class will be the puppet::install class which installs the Puppet client package.

```
class puppet::install {
  package { "puppet" :
    ensure => present,
  }
}
```

All of the operating systems we're installing on call the Puppet package puppet, so we're not going to use a variable here.

We do, however, need a couple of variables for our Puppet module, so we add a puppet::params class.

```
class puppet::params {
  $puppetserver = "puppet.example.com"
}
```

For the moment, this class only contains a Puppet server variable that specifies the fully-qualified domain name (FQDN) of our Puppet master.

Now we create our puppet::config class:

```
class puppet::config {

include puppet::params

  file { "/etc/puppet/puppet.conf":
    ensure = > present,
    content => template("puppet/puppet.conf.erb"),
    owner => "puppet",
    group => "puppet",
    require => Class["puppet::install"],
    notify => Class["puppet::service"],
  }
}
```

This class contains a single file resource that loads the puppet.conf.erb template. It also includes the puppet::params class so as to make available the variables defined in that class. Let's take a look at the contents of our template too:

```
[main]
    user = puppet
    group = puppet
    report = true
    reports = log,store
```

```
[master]
    certname = <%= puppetserver %>

[agent]
    pluginsync = false
    report = true
    server = <%= puppetserver %>
```

This is a very simple template, which we can then expand upon, or you can easily modify to add additional options or customize for your own purposes. You'll notice we've included configuration for both our master and the client. We're going to manage one puppet.conf file rather than a separate one for master and client. This is mostly because it's easy and because it doesn't add much overhead to our template.

We can then add the puppet::service class to manage the Puppet client daemon.

```
class puppet::service {
  service { "puppet":
    ensure => running,
    hasstatus => true,
    hasrestart => true,
    enable => true,
    require => Class["puppet::install"],
  }
}
```

We can then create an init.pp that includes the puppet class and the sub-classes we've just created:

```
class puppet {
  include puppet::install, puppet::config, puppet::service
}
```

Just stopping here would create a module that manages Puppet on all our clients. All we need to do, then, is to include this module on all of our client nodes, and Puppet will be able to manage itself. But we're also going to extend our module to manage the Puppet master as well. To do this, we're going to deviate slightly from our current design and put all the resources required to manage the Puppet master into a single class, called puppet::master:

```
class puppet::master {

include puppet
include puppet::params

package { "puppet-server":
  ensure => installed,
}

service { "puppetmasterd":
    ensure => running,
    hasstatus => true,
    hasrestart => true,
    enable => true,
```

```
    require => File["/etc/puppet/puppet.conf"],
  }
}
```

You can see that our class puppet::master includes the classes puppet and puppet::params. This will mean all the preceding Puppet configuration will be applied, in addition to the new package and service resources we've defined in this class.

We can now add this new module to our nodes, leaving them looking like this:

```
class base {
  include sudo, ssh, puppet
}

node 'puppet.example.com' {
  include base
  include puppet::master
}

node 'web.example.com' {
  include base
  include apache

  apache::vhost { 'www.example.com':
    port => 80,
    docroot => '/var/www/www.example.com',
    ssl => false,
    priority => 10,
    serveraliases => 'home.example.com',
  }
}

node 'db.example.com' {
  include base
  include mysql
}

node 'mail.example.com' {
  include base
  include postfix
}
```

We've added the puppet module to the base class we created earlier. This will mean it's added to all the nodes that include base. We've also added the puppet::master class, which adds the additional resources needed to configure the Puppet master, to the puppet.example.com node.

Summary

In this chapter, you've been introduced to quite a lot of Puppet's basic features and language, including:

- How to structure modules, including examples of modules to manage SSH, Postfix, MySQL and Apache.

- How to use language constructs like selectors, arrays and case statements

- A greater understanding of files and templates

- Definitions that allow you to manage configuration, such as Apache VirtualHosts

- Variable scoping

You've also seen how a basic Puppet configuration in a simple environment might be constructed, including some simple modules to manage your configuration. Also, Puppet Forge contains a large collection of pre-existing modules that you can either use immediately or modify to suit your environment.

In the next chapter, we'll look at how to scale Puppet beyond the basic Webrick server, using tools like Mongrel and Passenger and allowing you to manage larger numbers of hosts.

Resources

- Puppet Documentation: `http://docs.puppetlabs.com`

- Puppet Wiki: `http://projects.puppetlabs.com/projects/puppet/wiki`

- Puppet Forge: `http://forge.puppetlabs.com`

CHAPTER 3

■ ■ ■

Working with Environments

We've introduced you to installing and configuring Puppet. In this chapter, we show how you might integrate Puppet into your organization's workflow. This will allow you to use Puppet to make changes and manage your infrastructure in a logical and stable way.

To do this, we introduce a Puppet concept called "environments." Environments allow you to define, maintain and separate your infrastructure into appropriate divisions. In most organizations, you already have some of these divisions: development, testing, staging, pre-production and others. Just like a set of production, testing, and development systems, which are separated from one another to effectively isolate risky changes from production services, Puppet environments are designed to isolate changes to the configuration from impacting critical production infrastructure.

In this chapter we also build upon the concept of modules, which we introduced in Chapters 1 and 2. We show you how to configure environments on your Puppet masters and how to control which agents connect to which environment. Each agent can connect to a specific environment that will contain a specific set of configuration.

Finally, we exercise the workflow of making changes using our version control system, testing those changes in a safe and easy way using environments, then promoting the tested changes to the production environment in Puppet.

In order to demonstrate all of this to you, we create another host for the Example.com Pty Ltd organization we first introduced in Chapter 1. This new host is called mailtest.example.com. This host has been introduced to allow Example.com to test changes to their email server without impacting the production mail server. You can see the new node in Figure 3-1.

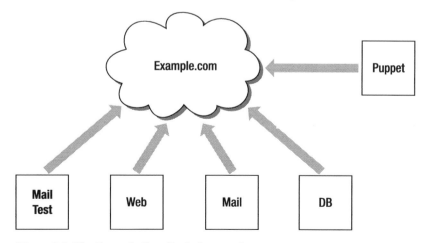

Figure 3-1. The Example.Com Pty Ltd network

65

To get started, we've installed the Red Hat Enterprise Linux operating system on mailtest.example.com in order to match the operating system Puppet already manages on mail.example.com. As we already have configuration to manage the mail.example.com host, we don't need to create any new manifests - we can re-use the existing ones to configure our new mailtest.example.com host.

■ **Note** This chapter starts to demonstrate the power of Puppet for re-using configuration: Rather than starting a new configuration from scratch, we can use existing Puppet manifests to create a new mail server.

Configuring Puppet Environments

To configure Puppet environments, you need to add them to the Puppet master's configuration. If you add each environment to the Puppet master, then each Puppet agent can request a specific environment when requesting a catalog from the master.

The first step to configure your Puppet master and agents to use environments is to add a stanza in the /etc/puppet.conf configuration file on the Puppet master for each environment you want to support. Let's do this now, by creating the three environments shown in Listing 3-1.

Listing 3-1. Puppet Master environments in puppet.conf

```
[main]
  modulepath = $confdir/modules
  manifest = $confdir/manifests/site.pp

[development]
  modulepath = $confdir/environments/development/modules
  manifest = $confdir/environments/development/manifests/site.pp

[testing]
  modulepath = $confdir/environments/testing/modules
  manifest = $confdir/environments/testing/manifests/site.pp
```

As you can see, each environment section of the puppet configuration file defines two settings, modulepath and manifest. The modulepath setting defines the path to the modules that will apply to each environment, and the manifest option specifies the site.pp file that applies to that environment. Recall from Chapter 1 that site.pp is the file that tells Puppet which configuration to load for our clients. These settings allow each environment to have a distinct set of modules and configuration.

■ **Note** When setting up environments, the Puppet master process should be restarted in order to activate configuration changes. As described in Chapter 1, the restart process depends on how Puppet is installed on the master. Most systems include an init script to accomplish this task.

In Chapters 1 and 2, we introduced you to building modules to store your Puppet configuration. In order to fully utilize environments, your Puppet manifests should be organized into modules. In this chapter, we use the modules we've created to manage our production environment, the main environment defined in Listing 3-1.

Populating the New Environments

Once you've defined the multiple environments on the Puppet master server, you need to populate these new search paths with the Puppet modules and manifests you've already created in production. In the "Version Controlling Your Modules" section of Chapter 2, our hypothetical company configured Puppet modules using the Git version control system. We'll expand on the file organization and introduce a strategy to manage and migrate changes between Puppet environments.

▨ **Note** If you have not yet installed Git and would like to do so now, please refer back to the Git installation information in Chapter 2.

We will use Git to make sure each of our three new environments; main (or production), development and testing will receive an identical copy of our production environment. The version control system will also allow us to easily keep these three environments synchronized when necessary, while also allowing them to diverge when we want to try out new changes. Three environments with identical modules and manifests will allow us to quickly make changes in the development or testing environment without impacting the production environment. If we're satisfied, we can easily merge the changes into production.

▨ **Note** Many organizations with multiple people committing changes to the Puppet configuration will benefit from a code review process. Information about the code review process used by the Puppet development community is available at: http://projects.puppetlabs.com/projects/puppet/wiki/Development_Development_ Lifecycle .

In Chapter 2, we initialized the /etc/puppet/modules directory as a Git repository. Once a Git repository exists, it may be cloned one or more times. Once there are multiple clones, changes to any of the repositories may be fetched and merged into any other repository.

Creating a Clone

Let's create a clone of the /etc/puppet/modules Git repository for the development and testing environments now.

First, you need to create the directory structure necessary to contain the new module search path:

```
$ cd /etc/puppet
$ mkdir -p environments/{development,testing}
```

Next, clone the original module repository you created in Chapter 2 into your development environment:

```
$ cd /etc/puppet/environments/development
$ git clone ../../modules
Initialized empty Git repository in /etc/puppet/environments/development/modules/.git/
```

This command makes a new copy of the Git repository, called a "clone," and automatically sets up a reference to the repository we cloned from. This reference, named "origin," refers to the original repository this repository was cloned from. The origin is actually the repository in the production Puppet environment, so you can add another name to be clear when you fetch updates:

```
$ cd /etc/puppet/environments/development/modules
$ git remote add production /etc/puppet/modules
$ git remote -v
production       /etc/puppet/modules (fetch)
production       /etc/puppet/modules (push)
```

As you can see, we've added a remote reference to the production environment module repository in the development environment's module repository. This remote reference allows Git to fetch changes.

Similar to the development environment you just set up, you'll also clone the production environment modules into a testing environment.

```
$ cd /etc/puppet/environments/testing
$ git clone ../../modules
Initialized empty Git repository in /etc/puppet/environments/testing/modules/.git/
$ cd modules
$ git remote add production /etc/puppet/modules
$ git remote add development /etc/puppet/environments/development/modules
```

Notice how we've also added the development repository as a remote in the testing environment repository. This will allow you to fetch changes you make in the development repository to the testing repository.

■ **Tip** For additional information on a branch and merge strategy using environments and Subversion rather than Git, please see `http://projects.puppetlabs.com/projects/1/wiki/Branch_Testing`.

Making Changes to the Development Environment

Now that you have your three environments populated with the same Puppet modules, you can make changes without affecting the production environment. We're going to use a basic workflow of editing and committing changes in the development branch first. This mirrors the common development life cycle of moving from development to testing and finally to production. We'll start with running a Puppet agent in the development environment to test the change we've made. Then, if everything goes well in the development environment, you can merge this change into testing or into production.

▓ **Tip** In large Puppet setups where changes from multiple groups of people need to be managed, it is common to run a selection of hosts against the testing environment. Periodically, the production environment repository will be synchronized against the testing environment.

We're going to edit the Postfix configuration file template we created in Chapter 2 to explore how Puppet isolates the three environments we've created. We'll edit the file main.cf.erb in the development environment and then run the Puppet agent in this environment to see the change. We'll also run the Puppet agent in the production environment, which we have not changed yet, and make sure our changes do not have any effect on production.

To start, edit the file main.cf.erb in /etc/puppet/environments/development/modules/postfix /templates/ using your favorite text editor and add a new line at the very top of the file to look like:

```
# This file managed by puppet: <%= this_will_fail %>
soft_bounce = no
command_directory = /usr/sbin
daemon_directory = /usr/libexec/postfix
mail_owner = postfix
myhostname = <%= hostname %>
mydomain = <%= domain %>
myorigin = $mydomain
mydestination = $myhostname, localhost.$mydomain, localhost, $mydomain
unknown_local_recipient_reject_code = 550
relay_domains = $mydestination
smtpd_reject_unlisted_recipient = yes
unverified_recipient_reject_code = 550
smtpd_banner = $myhostname ESMTP
setgid_group = postdrop
```

Now that you've made a change to the development environment, Git will let you know that the status of the repository has changed:

```
$ git status
# On branch master
# Changed but not updated:
#   (use "git add <file>..." to update what will be committed)
#   (use "git checkout -- <file>..." to discard changes in working directory)
#
#       modified:   main.cf.erb
#
no changes added to commit (use "git add" and/or "git commit -a")
```

Git has noticed that you've made a change to the main.cf.erb file and tells you this on the "modified" line. As we learned in Chapter 2, we must add files changed in the working directory to the index, and then commit the index to the repository. Before you do this, you should double-check to make sure the line you modified is what will actually be added in the new commit.

```
$ git diff
diff --git a/postfix/templates/main.cf.erb b/postfix/templates/main.cf.erb
index 3331237..2be61e0 100644
--- a/postfix/templates/main.cf.erb
+++ b/postfix/templates/main.cf.erb
@@ -1,3 +1,4 @@
+# This file managed by puppet: <%= this_will_fail %>
 soft_bounce = no
 command_directory = /usr/sbin
 daemon_directory = /usr/libexec/postfix
```

Notice the line beginning with the single plus sign. This indicates that you've added one line and this addition will be recorded when we commit the change, as we will with the git commit command:

```
$ git commit -a -m 'Updated postfix configuration template'
[master 0fb0463] Updated postfix configuration template
 1 files changed, 1 insertions(+), 1 deletions(-)
```

You've now successfully changed the development environment. But before testing the change on our mailtest.example.com system, let's review the environment configuration changes you've made to the Puppet Master.

- puppet.conf on the master now contains a development and testing section.

- The Puppet master process has been restarted to activate the change to puppet.conf.

- You updated modulepath and manifest in the development and testing section.

- You cloned the modules VCS repository to /etc/puppet/environments/{testing,development}/modules.

- You updated the postfix module and committed the change to the development repository.

Testing the New Environments with the Puppet Agent

Now that you have multiple environments configured on the Puppet master system and have made a change to the development environment, you're able to test this change using the Puppet agent.

In order to tell Puppet to use an environment other than production, use the environment configuration parameter or command line option:

```
$ puppet agent --noop --test --environment testing
```

▪ **Tip** Up through Puppet 2.6, the Puppet configuration on a node configures the environment that the node uses. The Puppet master does not directly control which environment a machine connects to. This may change in the future once issue #2834 is resolved; please watch `http://projects.puppetlabs.com/issues/2834` for up-to-date information. If you would like to manage the environment from the Puppet master, we recommend having Puppet manage the node's `puppet.conf` file and specify the `environment` parameter in the managed configuration file.

Running the Puppet agent on `mailtest.example.com` in the testing environment should produce the same results as running the agent in the production environment.

▪ **Tip** We recommend developing a habit of testing changes to Puppet using the `--noop` command line option. As mentioned in Chapter 1, the `--noop` option tells Puppet to check the current state of the system against the configuration catalog, but does it not manage the resources on the node. This provides a safe way determine if Puppet is going to make a change. It's also a unique feature of Puppet, compared to other tools.

You can switch between the production and testing environments by simply removing the environment command line option. The default environment is production (defined in the main stanza in the `puppet.conf` file); therefore, you need only leave the environment unspecified to switch back to the production environment.

```
$ puppet agent --noop --verbose -test
```

Notice how no resources are changing when switching between the two environments. This is because the testing environment is a clone of the production environment, and you have not made any changes to either of these two environments. In the last section, however, you made a change to Postfix module in the development environment, and we expect the Puppet agent to update the `main.cf` postfix configuration file with this change. Let's check the development environment now:

```
$ puppet agent --noop --verbose --test --environment development
err: Could not retrieve catalog from remote server: Error 400 on SERVER: Failed to parse↵
 template postfix/main.cf.erb: Could not find value for 'this_will_fail' at↵
 /etc/puppet/environments/development/modules/postfix/manifests/config.pp:17 on↵
 node mailtest.example.com
warning: Not using cache on failed catalog
err: Could not retrieve catalog; skipping run
```

Unlike the testing and production environment we ran the Puppet agent in, this run in the development environment resulted in an error. Such a bad error, in fact, that we didn't even receive a valid configuration catalog from the Puppet master. So what happened?

Notice that the error message returned by the Puppet master provides the exact line number in the manifest the error occurred on. On this line we're using the template we modified when we made a change to the development environment, and this change references a variable that we have not defined in the Puppet manifests. If we run the Puppet agent against the production environment, we can see everything is still OK:

```
$ puppet agent --test --noop
...
notice: Finished catalog run in 0.68 seconds
```

Let's go back and fix the problem with the ERB template by removing the reference to the undefined puppet variable this_will_fail. As you can see in the following file difference, we've fixed the problem in the first line of the template:

```
diff --git a/postfix/templates/main.cf.erb b/postfix/templates/main.cf.erb
index 3331237..241b4bb 100644
--- a/postfix/templates/main.cf.erb
+++ b/postfix/templates/main.cf.erb
@@ -1,3 +1,4 @@
+# This file managed by puppet.
 soft_bounce = no
 command_directory = /usr/sbin
 daemon_directory = /usr/libexec/postfix
```

Now, when we run Puppet agent in the development environment, we're no longer getting the error:

```
$ puppet agent --test --noop --environment development
```

This verification step allowed us to make changes and test them in an isolated environment without impacting Puppet nodes with their agent running against the production environment. Now that you're confident our change will not break production, you can commit the changes:

```
$  git add /etc/puppet/environments/development/modules/postfix/templates/main.cf.erb
$ git commit -m 'Added comment header, postfix main.cf is managed by puppet.'
Created commit d69bc30: Added comment header, postfix main.cf is managed by puppet.
 1 files changed, 2 insertions(+), 1 deletions(-)
```

In the next section, we examine the workflow of merging changes like this into the testing and production environments. This workflow helps teams of developers and system administrators work together while making changes to the system, without impacting production systems, through the use of Puppet environments.

Environment Branching and Merging

As you saw in the previous section, configuring multiple environments in Puppet requires three things:

- Modifying the puppet configuration file on the Puppet master

- Populating the directories specified in the modulepath

- Maintaining a set of version control working copies in each of those directories

One of the key benefits of version control systems is the ability to manage and organize the contributions from a group of people. In this section, we'll explore how a group of three people may use Puppet Environments, version control, and the concept of a "branch" to effectively coordinate and manage their changes to the configuration system. Branches are lines of independent development in a repository that share a common history. A branch could be a copy of our development environment with changes made to it; it shares a common history with the development environment but has a history of its own too. Branches allow multiple people to maintain copies of an environment, work on them independently and potentially combine changes between branches or back into the main line of development.

Expanding on our hypothetical company, imagine we have a small team of people working together: a system administrator, a developer and an operator. In this exercise, we'll explore how this team effectively makes changes that do not impact one another, can be merged into the main development and testing branch, and ultimately make their way to the production infrastructure.

Setting Up a Central Repository

Before the small group is able to work together in harmony, you'll need to make a few slight changes to the version control system. Git is unique compared to other version control systems, such as Subversion, in that each repository stands apart and is complete without the need to perform a checkout from a central repository. When working with a team, however, it is convenient to have a central place to store and track changes over time.

In this section, you'll clone a copy of the /etc/puppet/modules repository into /var/lib/puppet/git/modules.git and use this location as the "central" repository. It is central by convention only; there is technically nothing different about the repository that makes it any different from the other Git repositories we've been working with in this chapter. Once you have a repository designated as the central location, everyone will clone this repository and submit their changes back to it for review and testing. Let's go through this process now.

Creating a Bare Repository for the Modules

First, you need to create a "bare" repository containing your Puppet modules. A bare repository in Git is a repository with the history of commits, but no working copy. We want to create a bare repository to help make sure files aren't accidentally directly modified in the central location. Modifications should only happen through commits pushed to this location. We're going to perform these steps as the Puppet user, who is usually running as puppet, in order to help ensure file permissions and ownership remain consistent when different users are modifying the repository.

```
$ cd /var/lib/puppet
$ mkdir git
$ chown puppet:puppet git
$ sudo -H -u puppet -s
$ cd /var/lib/puppet/git
$ git clone --bare /etc/puppet/modules modules.git
Initialized empty Git repository in /var/lib/puppet/git/modules.git/
```

> ■ **Note** We recommend storing the central version control repository in the home directory of the Puppet user to start. This may vary from system to system, and may not be /var/lib/puppet on your platform.

Making Individual Changes

Once you have a central repository, it's time for everyone in the group to check out their own personal copies to work on. We recommend they do this in their home directories. Changes will be made there and submitted to the central repository for review. Let's first clone a repository for our system administrator, hereafter sysadmin:

```
sysadmin:~$ git clone puppet@puppet.example.com:git/modules.git
Initialized empty Git repository in ~/modules/.git/
remote: Counting objects: 36, done.
remote: Compressing objects: 100% (33/33), done.
remote: Total 36 (delta 0), reused 0 (delta 0)
Receiving objects: 100% (36/36), 5.58 KiB, done.
```

After cloning the repository from the central location, you can begin to make changes. In order to make sure you have the same changes you made to the main.cf.erb file in the previous section, pull the change made to the main.cf.erb file from the repository in /etc/puppet/environments/development/modules. You could directly fetch the change from the repository Puppet is using in /etc/puppet, but it may become confusing to manage what changes are located in which repositories.

To help coordinate with the rest of the team, instead push the change from the development repository into the central repository. This should be done using the puppet user account:

```
puppet:~$ cd /etc/puppet/environments/development/modules
puppet:development/modules$ git remote rm origin
puppet:development/modules$ git remote add origin puppet@puppet.example.com:git/modules.git
puppet:development/modules$ git push origin master:master
Counting objects: 9, done.
Compressing objects: 100% (4/4), done.
Writing objects: 100% (5/5), 499 bytes, done.
Total 5 (delta 2), reused 0 (delta 0)
To puppet@puppet.example.com:git/modules.git
   a13c3d8..d69bc30  master -> master

puppet:~$ cd /etc/puppet/environments/testing/modules
puppet:testing/modules$ git remote rm origin
puppet:testing/modules$ git remote add origin puppet@puppet.example.com:git/modules.git
puppet:~$ cd /etc/puppet/modules
puppet:/etc/puppet/modules$ git remote rm origin
puppet:/etc/puppet/modules$ git remote add origin puppet@puppet.example.com:git/modules.git
```

After executing these commands, you've updated each of the three Git repositories containing the production, testing, and development working copies to point at your fourth, central repository. The systems administrator now has a personal working copy which points to the central repository.

Developing a Change Using a Branch

In order to make a change, each team member should create a new Git branch for the topic he or she is working on and make their changes in this branch. A topic branch will allow other team members to easily fetch all of their work as a self-contained bundle, rather than requiring them to sort through each commit or set of commits. This will also make it easier to merge each team member's contributions into the master branch when necessary, as you can see in Listing 3-2.

Listing 3-2. Merging in changes

```
sysadmin:~$ cd modules

sysadmin:~/modules$ git fetch origin
From puppet@puppet.example.com:git/modules
   a13c3d8..d69bc30  master      -> origin/master

sysadmin:~/modules$ git checkout master
Already on "master"
Your branch is behind the tracked remote branch 'origin/master' by 1 commit,
and can be fast-forwarded.

sysadmin:~/modules$ git merge origin/master
Updating a13c3d8..d69bc30
Fast forward
 postfix/templates/main.cf.erb |    3 ++-
 1 files changed, 2 insertions(+), 1 deletions(-)
```

As you can see, we've pushed the change to main.cf.erb into the central repository. The sysadmin was able to update her personal copy with this change.

The sysadmin now has her copy and is able to push and pull changes in the central repository, but what about the developer and operator? They should each clone a copy of the central repository URL, puppet@puppet.example.com:git/modules.git, into their home directory. We'll run through the situation where the operator needs to make and test a change to the sshd configuration file, while the developer needs to make and test a change to the Postfix configuration files. These two changes will be tested independently in the development environment and then merged together in the testing environment.

■ **Tip** SSH Keys and Agent Forwarding should be employed when using Git in order to increase security, keep file ownership consistent, and manage the central code using the Puppet user. To accomplish this, people with authorization to change Puppet could have their public key added to ~puppet/.ssh/authorized_keys. For more information about SSH public keys, please see: http://www.debian-administration.org/articles/530

Making Changes to the sshd Configuration File

We'll go through the changes to Secure Shell or SSH the operator needs to make first. The operator is working specifically to make sure only members of certain groups are allowed to log in to the system using SSH.

To begin, you should create a topic branch to work on this problem. In Git, unlike other version control systems, a branch does not create a new directory path in the working directory of the repository. Instead, Git checks out the branch into the base directory of the repository.

Let's create a topic branch based on the current master branch in our central "origin" repository, like so:

```
operator:~/modules $ git checkout -b operator/ssh origin/master
Branch operator/ssh set up to track remote branch refs/remotes/origin/master.
Switched to a new branch "operator/ssh"
operator:~/modules $ git branch
* operator/ssh
  Master
```

Notice that the operator now has two branches in their personal ~/modules/ Git repository. Using a topic branch, we are free to modify things without worrying about impacting the work of the rest of the team. The branch provides a reference point to revert any of the changes we make to the Puppet configuration. Similarly, the development, production, and testing environments in the /etc/puppet directory on the Puppet master must explicitly check out this new branch in order for our changes to affect any of the Puppet agent systems. This strategy is much less risky and easier to coordinate with team members than directly editing the files contained in the /etc/puppet directory.

Now that the operator has his or her own branch, we're ready to make a change. We're going to add two lines using two commits to illustrate the history tracking features of a version control system.

First, add the groups who should have access to the machine. To start, only the wheel group should be allowed to log in, so add the following lines to the sshd_config template:

```
operator:~/modules $ git diff
diff --git a/ssh/files/sshd_config b/ssh/files/sshd_config
index 7d7f4b4..1fd84e5 100644
--- a/ssh/files/sshd_config
+++ b/ssh/files/sshd_config
@@ -3,4 +3,5 @@ Protocol 2
 SyslogFacility AUTHPRIV
 PermitRootLogin no
 PasswordAuthentication yes
+AllowGroups wheel adm
 UsePAM yes
```

As you can see, we've added a single line to the file ~/modules/ssh/files/sshd_config in the personal clone of the repository in the operator's home directory. We must commit and push this change into the central repository, but we haven't tested it yet so we should be careful and not merge the branch we're working on, operator/ssh, into the master branch yet.

```
operator:~/modules $ git commit -a -m 'Added AllowGroups to sshd_config'
Created commit eea4fbb: Added AllowGroups to sshd_config
 1 files changed, 1 insertions(+), 0 deletions(-)

operator:~/modules $ git push origin operator/ssh:operator/ssh
Counting objects: 9, done.
Compressing objects: 100% (4/4), done.
Writing objects: 100% (5/5), 454 bytes, done.
Total 5 (delta 2), reused 0 (delta 0)
```

```
To puppet@puppet.example.com:git/modules.git
 * [new branch]      operator/ssh -> operator/ssh
```

The git push command the operator used creates a new branch in the central repository with the same name as the topic branch the operator is working on in his or her home directory. This is important to prevent untested changes from making their way into the master branch. Once we've pushed the new branch to the central repository, we should test the new branch in the development environment.

▪ **Note** There is no limit to the number of environments you can configure on the central Puppet master. Many large teams find it beneficial to create per-contributor environments in addition to the standard development, testing and production environments. Per-contributor environments allow each person to test their own branches without interfering with the development environments of other individuals.

```
puppet:~ $ cd /etc/puppet/environments/development/modules
puppet:modules $ git fetch origin
remote: Counting objects: 14, done.
remote: Compressing objects: 100% (8/8), done.
remote: Total 10 (delta 4), reused 0 (delta 0remote: )
Unpacking objects: 100% (10/10), done.
From puppet@puppet.example.com:git/modules
   d69bc30..fa9812f  master      -> origin/master
 * [new branch]      operator/ssh -> origin/operator/ssh
puppet:modules $ git checkout -b operator/ssh origin/operator/ssh
Branch operator/ssh set up to track remote branch refs/remotes/origin/operator/ssh.
Switched to a new branch "operator/ssh"
```

Testing the Puppet Agent Against the sshd Configuration File

Now that we've switched to our new topic branch in the development environment, we're able to test the Puppet agent against the development environment.

```
puppet:~ $  puppet agent --test --environment development --noop
info: Caching catalog for scd.puppetlabs.vm
info: Applying configuration version '1289751259'
--- /etc/ssh/sshd_config       2010-11-14 08:16:45.000000000 -0800
+++ /tmp/puppet-file.13997.0    2010-11-14 08:16:57.000000000 -0800
@@ -3,4 +3,5 @@
 SyslogFacility AUTHPRIV
 PermitRootLogin no
 PasswordAuthentication yes
+AllowGroups wheel adm
 UsePAM yes
notice: /Stage[main]/Ssh::Config/File[/etc/ssh/sshd_config]/content: is↵
 {md5}9d4c3fba3434a46528b41a49b70b60e4, should be {md5}da54f2cdc309faf6d813a080783a31f6 (noop)
```

```
info: /Stage[main]/Ssh::Config/File[/etc/ssh/sshd_config]: Scheduling refresh of Service[sshd]
notice: /Stage[main]/Ssh::Service/Service[sshd]: Would have triggered 'refresh' from 1 events
notice: Finished catalog run in 0.39 seconds
```

Notice that this Puppet agent run is running in noop mode, and that the agent tells us it would have changed /etc/ssh/sshd_config by inserting the line we just committed to the branch operator/ssh and checked out in the development environment's repository on the Puppet master.

You're able to verify that the production environment remains unchanged, just like we did in the "Making Changes to the Development Environment" section when we updated the Postfix configuration file. Simply remove the environment command line option to cause the agent to execute in the default production environment again:

```
puppet:~ $ puppet agent --test --noop
info: Caching catalog for scd.puppetlabs.vm
info: Applying configuration version '1289752071'
notice: Finished catalog run in 0.33 seconds
```

Making Changes to the Postfix Configuration File

While the system operator is working on the change to the sshd_config file, the developer in our hypothetical company is working on a change to the Postfix configuration file. Just like the operator, he'll need a personal copy of the central repository we set up at puppet@puppet.example.com:git/modules.git in his home directory.

Once the developer has cloned his personal copy of the central repository, he's able to make his change to the Postfix configuration file. He'll also use a branch to track his changes and make it easy to merge into the testing branch for use in the testing environment. Finally, after testing, he'll use the tag feature of the version control system to cut a new release of the configuration used in production, then check out this tag in the repository used by the production Puppet environment.

To start, the developer creates his topic branch from the development branch named master. Note that the changes his teammate, the operator, has made have not yet been merged into the master branch, so the developer does not have them. We cover the process of merging multiple changes together when we merge both of these changes into the testing branch in the next section.

```
developer:~ $ cd ~/modules
developer:~/modules $ git checkout -b developer/postfix master
Switched to a new branch "developer/postfix"
```

Now that the developer has his own topic branch, he's free to change the code without impacting the work of anyone else on the team. His changes can be discarded or merged at a later point in time. Let's look at his changes to the Postfix configuration file and how he committed them into the version control system:

```
$ git log --abbrev-commit --pretty=oneline master..HEAD
7acf23d... Updated config.pp to use $module_name
0c164f6... Added manual change warning to postfix config
```

Using the git log command, you're able to see the developer has made two commits since he created his topic from the main master development branch. This specific command displays the series of commits from the master development branch to the tip of the current topic branch. You're able to use the git log command again to see exactly what the developer changed in these two commits, as shown in Listing 3-3.

Listing 3-3. Listing Git changes

```
developer:~/modules $ git log --summary -p --stat master..
commit 7acf23dc50774aee1139e43aec5b1e8f60fa9da9
Author: Devevloper <developer@example.com>
Date:   Sun Nov 14 09:45:16 2010 -0800

    Updated config.pp to use $module_name

    The $module_name variable has been introduced in Puppet
    2.6 and makes for easily renamed puppet modules without
    having to refactor much of the code.
---
 postfix/manifests/config.pp |    4 ++--
 1 files changed, 2 insertions(+), 2 deletions(-)

diff --git a/postfix/manifests/config.pp b/postfix/manifests/config.pp
index 9feb947..471822c 100644
--- a/postfix/manifests/config.pp
+++ b/postfix/manifests/config.pp
@@ -7,14 +7,14 @@ class postfix::config {

    file { "/etc/postfix/master.cf":
      ensure  => present,
-     source  => "puppet:///modules/postfix/master.cf",
+     source  => "puppet:///modules/${module_name}/master.cf",
      require => Class["postfix::install"],
      notify  => Class["postfix::service"],
    }

    file { "/etc/postfix/main.cf":
      ensure  => present,
-     content => template("postfix/main.cf.erb"),
+     content => template("${module_name/main.cf.erb"),
      require => Class["postfix::install"],
      notify  => Class["postfix::service"],
    }

commit 0c164f676da64cec5e6d02ac5cb8a60229e60219
Author: Developer <developer@example.com>
Date:   Sun Nov 14 09:42:17 2010 -0800

    Added manual change warning to postfix config
---
 postfix/files/master.cf |    4 +++-
 1 files changed, 3 insertions(+), 1 deletions(-)

diff --git a/postfix/files/master.cf b/postfix/files/master.cf
index 280f3da..7482d4c 100644
```

```
--- a/postfix/files/master.cf
+++ b/postfix/files/master.cf
@@ -1,3 +1,5 @@
+# This file managed by puppet.  Manual changes will be reverted.
+#
 #
 # Postfix master process configuration file.  For details on the format
 # of the file, see the master(5) manual page (command: "man 5 master").
```

Reviewing his changes, the developer notices he made a typographical mistake in the postfix configuration file and decides to fix this problem. In the second section of the diff output in the Postfix configuration file, the line containing template("${module_name/main.cf.erb") is missing a closing curly brace around the variable module_name. He decides to fix this and make a third commit to his topic branch. The output of git log now shows:

```
developer:~/modules $ git log --abbrev-commit --pretty=oneline master..
6b9f2b5... Fixup missing closing curly brace
7acf23d... Updated config.pp to use $module_name
0c164f6... Added manual change warning to postfix config
```

▓ **Tip** In order to help prevent typographical errors from being accepted into the repository, it is a good idea to execute puppet --parseonly as a pre-commit hook in your version control system. Most version control systems support hook scripts to accept or deny a commit. If you use Subversion or Git, example pre-commit hooks are available online at http://projects.puppetlabs.com/projects/1/wiki/Puppet_Version_Control.

The developer is satisfied with his changes to Postfix, and he would like to try them out in the development environment in a similar way the operator tested out her changes. The overall workflow the developer follows is to push their topic branch to the central repository, fetch the changes in the development environment's repository, check out the topic branch, then run the Puppet agent against the development environment.

Before publishing his topic branch to a different repository, he decides to clean up his commit history to remove the entire commit that he created simply to fix a single character mistake he introduced. The git rebase command allows him to quickly and easily modify his topic branch to clean up this mistake.

```
developer:~modules/ $ git rebase -i master
```

This command will open, in your default text editor, a list of commits to the topic branch since it diverged from the master development branch. In order to clean up the commit history, the developer replaces "pick" with "squash" in the line listing his commit to add the missing curly brace. This will effectively combine this commit with the commit above it, where the curly brace should have been present in the first place.

```
pick 0c164f6 Added manual change warning to postfix config
pick 7acf23d Updated config.pp to use $module_name
squash 6b9f2b5 Fixup missing closing curly brace
```

```
# Rebase fa9812f..6b9f2b5 onto fa9812f
#
# Commands:
#  pick = use commit
#  edit = use commit, but stop for amending
#  squash = use commit, but meld into previous commit
#
# If you remove a line here THAT COMMIT WILL BE LOST.
# However, if you remove everything, the rebase will be aborted.
```

Once the developer makes this change, he saves the file and quits the editor. git rewrites history for him, giving him the option to change the commit message of the freshly cleaned commit:

```
".git/COMMIT_EDITMSG" 17L, 524C written
Created commit e4e27c7: Updated config.pp to use $module_name
 1 files changed, 2 insertions(+), 2 deletions(-)
Successfully rebased and updated refs/heads/developer/postfix
```

The developer is now ready to publish his topic branch to the rest of his colleagues and to the puppet master system itself, in order to check out the topic branch in the /etc/puppet/environments/development/modules repository.

```
developer:~/modules $ git push origin developer/postfix:developer/postfix
Counting objects: 21, done.
Compressing objects: 100% (14/14), done.
Writing objects: 100% (15/15), 1.79 KiB, done.
Total 15 (delta 3), reused 0 (delta 0)
To puppet@puppet.example.com:git/modules.git
 * [new branch]      developer/postfix -> developer/postfix
```

Next, he logs into the puppet master system as the user puppet, fetches his topic branch from the central repository, and then checks out his topic branch in the development environment. This process will switch the current development environment away from whatever branch it was previously on. This could potentially interfere with the work of the operator. If this becomes a common problem, it is possible to set up more environments to ensure each contributor has their own location to test their changes without interfering with others.

```
puppet:~ $ cd /etc/puppet/environments/development/modules
ppuppet:modules $ git fetch origin
remote: Counting objects: 21, done.
remote: Compressing objects: 100% (14/14), done.
remote: Total 15 (delta 3), reused 0 (delta 0)
Unpacking objects: 100% (15/15), done.
From puppet@puppet.example.com:git/modules
 * [new branch]      developer/postfix -> origin/developer/postfix
puppet:modules $ git checkout -b developer/postfix origin/developer/postfix
Branch developer/postfix set up to track remote branch refs/remotes/origin/developer/postfix.
Switched to a new branch "developer/postfix"
```

The developer's topic branch has now been checked out in the location the Puppet master is using for the development environment.

Testing the Puppet Agent Against the Postfix Configuration File

You can run the Puppet agent against the development environment, as we have previously and as shown in Listing 3-4, to verify your changes.

Listing 3-4. Testing the Puppet

```
agentroot:~ # puppet agent --test --noop --environment development
info: Caching catalog for scd.puppetlabs.vm
info: Applying configuration version '1289764649'
--- /etc/ssh/sshd_config      2010-11-14 12:11:28.000000000 -0800
+++ /tmp/puppet-file.25961.0   2010-11-14 12:11:40.000000000 -0800
@@ -3,5 +3,4 @@
 SyslogFacility AUTHPRIV
 PermitRootLogin no
 PasswordAuthentication yes
-AllowGroups wheel adm
 UsePAM yes
notice: /Stage[main]/Ssh::Config/File[/etc/ssh/sshd_config]/content: is {md5}da5
4f2cdc309faf6d813a080783a31f6, should be {md5}9d4c3fba3434a46528b41a49b70b60e4 (
noop)
info: /Stage[main]/Ssh::Config/File[/etc/ssh/sshd_config]: Scheduling refresh of
 Service[sshd]
notice: /Stage[main]/Ssh::Service/Service[sshd]: Would have triggered 'refresh'
from 1 events
--- /etc/postfix/master.cf    2010-11-14 11:54:37.000000000 -0800
+++ /tmp/puppet-file.22317.0   2010-11-14 11:58:15.000000000 -0800
@@ -1,3 +1,5 @@
+# This file managed by puppet.  Manual changes will be reverted.
+#
 #
 # Postfix master process configuration file.  For details on the format
 # of the file, see the master(5) manual page (command: "man 5 master").
notice: /Stage[main]/Postfix::Config/File[/etc/postfix/master.cf]/content: is↵
{md5}3b4d069fa7e4eb6570743261990a0d97, should be {md5}710171facd4980c2802a354ee4cb4a4e (noop)
info: /Stage[main]/Postfix::Config/File[/etc/postfix/master.cf]: Scheduling refresh of↵
 Service[postfix] notice: /Stage[main]/Postfix::Service/Service[postfix]: Would have↵
 triggered 'refresh' from 1 events
notice: Finished catalog run in 0.61 seconds
```

The Puppet agent run against the development environment shows us that Puppet will update the Postfix configuration file and notify the Postfix service as a result. Notice how the changes we've made to this system by trying out the operator/ssh branch will now be reverted. This is because the developer created his branch from the master branch and the operator has not yet merged her operator/ssh branch back into master, therefore her changes are not present.

At this point, both the changes of the operator and the developer have been tried in using the development environment. It's now time to merge both change lists into a testing branch and make them both available in the testing Puppet environment.

Merging Changes into a Testing Environment

Unlike the development Puppet environment, where anything goes and people may perform a checkout on their branches to quickly try out their changes and topic branches, the testing environment should change less frequently. The process of merging topic branches from the master development branch into a testing branch periodically, once every two weeks for example, has worked well for many projects and companies. In this section, we work through the process of merging change lists into the testing branch with the goal of ultimately promoting the testing branch to a production release.

Creating the Testing Branch

First, our system administrator will create a new branch, called "testing," based on the current master branch we started with. When starting out with Puppet, this testing branch and the process of merging change lists should be set early on in order to provide a good reference point. It also provides and staging area that's not quite as risky as the development environment, and does not require a release process like the production environment does.

The system administrator creates the new testing branch in a manner similar to how the operator and developer created their topic branches. This should be done in the personal repository the system administrator has in her home directory:

```
sysadmin:~modules/ $ git checkout testing master
Switched to a new branch "testing"
```

■ **Note** There is no technical difference between a topic branch and a testing branch the system administrator creates for the testing environment. The team is simply using a convention of treating the testing branch as a long-lived branch to merge change lists into. Similarly, the master branch is the branch where current development happens.

Merging the Changes into the Development Branch

Before checking out the testing branch on the Puppet master, the system administrator decides to merge the change lists from the operator and the developer into the main development branch. This keeps the main development branch in sync with the testing branch and allows the system administrator to advance the master development branch with additional changes without affecting the testing environment, which will only be updated on the Puppet master periodically.

```
sysadmin:~modules/ $ git fetch origin
From puppet@puppet.example.com:git/modules
 * [new branch]      developer/postfix -> origin/developer/postfix
 * [new branch]      operator/ssh -> origin/operator/ssh

sysadmin:~modules/ $ git merge --no-ff origin/developer/postfix
Merge made by recursive.
 postfix/files/master.cf    |    4 +++-
 postfix/manifests/config.pp |    4 ++--
```

```
2 files changed, 5 insertions(+), 3 deletions(-)

sysadmin:~modules/ $ git merge --no-ff origin/operator/ssh
Merge made by recursive.
 ssh/files/sshd_config |    1 +
 1 files changed, 1 insertions(+), 0 deletions(-)
```

▓ **Tip** It is a good idea to perform a `git fetch origin` to see if there are any changes in the central repository prior to merging topic branches. If there are, then performing `git merge origin/master` while on the master branch will bring those changes into the local repository.

The system administrator has merged the changes using the `--no-ff` option in order to create a merge commit for each of the two topic branches. In the future, this merge commit will allow the team to refer back to the change list as a whole rather than having to tease apart which commit is associated with which topic. We're able to verify that both the changes from the operator and the developer are now in the master branch of the system administrator's repository, by using the `git log` command:

```
sysadmin:~modules/ $ git log --abbrev-commit --pretty=oneline origin/master..
1bbda50... Merge commit 'origin/operator/ssh'
9b41d49... Merge commit 'origin/developer/postfix'
e4e27c7... Updated config.pp to use $module_name
0c164f6... Added manual change warning to postfix config
eea4fbb... Added AllowGroups to sshd_config
```

Notice that this time, the system administrator has used the `git log` command to display abbreviated log messages from the current head of the `origin/master` branch to the current head of the local checked out branch. He chose `origin/master` because he has not pushed the newly merged changes to the central repository and this command therefore shows a list of changes that will be pushed if he decides to do so.

Everything looks good, as he expected. He also doesn't see the commit the developer made on his own topic branch to add the missing curly brace, because the developer chose to rebase his topic branch against the master branch before publishing his change list.

Merging into the Testing Branch

The team members decide to make the newly merged master branch the first testing branch, and they decide to continue developing on the master branch over the next couple of weeks. In a few days or weeks, the team will come together and decide on which of the change lists that each member has contributed are ready for merging into the testing branch. The system administrator starts this process by merging the changes he just made to the master branch into the testing branch, then pushing all of these changes to the central repository:

```
sysadmin:~modules/ $ git checkout testing
Switched to branch "testing"
```

```
sysadmin:~modules/ $ git merge master
Updating fa9812f..1bbda50
Fast forward
 postfix/files/master.cf    |    4 +++-
 postfix/manifests/config.pp |   4 ++--
 ssh/files/sshd_config      |    1 +
 3 files changed, 6 insertions(+), 3 deletions(-)

sysadmin:~modules/ $ git push origin
Counting objects: 6, done.
Compressing objects: 100% (3/3), done.
Writing objects: 100% (3/3), 494 bytes, done.
Total 3 (delta 1), reused 0 (delta 0)
To puppet@puppet.example.com:git/modules.git
    fa9812f..1bbda50  master -> master

sysadmin:~modules/ $ git push origin testing:testing
Total 0 (delta 0), reused 0 (delta 0)
To puppet@puppet.example.com:git/modules.git
 * [new branch]      testing -> testing
```

Notice that the system administrator executes two different push commands: one plain git push origin, and one git push origin testing:testing. This is because git push, by default, will only push the changes made to local branches into a remote repository if there is a branch with the same name in both locations.

Performing Checkout on the Testing Branch

Previously, the operator and developer logged into the puppet master and activated their changes by checking out their code in /etc/puppet/environments/development/modules. Similarly, the system administrator needs to fetch and checkout the new testing branch into the /etc/puppet/environments/testing/modules repository to activate the new configuration in the testing environment. Before doing so, he verifies that the remote named "origin" is configured to connect to the central repository at puppet@puppet.example.com:git/modules.git:

```
puppet:~ $ cd /etc/puppet/environments/testing/modules/
puppet:modules/ $ git remote -v
origin  /etc/puppet/modules/.git

puppet:modules/ $ git remote rm origin
puppet:modules/ $ git remote add origin puppet@puppet.example.com:git/modules.git
puppet:modules/ $ git fetch origin
remote: Counting objects: 39, done.
remote: Compressing objects: 100% (24/24), done.
remote: Total 28 (delta 9), reused 0 (delta 0)
Unpacking objects: 100% (28/28), done.
From puppet@puppet.example.com:git/modules
 * [new branch]      developer/postfix -> origin/developer/postfix
 * [new branch]      master    -> origin/master
```

```
* [new branch]      operator/ssh -> origin/operator/ssh
* [new branch]      testing    -> origin/testing
```

Now that the testing environment repository has an up-to-date list of the branches, including the new testing branch, the system administrator performs a git checkout to activate the new changes on the system:

```
puppet:modules/ $ git checkout -b testing --track origin/testing
Branch testing set up to track remote branch refs/remotes/origin/testing.
Switched to a new branch "testing"
```

Testing the Changes

The system administrator is finally able to test a Puppet agent against the new testing environment, which now contains both changes: the SSH contribution from the operator, and the Postfix contribution from the developer. The testing environment is the only place where both changes are currently active in the configuration management system.

```
root:~ # puppet agent --test --noop --environment testing
info: Caching catalog for scd.puppetlabs.vm
info: Applying configuration version '1289770137'
…
info: /Stage[main]/Ssh::Config/File[/etc/ssh/sshd_config]: Scheduling refresh of Service[sshd]
notice: /Stage[main]/Ssh::Service/Service[sshd]: Triggered 'refresh' from 1 events
notice: Finished catalog run in 2.77 seconds
```

Production Environment Releases

Our team of Puppet contributors at Example.com has been effectively making changes to the configuration management system. Using Puppet Environments and a version control system, they're able to work efficiently and independently of one another without creating conflicts or obstructing another person's work. We've seen how the operator and the developer were able to make two changes in parallel, publishing those changes in a branch in the central version control repository for the system administrator to merge into a testing branch.

The team has also tested a number of machines using the Puppet agent in the testing environment, and is now ready to release the configuration to the production systems. This section covers how the team creates their first release, and provides a process to follow for subsequent releases.

You'll also see how a Git feature called "tagging" is useful to provide a method of referring to a specific point in time when the production configuration was active. You'll see how tags provide the ability to quickly roll back changes that might not be desirable in the production environment.

First, the team decides to release the current testing branch into production. Before doing so, the system administrator creates a tag so this release can be easily referred back to in the future. The system administrator does this in his own personal repository in his home directory:

```
sysadmin:~ $ cd ~/modules/
sysadmin:~modules/ $ git checkout testing
Switched to branch "testing"
sysadmin:~modules/ $ git tag -m 'First release to production' 1.0.0
sysadmin:~modules/ $ git push --tags origin
Counting objects: 1, done.
```

```
Writing objects: 100% (1/1), 177 bytes, done.
Total 1 (delta 0), reused 0 (delta 0)
To puppet@puppet.example.com:git/modules.git
 * [new tag]         1.0.0 -> 1.0.0
```

The process of creating a tag is often called "cutting a release." The system administrator has done just this, tagged the current testing branch as a release to production, and then published the new tagged release into the central repository.

New branches, such as the testing or topic branches, were activated in the development and testing environments in the previous section. The process of activating a new production release is very similar, except instead of checking out a branch, which may change over time, a specific tag is checked out, which is static and refers to a very specific point in the history of configuration changes.

To activate the new production release, the system administrator logs into the Puppet master system as the user puppet, fetches the new tag from the central repository, and then checks out the tagged production release. Unlike the development and testing environments, Example.com has chosen to configure the production environment to use the working copy at /etc/puppet/modules rather than as a sub directory of /etc/puppet/environments where the development and testing active working copies reside.

```
puppet:~ $ cd /etc/puppet/modules
puppet:modules/ $ git fetch origin
remote: Counting objects: 21, done.
remote: Compressing remote: objects: 100% (13/13), done.
remote: Total 14 (delta 3), reused 0 (delta 0)
Unpacking objects: 100% (14/14), done.
From puppet@puppet.example.com:git/modules
 * [new branch]      developer/postfix -> origin/developer/postfix
   fa9812f..1bbda50  master      -> origin/master
 * [new branch]      testing     -> origin/testing
 * [new tag]         1.0.0       -> 1.0.0
```

Remember that the git fetch command does not affect the currently checked out configuration; it only updates the internal git index of data. The system administrator then checks out the newly-released production environment using the same familiar syntax we've seen so far:

```
puppet:modules/ $ git checkout tags/1.0.0
git checkout tags/1.0.0
Note: moving to "tags/1.0.0" which isn't a local branch
If you want to create a new branch from this checkout, you may do so
(now or later) by using -b with the checkout command again. Example:
  git checkout -b <new_branch_name>
HEAD is now at 1bbda50... Merge commit 'origin/operator/ssh'
```

The note about moving to a non-local branch may be safely ignored. A tag is static reference, and the team should not have any need to directly modify the files in /etc/puppet/modules or make commits from the active production environment repository.

After executing the git checkout command to place the 1.0.0 release of the configuration into the production environment, everything is now active for the puppet agents. The system administrator verifies this by executing puppet agent in the default environment:

```
root:~ # puppet agent --test --noop
info: Caching catalog for scd.puppetlabs.vm
info: Applying configuration version '1289772102'
notice: Finished catalog run in 0.53 seconds
```

You will also remember that the default environment is the production environment, and as such, the system administrator did not need to set the --environment command line option. If something were to have gone wrong in the production environment, a previous tag may be activated quickly, rolling back the changes introduced by the release of a new production configuration. One of the team members simply needs to execute git checkout tags/x.y.z to roll back the configuration.

The changes and workflow we've seen the operator, developer, and system administrator undertake in this chapter may now be repeated in a cycle. This development, testing, and release cycle provides an effective method to make changes to the configuration management system in a safe and predictable manner. Changes to the production system can be made with confidence: They've been vetted through the development and testing phases of the release process, they've been explicitly tagged in a release, and they can be quickly and easily backed out if things go awry.

Summary

You've seen how Puppet environments enable a team of contributors to work effectively and efficiently. Puppet environments, combined with a modern version control system, enable three people to make changes simultaneously and in parallel without obstructing each other's work. Furthermore, the tagging and branching features of modern version control systems provide an effective release management strategy. The process a single team member may follow in order to make changes is summarized as:

- Develop changes in a local topic branch

- Rebase against the master branch to remove any unnecessary commits

- Publish the topic branch to the central repository

- Activate and try the changes in the development puppet environment

- Periodically merge and activate change lists from multiple people into a testing branch

- Periodically cut a release of the testing branch using version control tags.

Resources

- Debian stable, testing, unstable releases and distributions - http://www.debian.org/doc/FAQ/ch-ftparchives.en.html

- Puppet Labs Environments Curated Documentation - http://docs.puppetlabs.com/guides/environment.html

- Puppet Labs Environments Wiki Article - http://projects.puppetlabs.com/projects/1/wiki/Using_Multiple_Environments

CHAPTER 4

■■■

Puppet Scalability

We've seen that the Puppet agent and master require very little work to get up and running on a handful of nodes using the default configuration. It is, however, a significantly more involved undertaking to scale Puppet to handle hundreds of nodes. Yet many installations are successfully using Puppet to manage hundreds, thousands and tens of thousands of nodes. In this chapter, we cover a number of proven strategies that are employed to scale Puppet.

In this chapter you'll see how to enable a single Puppet master system to handle hundreds of nodes using the Apache web server. We also demonstrate how to configure more than one Puppet master system to handle thousands of nodes using a load balancer. Throughout, we make a number of recommendations to help you avoid the common pitfalls related to performance and scalability.

Finally, you'll learn how to measure the performance of the Puppet master infrastructure in order to determine when it's time to add more capacity. We also provide two small scripts to avoid the "thundering herd effect" and to measure catalog compilation time.

First, though, we need review some of the challenges you'll be facing along the way.

Identifying the Challenges

Earlier in the book, you learned a bit about Puppet's client-server configuration and the use of SSL to secure connections between the agent and the master. Puppet uses SSL, specifically the HTTPS protocol, to communicate. As a result, when we're scaling Puppet we are in fact scaling a web service, and many of the problems (and the solutions) overlap with traditional web scaling. Consequently, the two challenges we're going to need to address when scaling Puppet are:

- Scaling the transport
- Scaling SSL

The first challenge requires that we increase the performance and potential number of possible master and agent connections. The second challenge requires that we implement good management of the SSL certificates that secure the connection between the master and the agent. Both challenges require changes to Puppet's "out-of-the-box" configuration.

In Chapter 1 we started the Puppet Master using the puppet master command. The default puppet master configuration makes use of the WEBRick Ruby-based HTTP server. Puppet ships WEBRick to eliminate the need to set up a web server like Apache to handle the HTTPS requests out of the box. While the WEBrick server provides quick and easy testing, it does not provide a scalable solution and should not be used except to evaluate, test and develop Puppet. In production situations, a more robust web server such as Apache or Nginx is necessary to handle the number of client requests.

Therefore, the first order of business when scaling Puppet is to replace the default WEBRick HTTP server. In the following section, we first replace WEBRick with the Apache web server on a single Puppet master system and then show how this strategy can be extended to multiple Puppet master systems working behind a load balancer.

The second change to Puppet's out-of-the-box configuration is the management of the SSL certificates that Puppet uses to secure the connection between agent and master. The Puppet master stores a copy of every certificate issued, along with a revocation list. This information needs to be kept in sync across the Puppet worker nodes. So, together with the transport mechanism between the agent and master, we'll explore the two main options of handling SSL certificates in a scalable Puppet deployment:

- Using a single Certificate Authority Puppet master

- Distributing the same Certificate Authority across multiple Puppet masters

Running the Puppet Master with Apache and Passenger

The first scaling example we're going to demonstrate is the combination of the Apache web server with a module called Phusion Passenger, which is also known as mod_rails, mod_passenger, or just Passenger. Passenger is an Apache module that allows the embedding of Ruby applications, much like mod_php or mod_perl allow the embedding of PHP and Perl applications. The Passenger module is not a standard module that ships with Apache web server, and as a result, must be installed separately. Passenger is available as a Ruby gem package, or may be downloaded and installed from http://www.modrails.com/.

For networks of one to two thousand Puppet managed nodes, a single Puppet master system running inside of Apache with Passenger is often sufficient. Later in this chapter, we examine how to run multiple Puppet master systems if you want a highly available system or support for an even larger number of Puppet-managed nodes. These more complex configurations all build on the basic Apache and Passenger configuration we introduce to you. We also build upon the Puppet master configuration we created in Chapter 2 and the environment structure we introduced in Chapter 3.

First, you need to install Apache and Passenger, then configure Apache to handle the SSL authentication and verification of the Puppet agent, and finally connect Apache to the Puppet master and ensure everything is working as expected.

As we scale Puppet up, it is important to draw the distinction between the idea of a front-end HTTP request handler and a back-end Puppet master worker process. The front-end request handler is responsible for accepting the TCP connection from the Puppet agent, selecting an appropriate back-end worker, routing the request to the worker, accepting the response and finally serving it back to the Puppet agent. This distinction between a front-end request handler and a back-end worker process is a common concept when scaling web services.

Installing Apache and Passenger on Enterprise Linux

To get started, you need to install Apache and Passenger. Apache and Passenger are a relatively simple and easy to set up. Pre-compiled Passenger packages may not be available for your platform, however, making configuration a little more complex. This section covers the installation of Apache and Passenger on the Enterprise Linux family of systems such as CentOS, RedHat Enterprise Linux, and Oracle Enterprise Linux.

In Listing 4-1, we've used the puppet resource command to ensure that Apache and the Apache SSL libraries are installed. We've also ensured that the Apache service is not currently running. The next step is to obtain Passenger, which is implemented as an Apache loadable module, similar to mod_ssl or mod_perl.

Listing 4-1. Installing Apache on Enterprise Linux

```
# puppet resource package httpd ensure=present
notice: /Package[httpd]/ensure: created
```

```
package { 'httpd':
    ensure => '2.2.3-43.el5.centos'
}
# puppet resource package mod_ssl ensure=present
notice: /Package[mod_ssl]/ensure: created
package { 'mod_ssl':
    ensure => '2.2.3-43.el5.centos'
}
# puppet resource service httpd ensure=stopped
notice: /Service[httpd]/ensure: ensure changed 'running' to 'stopped'
service { 'httpd':
    ensure => 'running'
}
```

In order to install Passenger on our Enterprise Linux system, configure yum to access a local yum repository with packages for Puppet and rubygem_passenger. An example of the yum repository configuration for the x86_64 architecture is:

```
root:~ # yum list rubygem-passenger
Available Packages
rubygem-passenger.x86_64                    2.2.11-3.el5                    localyum
```

We've verified that the rubygem-passenger package is now available on this system, so we're able to install the package using puppet resource, as shown in Listing 4-2.

Listing 4-2. Installing Phusion Passenger on Enterprise Linux

```
# puppet resource package rubygem-passenger ensure=present
notice: /Package[rubygem-passenger]/ensure: created
package { 'rubygem-passenger':
    ensure => '2.2.11-3.el5'
}
```

Installing Apache and Passenger on Debian-Based Systems

At the time of writing, Passenger packages are available in Debian 5, "Lenny." The packages available in the stable repository have known issues, however, and we recommend installing version 2.2.11 of Passenger from the backports package repository.

DEBIAN BACKPORTS

Debian backports provide the means to install packages that are available in the testing and unstable branch in a stable system. The packages are designed to link against libraries provided in Debian stable to minimize compatibility issues. More information about using Debian backports is available at http://backports.debian.org/

Installing Apache on Debian is very straightforward (see Listing 4-3). The packages available in the stable release of the Debian operating system work extremely well with Puppet. Please ensure you've enabled Debian backports as per the instructions at http://backports.debian.org/ before attempting to install the passenger package.

Listing 4-3. Installing Apache and Passenger on Debian / Ubuntu

```
# puppet resource package apache2 ensure=present
notice: /Package[apache2]/ensure: created
package { apache2:
    ensure => '2.2.9-10+lenny8'
}

# puppet resource package libapache2-mod-passenger ensure=present
notice: /Package[libapache2-mod-passenger]/ensure: created
package { libapache2-mod-passenger:
  ensure => '2.2.11debian-1~bpo50+1'
}
```

As an alternative to the Puppet resource commands shown in Listing 4-3, Passenger may be installed from Debian backports using the command `aptitude -t lenny-backports install libapache2-mod-passener`.

Installing Passenger Using Ruby Gems

Compiled binary packages of Passenger 2.2.11 are available for some platforms, but not all. Ruby Gems provide an alternative way to install the Passenger module. The passenger gem behaves slightly differently from most binary packages; the source code for Passenger is installed using the Gem format complete with a shell script to assist in the compilation of the Apache module.

For this installation method to succeed, the Apache development packages for your platform will need to be installed and present. The Passenger build scripts will link the library using the available version of Apache development libraries (Listing 4-4).

Listing 4-4. Installing Passenger using Rubygems

```
# gem install rack -v 1.1.0
# gem install passenger -v 2.2.11
# passenger-install-apache2-module
```

The output of the passenger-install-apache2-module script is quite long and has been truncated. For additional information and troubleshooting tips related to installing Passenger using Ruby Gems please see: http://www.modrails.com/install.html

---

▓ **Tip** Up-to-date information about Passenger versions known to work with Puppet is available online at: http://projects.puppetlabs.com/projects/1/wiki/Using_Passenger

---

Configuring Apache and Passenger

If you haven't already done so, make sure you've started the Puppet master at least once to create the SSL certificates you're going to configure Apache to use. Apache will then verify that the Puppet agent certificate is signed with the generated Puppet CA, and present a certificate that the Puppet agent uses to verify the authenticity of the server. Once you have you SSL certificates in place, configure Apache by enabling the Passenger module and creating an Apache virtual host for the Puppet master service.

First, enable mod_passenger with the following configuration provided in Listing 4-5.

Listing 4-5. The Apache Passenger configuration file

```
# /etc/httpd/conf.d/10_passenger.conf

# The passenger module path should match ruby gem version
LoadModule passenger_module /usr/lib/ruby/gems/1.8/gems/passenger-
2.2.11/ext/apache2/mod_passenger.so
PassengerRoot /usr/lib/ruby/gems/1.8/gems/passenger-2.2.11
PassengerRuby /usr/bin/ruby

# Recommended Passenger Configuration
PassengerHighPerformance on
PassengerUseGlobalQueue on
# PassengerMaxPoolSize control number of application instances,
# typically 1.5x the number of processor cores.
PassengerMaxPoolSize 6
# Restart ruby process after handling specific number of request to resolve MRI memory leak.
PassengerMaxRequests 4000
# Shutdown idle Passenger instances after 30 min.
PassengerPoolIdleTime 1800
# End of /etc/httpd/conf.d/10_passenger.conf
```

■ **Tip** For more information about tuning Passenger, please see:
http://www.modrails.com/documentation/Users%20guide%20Apache.html

The second aspect of the Apache configuration is the Apache virtual host stanza. The virtual host configures Apache to listen on TCP port 8140 and to encrypt all traffic using SSL and the certificates generated for use with the Puppet master. The virtual host also configures Passenger to use the system's Ruby interpreter and provides the path to the Rack configuration file named config.ru (Listing 4-6).

Listing 4-6. Apache Puppet master configuration file

```
# /etc/httpd/conf.d/20_puppetmaster.conf
# Apache handles the SSL encryption and decryption. It replaces webrick and listens by default
on 8140
Listen 8140
<VirtualHost *:8140>
```

```
SSLEngine on
SSLProtocol -ALL +SSLv3 +TLSv1
SSLCipherSuite ALL:!ADH:RC4+RSA:+HIGH:+MEDIUM:-LOW:-SSLv2:-EXP
# Puppet master should generate initial CA certificate.
# ensure certs are located in /var/lib/puppet/ssl
# Change puppet.example.com to the fully qualified domain name of the Puppet master, i.e.
$(facter fqdn).
SSLCertificateFile /var/lib/puppet/ssl/certs/puppet.example.com.pem
SSLCertificateKeyFile /var/lib/puppet/ssl/private_keys/puppet.example.com.pem
SSLCertificateChainFile /var/lib/puppet/ssl/certs/ca.pem
SSLCACertificateFile /var/lib/puppet/ssl/ca/ca_crt.pem
# CRL checking should be enabled
# disable next line if Apache complains about CRL
SSLCARevocationFile /var/lib/puppet/ssl/ca/ca_crl.pem
# optional to allow CSR request, required if certificates distributed to client during
provisioning.
SSLVerifyClient optional
SSLVerifyDepth 1
SSLOptions +StdEnvVars

# The following client headers record authentication information for down stream workers.
RequestHeader set X-SSL-Subject %{SSL_CLIENT_S_DN}e
RequestHeader set X-Client-DN %{SSL_CLIENT_S_DN}e
RequestHeader set X-Client-Verify %{SSL_CLIENT_VERIFY}e

RackAutoDetect On
DocumentRoot /etc/puppet/rack/puppetmaster/public/
<Directory /etc/puppet/rack/puppetmaster/>
    Options None
    AllowOverride None
    Order allow,deny
    allow from all
</Directory>
</VirtualHost>
# /etc/httpd/conf.d/20_puppetmaster.conf
```

This configuration file may appear a little overwhelming. In particular, the RequestHeader statements are the source of much confusion among Puppet newcomers and veterans alike. When using this configuration file example, make sure to replace puppet.example.com with the fully qualified domain name of your own Puppet master system. The fully qualified domain name is easily found with the command:

```
$ facter fqdn.
```

The first section of the configuration file makes sure Apache is binding and listening on TCP port 8140, the standard port for a Puppet master server.

Next, the virtual host stanza begins with <VirtualHost *:8140>. Please refer to the Apache version 2.2 configuration reference (http://httpd.apache.org/docs/2.2/) for more information about configuring Apache virtual hosts.

SSL is enabled for the Puppet master specific virtual host using SSLEngine on and setting the SSLCipherSuite parameters. In addition to enabling SSL encryption of the traffic, certificates are provided to prove the identity of the Puppet master service. Next, revocation is enabled using the

SSLCARevocationFile parameter. The puppet cert command will automatically keep the ca_crl.pem file updated as we issue and revoke new Puppet agent certificates.

Finally, Apache is configured to verify the authenticity of the Puppet agent certificate. The results of this verification are stored in the environment as a standard environment variable. The Puppet master process running inside Passenger will check the environment variables set by the SSLOptions +StdEnvVars configuration in order to authorize the Puppet agent.

In the section immediately following the SSL configuration, the results of verifying the Puppet agent's certificate are stored as client request headers as well as in standard environment variables. Later in this chapter, you'll see how Client Request Headers may be consulted by downstream workers in order to provide authentication using standard environment variables.

The last section of the Puppet master virtual host is the Rack configuration. Rack provides a common API for web servers to exchange requests and responses with a Ruby HTTP service like Puppet. Rack is commonly used to allow web applications like the Puppet Dashboard to be hosted on multiple web servers. This stanza looks for a special file called config.ru in /etc/puppet/rack/puppetmaster/ (see Listing 4-7).

Listing 4-7. Puppet master Rack configuration file

```
# /etc/puppet/rack/puppetmaster/config.ru
# a config.ru, for use with every rack-compatible webserver.
$0 = "master"
# if you want debugging:
# ARGV << "--debug"
ARGV << "--rack"
require 'puppet/application/master'
run Puppet::Application[:master].run
# EOF /etc/puppet/rack/puppetmaster/config.ru
```

■ **Tip** If you installed Puppet from packages, check your "share" directory structure for a config.ru example provided by the package maintainer, often located at /usr/share/puppet/ext/rack/files/config.ru. For up to date Rack configuration files, check the ext directory in the most recently released version of Puppet. This may be found online at https://github.com/puppetlabs/puppet/tree/master/ext/rack/files

Before creating this configuration file, you may need to create the skeleton directory structure for Rack and the Puppet master rack application instance. To do so, you could execute the command:

```
mkdir -p /etc/puppet/rack/puppetmaster/{public,tmp}.
```

■ **Note** The config.ru Rack configuration file should be owned by the puppet user and group. Passenger will inspect the owner of this file and switch from the root system account to this less privileged puppet service account when Apache is started.

Testing the Puppet Master in Apache

We've covered the steps required to install and configure Apache and Passenger. You're now ready to test your changes by starting the Apache service. Before doing so, make sure to double check the ownership of the config.ru file. If there is a certificate problem, make sure the existing SSL certificates are configured in the Puppet master Apache virtual host configuration file, as shown in Listing 4-6. You also want to make sure the Puppet master is not already running.

In order to start Apache and the new Puppet master service, you can again use the puppet resource command:

```
# puppet resource service httpd ensure=running enable=true hasstatus=true
service { 'httpd':
    ensure => 'running',
    enable => 'true'
}
```

Running the Puppet agent against the Apache Puppet master virtual host will allow you to test the system:

```
# puppet agent --test
info: Caching catalog for puppet.example.lan
info: Applying configuration version '1290801236'
notice: Passenger is setup and serving catalogs.
notice: /Stage[main]//Node[default]/Notify[Passenger]/message: defined 'message' as 'Passenger
is setup and serving catalogs.'
notice: Finished catalog run in 0.38 seconds
```

The Puppet agent does not provide any indication that the Puppet master service has switched from WEBrick to Apache. The best way to tell if everything is working is to use to Apache access logs (see Listing 4-8). The Puppet master virtual host will use the combined access logs to record incoming requests from the Puppet agent.

Listing 4-8. Puppet requests in the Apache access logs

```
# tail /var/log/httpd/access_log
127.0.0.1 - - [24/Nov/2010:20:48:11 -0800] "GET
/production/catalog/puppet.example.com?facts=…& A&facts_format=b64_zlib_yaml HTTP/1.1" 200
1181 "-" "-"
127.0.0.1 - - [24/Nov/2010:20:48:12 -0800] "PUT /production/report/puppet.example.com
HTTP/1.1" 200 14 "-" "-"
```

In the access_log file we can see that the Puppet agent issues a HTTP GET request using the URI /production/catalog/puppet.example.com. We can also see the Puppet agent sends the list of facts about itself in the request URI. The Puppet master compiles the modules and manifests into a configuration catalog and provides this catalog in the HTTP. The "200" status code indicates that this operation was successful. Following the catalog run, the Puppet agent submits a report using the PUT request to the URI /production/report/puppet.example.com. We cover more information about reports and reporting features in Puppet in Chapter 10.

In addition to the Apache access_log, the Puppet master process itself continues to log information about itself to the system log. This information is available in /var/log/messages on Enterprise Linux bases systems and in /var/log/daemon on Ubuntu/Debian systems.

And that's it! You've added an Apache and Passenger front-end to your Puppet master that will allow you to scale to a much larger number of hosts.

Load-Balancing Multiple Puppet Masters

You've replaced the WEBrick HTTP server with the Apache web server. Sometimes, though, you need more capacity than a single machine can provide alone. In this case, you can scale the Puppet master horizontally rather than vertically. Horizontal scaling uses the resources of multiple Puppet masters in a cluster to get more capacity than any one system can provide. This configuration can cater for environments with tens of thousands of managed nodes.

There are many options and strategies available to provide a front-end request handler. We're going to use HTTP load balancing to direct client requests to available back-end services. Each Puppet master worker is configured independently, using different Apache virtual host configurations bound to different ports on the loopback interface 127.0.0.1. This allows multiple Puppet master workers to be configured and tested on the same operating system instance and easily redistributed to multiple hosts; all you have to do is change the listening IP address and port numbers in the load balancer and worker configuration files.

Load Balancing

For an introduction into the general problem of load balancing and scalable web architectures, we recommend the Wikipedia article titled Load balancing (computing) at - http://en.wikipedia.org/wiki/Load_balancing_(computing). In particular, the idea of horizontal and vertical scaling is an important one to consider. The Puppet master scales well both horizontally and vertically, either by adding more systems working in parallel or by increasing the amount of memory and processor resources.

HTTP Load Balancing

The problem of scaling HTTP-based web services to tens of thousands of clients has been around for quite some time. There are many technical solutions provided by commercial products like Citrix NetScaler, Cisco IOS, and F5 BIG-IP. Many open-source software projects also exist, including Apache itself, HAProxy, Nginx, and Pound. Puppet fits into the overall problem of HTTP load balancing nicely because of its use of SSL and HTTP for communication.

We're going to build upon the single Puppet master configuration we just created and then split the work across two Puppet master systems. We'll use the Apache Web server to handle the incoming Puppet agent requests and route them to an available back-end Puppet master. If we require additional capacity, we can add additional Puppet master processes. This configuration has the added benefit of high availability. If a particular Puppet master system has trouble or needs to be taken out of service, the front-end load balancer will stop routing Puppet agent requests to that master process.

We're going to configure two Puppet master Apache virtual hosts, much like the virtual host we created in the previous section. However, there is one important difference: we will disable SSL for the Apache virtual hosts. Instead, we'll configure a new front-end Apache virtual host to authorize incoming Puppet agent requests and handle the SSL encryption and decryption of the traffic. This front-end load balancer will terminate the SSL connection, be responsible for authenticating the Puppet agent request and then present this authentication information to the back-end Puppet master workers for authorization.

You'll see how Apache is able to pass the authentication information along through the use of client request headers, and how the back-end virtual hosts are able to set environment variables for the Puppet master based on the values of these client request headers.

■ **Caution** It is important to keep in mind that the load-balancing configuration discussed in this section authorizes and terminates SSL connections at the load balancer. All traffic between the front-end load balancer and the back-end Puppet master systems are therefore unencrypted and in plain text. Requests directly to the worker virtual hosts may easily be forged and should only be allowed from the load balancer. If this is an unacceptable configuration for your environment, please consider using a TCP load balancer in order to preserve and pass through the SSL encryption to the back-end Puppet master virtual hosts.

Puppet Master Worker Configuration

When running the Puppet master behind a load balancer, there will be multiple Puppet master processes running on different hosts behind the load balancer. The load balancer will listen on the Puppet port of 8140. Incoming requests will be dispatched to available back-end worker processes, as illustrated in Figure 4-1. The example configuration presented in this chapter configures the Puppet CA and workers all on the same host using unique TCP ports bound to the loopback interface.

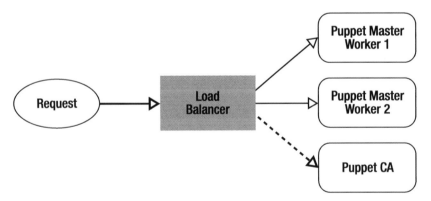

Figure 4-1. Puppet master workers

To get started with our load-balancing configuration, you'll copy the existing Puppet master virtual host we configured in the previous section into two additional virtual host configurations. Each of these two virtual hosts will have SSL disabled. You'll then create a third virtual host listening on the standard Puppet master port of 8140 with SSL enabled. This virtual host will forward a request to any available back-end virtual host.

First, move the existing Puppet master to port 8141 to free up port 8140 for the new front-end load balancer virtual host. To do this, update the Listen and VirtualHost configuration items in the Apache Puppet master configuration, in our case in the 20_puppetmaster.conf file we created earlier:

```
Listen 8141
# Moved the Puppet master stand alone to port 8141.
# The Load balancer listens on the standard Puppet master port
<VirtualHost *:8141>
```

This change to the virtual host only required two small edits to the TCP port configuration in 20_puppetmaster.conf.

Next, create a new Puppet master virtual host configuration for the first back-end worker in /etc/httpd/conf.d/40_puppetmaster_worker_18140.conf.

In Listing 4-9, we configure a unique Rack DocumentRoot in order to uniquely identify the first Puppet master worker. Commands such as passenger-status identify processes by their configured DocumentRoot.

Listing 4-9. *First Apache Puppet master worker virtual host configuration file*

```
# cat 40_puppetmaster_worker_18140.conf
Listen 18140
<VirtualHost 127.0.0.1:18140>
SSLEngine off

# Obtain Authentication Information from Client Request Headers
SetEnvIf X-Client-Verify "(.*)" SSL_CLIENT_VERIFY=$1
SetEnvIf X-SSL-Client-DN "(.*)" SSL_CLIENT_S_DN=$1

RackAutoDetect On
DocumentRoot /etc/puppet/rack/puppetmaster_18140/public/
<Directory /etc/puppet/rack/puppetmaster_18140/>
    Options None
    AllowOverride None
    Order allow,deny
    allow from all
</Directory>
</VirtualHost>
```

In addition to the configuration file, you need to duplicates the Rack configuration directory into the new DocumentRoot location (see Listing 4-10).

Listing 4-10. *Create the first Puppet master worker rack configuration*

```
# rsync -avxH /etc/puppet/rack/puppetmaster{,_18140}/
building file list ... done
created directory /etc/puppet/rack/puppetmaster_18140
./
config.ru
public/
tmp/
sent 621 bytes   received 60 bytes  1362.00 bytes/sec
total size is 431   speedup is 0.63
```

Note the trailing slash in the rsync command, which is important and ensures that the directory contents are copied into one another.

■ **Caution** The back-end worker process is listening on the local interface of 127.0.0.1. This prevents network systems from reaching the unencrypted, plain text back-end worker virtual host. In a production deployment, the back-end virtual host is often on a different machine than the front-end load balancer. Care must be taken to ensure the unencrypted traffic is secure and protected. In general, the back-end virtual host should not accept connections from any machine other than the front-end load balancer.

Front End Load Balancer Configuration

After we configure the first back-end Puppet master worker, we need to configure the front-end virtual host. This front-end virtual host is going to perform a number of tasks:

1. Terminate the SSL connection

2. Authenticate the client request

3. Set the authentication information in client request headers

4. Pass the request along to one of the available back-end worker processes.

The configuration file for the front-end load balancer is very similar to the original Apache Passenger configuration file with the addition of a reverse proxy stanza and the removal of the Passenger and Rack configuration stanzas (Listing 4-11).

Listing 4-11. Apache front-end load balancer configuration file

```
# cat 30_puppetmaster_frontend_8140.conf
# Available back-end worker virtual hosts
# NOTE the use of cleartext unencrypted HTTP.
<Proxy balancer://puppetmaster>
  BalancerMember http://127.0.0.1:18140
  BalancerMember http://127.0.0.1:18141
</Proxy>

Listen 8140
<VirtualHost *:8140>
SSLEngine on
# SSLCipherSuite SSLv2:-LOW:-EXPORT:RC4+RSA
SSLProtocol -ALL +SSLv3 +TLSv1
SSLCipherSuite ALL:!ADH:RC4+RSA:+HIGH:+MEDIUM:-LOW:-SSLv2:-EXP
# Puppet master should generate initial CA certificate.
# ensure certs are located in /var/lib/puppet/ssl
SSLCertificateFile /var/lib/puppet/ssl/certs/puppet.example.com.pem
SSLCertificateKeyFile /var/lib/puppet/ssl/private_keys/puppet.example.com.pem
SSLCertificateChainFile /var/lib/puppet/ssl/certs/ca.pem
SSLCACertificateFile /var/lib/puppet/ssl/ca/ca_crt.pem
# CRL checking should be enabled
# disable next line if Apache complains about CRL
SSLCARevocationFile /var/lib/puppet/ssl/ca/ca_crl.pem
```

```
# optional to allow CSR request, required if certificates distributed to client during
provisioning.
SSLVerifyClient optional
SSLVerifyDepth 1
SSLOptions +StdEnvVars

# The following client headers record authentication information for down stream workers.
RequestHeader set X-SSL-Subject %{SSL_CLIENT_S_DN}e
RequestHeader set X-Client-DN %{SSL_CLIENT_S_DN}e
RequestHeader set X-Client-Verify %{SSL_CLIENT_VERIFY}e

<Location />
  SetHandler balancer-manager
  Order allow,deny
  Allow from all
</Location>

ProxyPass / balancer://puppetmaster/
ProxyPassReverse / balancer://puppetmaster/
ProxyPreserveHost On

</VirtualHost>
```

There are three main differences between the front-end load balancer configuration file in Listing 4-11 and the stand-alone Apache Puppet master configuration in Listing 4-6. At the top of the load balancer virtual host configuration, a pool of back-end virtual hosts is defined in the Proxy stanza. Notice that two virtual hosts are listed, port 18140 and port 18141, even though we have only configured the one listening on port 18140 so far.

Part of the responsibility of the front-end load balancer is to determine if each back-end worker is online and available to handle requests. Since no worker virtual host is available on port 18141 yet, the front-end virtual host will automatically take http://127.0.0.1:18141 out of rotation until it becomes available. The Puppet agent nodes will not see an error message unless all back-end worker virtual hosts are marked as offline.

In addition to defining the list of back-end worker virtual hosts, the Proxy stanza gives the name balancer://puppetmaster to the collection. When additional back-end virtual hosts are added to the system, they should be listed using the BalancerMember keyword in the Proxy stanza. Once listed, they'll automatically be added to the rotation of back-end workers used by the front-end virtual host listening on port 8140.

The second important section of the front-end virtual host configuration file is the three RequestHeader lines. These three configuration statements configure the front-end load balancer to set three client request headers containing authentication information. When a back-end Puppet master virtual host receives a client request from the load balancer, it will inspect these client request headers and set environment variables based on their contents. The Puppet master process will look to these environment variables while authorizing the Puppet agent request.

For the Puppet agent running on mail.example.com, the client request headers used for authentication look as shown in Listing 4-12.

Listing 4-12. Puppet agent authentication and authorization request headers

```
X-SSL-Subject: /CN=mail.example.com
X-Client-DN: /CN=mail.example.com
X-Client-Verify: SUCCESS
```

The X-SSL-Subject and X-Client-DN headers contain the same information, the common name from the verified SSL certificate presented by the Puppet agent. This information is provided in two headers to support back-end HTTP servers other than Apache. The X-Client-Verify header indicates to the back-end worker whether or not the load balancer was able to verify the authenticity of the client SSL certificate. This value will be SUCCESS in Apache if the client certificate is signed by a trusted Certificate Authority, is not listed in the Certificate Revocation List, and has not expired.

The information set in the client request headers directly matches the SetEnvIf configuration lines configured in the back-end Puppet master virtual host. We can see these lines in /etc/httpd/conf.d/40_puppetmaster_worker_18140.conf as we configured them in Listing 4-9:

```
# Obtain Authentication Information from Client Request Headers
SetEnvIf X-Client-Verify "(.*)" SSL_CLIENT_VERIFY=$1
SetEnvIf X-SSL-Client-DN "(.*)" SSL_CLIENT_S_DN=$1
```

The authentication information in a load-balanced Puppet master configuration is passed from the load balancer to the back-end workers using client request headers. This design allows heterogeneous front-end and back-end HTTP systems to work together as long as the back-end HTTP server is able to read the Puppet agent certificate common name and determine whether or not the certificate is currently valid. Once read from the headers, the back-end HTTP server sets this information in two environment variables for Puppet to reference.

The third important section in the front-end load balancer configuration in Listing 4-11 tells Apache to route all requests to the pool of Puppet master virtual hosts. This section is composed of the three lines, ProxyPass, ProxyPassReverse, ProxyPreserveHost. These three statements tell Apache the virtual host listening on port 8140 should forward all Puppet agent requests to the pool of Puppet master workers named balancer://puppetmaster.

■ **Tip** Detailed information about mod_proxy and additional configuration options are available online at http://httpd.apache.org/docs/2.0/mod/mod_proxy.html.

Testing the Load Balancer Configuration

We're now almost ready to test the new Puppet master configuration using the Puppet agent. Before doing so, you need to make sure each virtual host is logging information in a clearly defined location. This will allow you to trace the Puppet agent request as it passes through the front-end load balancer to the back-end worker virtual host.

To make it easier, let's separate out the logging events for each virtual host by adding ErrorLog and CustomLog configuration options to each configuration file, as shown in Listing 4-13.

Listing 4-13. Configuring front-end logging

```
ErrorLog /var/log/httpd/balancer_error.log
CustomLog /var/log/httpd/balancer_access.log combined
CustomLog /var/log/httpd/balancer_ssl_requests.log "%t %h %{SSL_PROTOCOL}x %{SSL_CIPHER}x
\"%r\" %b"
```

Only three lines need to be inserted into the <VirtualHost>…</VirtualHost> stanza to enable logging on the front end. Every request coming into the Puppet master infrastructure will pass through the front-end virtual host and will be logged to the balancer_access.log file.

Worker virtual hosts do not handle SSL encrypted traffic and only require two configuration lines to be inserted into the VirtualHost stanza. Every request routed to a specific worker will be logged into that worker's access log file. In Listing 4-14, we've included the TCP port number of the worker to uniquely identify the log file and the associated worker.

Listing 4-14. Configuring worker logging

```
ErrorLog /var/log/httpd/puppetmaster_worker_error_18140.log
CustomLog /var/log/httpd/puppetmaster_worker_access_18140.log combined
```

Once the front-end load balancer and back-end worker virtual hosts have been configured to log to their own log files, you need to restart Apache and makes sure the log files were created properly.

```
# service httpd restart
ls -l {balancer,puppetmaster}*.log
-rw-r--r-- 1 root root 0 Nov 26 15:36 balancer_access.log
-rw-r--r-- 1 root root 0 Nov 26 15:36 balancer_error.log
-rw-r--r-- 1 root root 0 Nov 26 15:36 balancer_ssl_requests.log
-rw-r--r-- 1 root root 0 Nov 26 15:36 puppetmaster_worker_access_18140.log
-rw-r--r-- 1 root root 0 Nov 26 15:36 puppetmaster_worker_error_18140.log
```

With the appropriate log files in place, you can now test the load balancer and the single back-end worker using puppet agent:

```
# puppet agent --test
info: Caching catalog for puppet.example.com
info: Applying configuration version '1290814852'
notice: Passenger is setup and serving catalogs.
notice: /Stage[main]//Node[default]/Notify[Passenger]/message: defined 'message' as 'Passenger
is setup and serving catalogs.'
notice: Finished catalog run in 0.43 seconds
```

Here we've run the puppet agent command and obtained a catalog from the Puppet master. The Apache load-balancing virtual host listened on puppet.example.com port 8140 and received the Puppet agent request, forwarded it along to the back-end Puppet master virtual host listening on port 18140, and then provided the response back to the Puppet agent.

We can check the Apache logs to verify that this is what actually happened, as shown in Listings 4-15 through 4-17.

Listing 4-15. Load balancer request log

```
# less balancer_access.log
127.0.0.1 - - [26/Nov/2010:15:40:51 -0800] "GET /production/catalog/puppet.example.com?facts=…
&facts_format=b64_zlib_yaml HTTP/1.1" 200 944 "-" "-"
127.0.0.1 - - [26/Nov/2010:15:40:53 -0800] "PUT /production/report/puppet.example.com
HTTP/1.1" 200 14 "-" "-"
```

Listing 4-16. Load balancer error log

```
root:/var/log/httpd # less balancer_error.log
[Fri Nov 26 15:40:53 2010] [error] (111)Connection refused: proxy: HTTP: attempt to connect to
127.0.0.1:18141 (127.0.0.1) failed
[Fri Nov 26 15:40:53 2010] [error] ap_proxy_connect_backend disabling worker for (127.0.0.1)
```

Listing 4-17. First Puppet master worker request log

```
# less puppetmaster_worker_access_18140.log
127.0.0.1 - - [26/Nov/2010:15:40:51 -0800] "GET /production/catalog/puppet.example.lan?facts=…
&facts_format=b64_zlib_yaml HTTP/1.1" 200 944 "-" "-"
127.0.0.1 - - [26/Nov/2010:15:40:53 -0800] "PUT /production/report/puppet.example.lan
HTTP/1.1" 200 14 "-" "-"
```

In Listing 4-15, you can see the incoming Puppet agent catalog request at 3:40:51 PM. The front-end load balancer receives the request and, according to the balancer_error.log shown in Listing 4-16, disables the worker virtual host on Port 18141. This leaves one additional worker in the balancer://puppetmaster pool, which receives the request, as indicated in puppetmaster_worker_access_18140.log shown in Listing 4-17. Finally, the Puppet agent uploads the catalog run report a few seconds later.

What happens, however, if all the back-end workers are disabled? Well, let's see. To do this, disable the Puppet master virtual host by renaming the configuration file:

```
# mv 40_puppetmaster_worker_18140.conf{,.disabled}
```

Restarting Apache:

```
# service httpd restart
Stopping httpd:                                          [  OK  ]
Starting httpd:                                          [  OK  ]
```

And then running the Puppet agent again:

```
# puppet agent --test
err: Could not retrieve catalog from remote server: Error 503 on SERVER …
warning: Not using cache on failed catalog
err: Could not retrieve catalog; skipping run
err: Could not send report: Error 503 on SERVER …
```

We've discovered that the Puppet agent receives error 503 when no back-end Puppet master worker virtual hosts are available. The front-end load balancer runs through its list of back-end workers defined in the Proxy balancer://puppetmaster section of 30_puppetmaster_frontend_8140.conf file. Finding no available back-end workers, the front-end returns HTTP error code 503, Service Temporarily Unavailable to the client. This HTTP error code is also available in the front-end load balancer's error log file (Listing 4-18).

Listing 4-18. Apache front end load balancer error log

```
# less balancer_error.log
[Fri Nov 26 15:59:01 2010] [error] (111)Connection refused: proxy: HTTP: attempt to connect to
127.0.0.1:18140 (127.0.0.1) failed
[Fri Nov 26 15:59:01 2010] [error] ap_proxy_connect_backend disabling worker for (127.0.0.1)
[Fri Nov 26 15:59:01 2010] [error] (111)Connection refused: proxy: HTTP: attempt to connect to
127.0.0.1:18141 (127.0.0.1) failed
[Fri Nov 26 15:59:01 2010] [error] ap_proxy_connect_backend disabling worker for (127.0.0.1)
[Fri Nov 26 15:59:01 2010] [error] proxy: BALANCER: (balancer://puppetmaster). All workers
are in error state
```

Now that you've seen one and no back-end masters working, let's bring back both workers back online. In doing so, you will configure the second Puppet master worker.

The second back-end worker running on TCP port 18141 is almost identical to the first worker virtual host configuration, except the port number is incremented by one. First re-enable the first back-end worker, and then define the second back-end worker:

```
# mv 40_puppetmaster_worker_18140.conf{.disabled,}
```

This command renamed the disabled configuration file back to the original name of 40_puppetmaster_worker_18140.conf, effectively re-enabling the worker virtual host listening on port 18140.

```
# sed s/18140/18141/ 40_puppetmaster_worker_18140.conf \
  > 41_puppetmaster_worker_18141.conf
```

This command reads the configuration file of the first worker and writes out a new configuration file for the second worker. While the original file is being read and the new file written, the sed command is performing a search-and-replace, replacing all instances of "18140" with "18141." The results are two nearly identical worker virtual hosts, the only difference being the port and the log files:

```
# rsync -axH /etc/puppet/rack/puppetmaster{,_18141}/
```

The Rack configuration for each worker process is identical and needs no modification when bringing additional workers online. Using the rsync command, we're able to create an identical copy of the existing Puppet rack configuration for use with the new worker virtual host.

Using the diff command, we're able to easily visualize the lines modified by the sed command. As you can see in Listing 4-19, the difference between the two worker configuration files is only a matter of the listening port and the log files.

Listing 4-19. Comparison of two Puppet master worker virtual host configurations

```
# diff -U2 4{0,1}*.conf
--- 40_puppetmaster_worker_18140.conf    2010-11-26 16:19:21.000000000 -0800
+++ 41_puppetmaster_worker_18141.conf    2010-11-26 16:19:31.000000000 -0800
@@ -1,4 +1,4 @@
-Listen 18140
-<VirtualHost 127.0.0.1:18140>
+Listen 18141
+<VirtualHost 127.0.0.1:18141>
 SSLEngine off

@@ -8,6 +8,6 @@

 RackAutoDetect On
-DocumentRoot /etc/puppet/rack/puppetmaster_18140/public/
-<Directory /etc/puppet/rack/puppetmaster_18140/>
+DocumentRoot /etc/puppet/rack/puppetmaster_18141/public/
+<Directory /etc/puppet/rack/puppetmaster_18141/>
    Options None
    AllowOverride None
@@ -16,6 +16,6 @@
 </Directory>

-ErrorLog /var/log/httpd/puppetmaster_worker_error_18140.log
-CustomLog /var/log/httpd/puppetmaster_worker_access_18140.log combined
+ErrorLog /var/log/httpd/puppetmaster_worker_error_18141.log
+CustomLog /var/log/httpd/puppetmaster_worker_access_18141.log combined
</VirtualHost>
```

As you can see, we configure a unique Rack DocumentRoot for each back-end Puppet master worker process. This is important to allow Passenger to track and identify each of the multiple Puppet masters. After configuring the second back-end worker virtual host, restart Apache:

```
# service httpd restart
Stopping httpd:                                           [  OK  ]
Starting httpd:                                           [  OK  ]
```

And test the Puppet agent again:

```
# puppet agent --test
info: Caching catalog for puppet.example.lan
info: Applying configuration version '1290817197'
notice: Passenger is setup and serving catalogs.
notice: /Stage[main]//Node[default]/Notify[Passenger]/message: defined 'message' as 'Passenger
is setup and serving catalogs.'
notice: Finished catalog run in 0.44 seconds
```

Both back-end Puppet master virtual hosts are now online and responding to requests. You can check the status of the Ruby processes Passenger has started using the passenger-status command. The passenger-status command indicates that the Puppet master process IDs started by Passenger when Puppet agent requests are routed to the back-end worker virtual hosts (see Listing 4-20).

Listing 4-20. The passenger-status command

```
# passenger-status
----------- General information -----------
max      = 6
count    = 2
active   = 0
inactive = 2
Waiting on global queue: 0

----------- Domains -----------
/etc/puppet/rack/puppetmaster_18140:
  PID: 25329   Sessions: 0   Processed: 1      Uptime: 27s

/etc/puppet/rack/puppetmaster_18141:
  PID: 25341   Sessions: 0   Processed: 1      Uptime: 25s
```

You can see the two Passenger processes servicing the front-end. With that, we've configured a simple and very scalable Puppet master implementation. To scale it further, all you now need to do is follow a subset of these steps to add additional back-end workers to the configuration and into the pool.

We also chose to configure the front-end and back-end virtual hosts all on the same system, as we can see through the use of 127.0.0.1 in each of the back-end configuration files and the Proxy section of the front-end virtual host. The choice to run all of the worker processes on the same host has greatly simplified the signing of SSL certificates when connecting new Puppet agent nodes. As mentioned previously in this chapter, the serial number and certificate revocation lists must be kept in sync across Puppet master systems that issue new client certificates. In the next section, you'll see how to manage back-end worker processes on separate systems.

Puppet CA Load Balancing Configuration

Thus far in this chapter, you've configured the Puppet master service in a stand-alone Apache virtual host. Scaling the Puppet master system horizontally, you configured a number of Apache virtual hosts working together behind a reverse proxy load balancer. In both configurations, all of the Puppet master worker virtual hosts are running on the same host.

With multiple Puppet master workers running on the same system, all workers write Puppet certificates to the same file system location. For this reason, you don't need to worry which worker accepts the certificate signing requests. But if you'd like to scale even further than what we've already done, and spread our Puppet master workers onto multiple systems, then management of certificates becomes an issue that you need to address.

There are a couple of ways you can address this issue:

- Synchronize the Puppet CA directory across all of the worker systems

- Make one worker system the active Puppet CA service and a second worker system the hot standby Puppet CA service

We're going to show you how to use a hot (active) standby CA model to keep your certificate data synchronized. This architecture allows you to keep all Puppet CA data in one place, thereby minimizing the effort needed to maintain the Puppet master infrastructure (see Figure 4-2).

To do this, you will configure a second system to periodically synchronize the Puppet CA files. If the active Puppet CA system falls offline, the front-end load balancer will automatically redirect certificate requests to the hot standby. With the CA kept in sync, the hot standby will be ready to serve certificate-signing requests for new hosts.

The hot standby model requires the front-end Apache load balancer to redirect all certificate requests from all Puppet agent nodes to a specific set of Puppet master workers. We'll demonstrate how to do this and see how to test the new configuration. Finally, we'll show how to take the primary Puppet CA offline for maintenance and back online again, including handling if Puppet agents have submitted certificate requests to the hot standby.

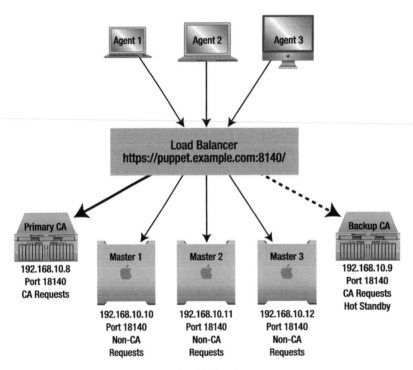

Figure 4-2. Puppet agent HTTPS load balancing

Puppet CA Worker Configuration

The first step to take when scaling the Puppet master infrastructure across multiple worker systems is to add two additional work virtual hosts for the Puppet CA service. While developing and testing, we're going to configure these using the 127.0.0.1 local host address. In a production configuration, the addresses of each Puppet master and Puppet CA worker should be on different hosts.

First create two new virtual hosts using the existing configurations of the two we created earlier. The virtual host workers listening on port 18142 and 18143 will be specifically for the active and hot standby Puppet CA service:

```
# sed s/18140/18142/ 40_puppetmaster_worker_18140.conf \
  > 42_puppetmaster_worker_18142.conf
```

Substitute all instances of the string "18140" with the string "18142" and write the output to the new configuration file named 42_puppetmaster_worker_18142.conf. This configuration file is the virtual host for the Puppet CA.

```
# rsync -axH /etc/puppet/rack/puppetmaster{,_18142}/
```

Next, copy the entire contents of the original Rack configuration from Listing 4-7 without modification. This configuration will use the default SSL directory:

```
# sed s/18140/18143/ 40_puppetmaster_worker_18140.conf \
  > 43_puppetmaster_worker_18143.conf
# rsync -axH /etc/puppet/rack/puppetmaster{,_18143}/
```

Repeat the process of searching and replacing the port number for the standby Puppet CA worker. The virtual host listening on port 18142 will become the active Puppet CA back-end worker. The virtual host listening on port 18143 will become the hot standby Puppet CA back-end worker.

In order to simulate the two different Puppet CA workers living on two different systems, you'll need to duplicate the existing CA directory into a new location. This configuration prevents the two Puppet CA systems from sharing the same CA directory and certificate revocation list:

```
# rsync -axH /var/lib/puppet/ssl/ca{,.standby}/
```

The rsync command duplicates the existing Puppet CA directory into a new directory at /var/lib/puppet/ssl/ca.standby/:

```
# vim /etc/puppet/rack/puppetmaster_18143/config.ru
```

We're editing the file to add a single line immediately above the existing "ARGV" line. The new line contains ARGV << "--cadir" << "/var/lib/puppet/ssl/ca.standby". A complete listing of the standby CA's Rack configuration is provided in Listing 4-21.

Listing 4-21. Standby Puppet CA Rack configuration

```
$0 = "master"
# if you want debugging:
# ARGV << "--debug"
ARGV << "--cadir" << "/var/lib/puppet/ssl/ca.standby"
ARGV << "--rack"
require 'puppet/application/master'
run Puppet::Application[:master].run
```

Using this configuration, the Active Puppet CA worker will continue to use /var/lib/puppet/ssl/ca/ while the standby worker will use /var/lib/puppet/ssl/ca.standby/.

We should now restart the Apache service to make sure the changes are valid but at this point the front-end HTTPS reverse proxy has not yet been configured to route any requests to either of these two Puppet CA workers.

We now need to configure the front-end load balancer to redirect all certificate related requests to the new port 18142 worker. We also configure the load balancer to fall back to the hot standby running at 18143 if the primary Puppet CA worker is offline (see Listing 4-22).

Listing 4-22. Standby Puppet CA Load Balancer configuration

```
# vim 30_puppetmaster_frontend_8140.conf
<Proxy balancer://puppetmasterca>
  # Puppet CA Active Worker
  BalancerMember http://127.0.0.1:18142
  # Puppet CA Hot Standby
  BalancerMember http://127.0.0.1:18143 status=+H
</Proxy>
```

As we can see in Listing 4-22, a new Proxy section configures the load balancer to first connect to http://127.0.0.1:18142, and then connect to http://127.0.0.1:18143 when a request is sent to the balancer named puppetmasterca. The option status=+H tells the front end that the second member is a hot standby.

With the back-end Puppet CA workers configured, the load balancer must now be configured to route certificate requests, and only certificate requests, to the two member workers. This configuration listing goes in the main Apache front-end virtual host block, as shown in Listing 4-23.

Listing 4-23. Load Balancer certificate request routing configuration

```
# Ordering of ProxyPass directives is important
# Direct all Puppet agent CA requests to a specific set of workers.
ProxyPassMatch ^(/.*?)/(certificate.*?)/(.*)$ balancer://puppetmasterca
ProxyPassReverse ^(/.*?)/(certificate.*?)/(.*)$ balancer://puppetmasterca
# Direct all other Puppet agent requests to the default set of workers.
 ProxyPass / balancer://puppetmaster/
 ProxyPassReverse / balancer://puppetmaster/

ProxyPreserveHost On
```

Here, we configured the load balancer to handle requests matching a pattern indicating they are certificate-related. We configured the load balancer to direct these requests to the group of workers named balancer://puppetmasterca, which were defined in Listing 4-22. Using this group of workers guarantees that the load balancer will send the request to the worker on 18142 if it is online, and 18143 if 18142 is down, and return HTTP status 503 Temporarily Unavailable if neither is available.

The ProxyPassMatch directive configures a regular expression to match against the request URI of the Puppet agent. In this case, we have configured the URI containing certificate in the second path element as a match. This ensures that certificate requests are directed appropriately, regardless of the environment or the Puppet agent name.

After configuring the two back-end Puppet CA worker virtual hosts on ports 18142 and 18143, you need to restart Apache:

```
# service httpd restart
Stopping httpd:                                    [  OK  ]
Starting httpd:                                    [  OK  ]
```

Let's test the new configuration, with a new system named mock.example.com:

```
# puppet agent --test
info: Creating a new SSL key for mock.example.com
info: Caching certificate for ca
info: Creating a new SSL certificate request for mock.example.com
info: Certificate Request fingerprint (md5): 3C:56:A1:FD:6A:4B:2F:C5:72:8C:66:1E:39:D2:99:AB
Exiting; no certificate found and waitforcert is disabled
```

Once the new Puppet agent creates a certificate-signing request and submits it to the load balancer, we can check the Apache logs to make sure that CA requests are being routed properly to the worker listening on port 18142.

In Listing 4-24, you can see a number of HTTP 404 status results on the second and third line of the logs. Apache is returning status 404 "Not Found" because the Puppet node mock.example.com is a new node and no signed certificates or certificate requests exist for this system. Until we sign the new certificate request using the puppet cert --sign command, the Puppet CA worker will continue to return 404 "Not Found" status codes to the Puppet agent on mock.example.com.

Listing 4-24. HTTP 404 status results due to certificate errors

```
# less puppetmaster_worker_access_18142.log
127.0.0.1 - - [27/Nov/2010:15:04:05 -0800] "GET /production/certificate/ca HTTP/1.1" 200 839
"-" "-"
127.0.0.1 - - [27/Nov/2010:15:04:06 -0800] "GET /production/certificate/mock.example.com
HTTP/1.1" 404 43 "-" "-"
127.0.0.1 - - [27/Nov/2010:15:04:06 -0800] "GET
/production/certificate_request/mock.example.com HTTP/1.1" 404 51 "-" "-"
127.0.0.1 - - [27/Nov/2010:15:04:06 -0800] "PUT
/production/certificate_request/mock.example.com HTTP/1.1" 200 4 "-" "-"
127.0.0.1 - - [27/Nov/2010:15:04:06 -0800] "GET /production/certificate/mock.example.com
HTTP/1.1" 404 43 "-" "-"
127.0.0.1 - - [27/Nov/2010:15:04:06 -0800] "GET /production/certificate/mock.example.com
HTTP/1.1" 404 43 "-" "-"
```

To make sure the Puppet agent is routed to the correct worker system, you need to sign the new certificate request:

```
puppetca --sign mock.example.com
notice: Signed certificate request for mock.example.com
notice: Removing file Puppet::SSL::CertificateRequest mock.example.com \
  at '/var/lib/puppet/ssl/ca/requests/mock.example.com.pem'
```

Note that the primary Puppet CA worker is using the default CA directory. If the active worker falls offline, requests will be redirected to the Puppet CA worker on 18143 and therefore the /var/lib/puppet/ssl/ca.standby/ directory.

Once the certificate has been signed, you can run the Puppet agent on the new node again to make sure the agent is able to download its signed certificate from the master.

```
# puppet agent --test
info: Caching certificate for mock.example.com
info: Caching certificate_revocation_list for ca
info: Caching catalog for mock.example.com
```

```
info: Applying configuration version '1290900612'
notice: Passenger is setup and serving catalogs.
notice: /Stage[main]//Node[default]/Notify[Passenger]/message: defined 'message' as 'Passenger
is setup and serving catalogs.'
notice: Finished catalog run in 0.06 seconds
```

You can also check the logs again to make sure HTTP Status 200 is present, now that the Puppet agent has the signed certificate:

```
# tail -2 puppetmaster_worker_access_18142.log
127.0.0.1 - - [27/Nov/2010:15:04:31 -0800] "GET /production/certificate/mock.example.com
HTTP/1.1" 200 875 "-" "-"
127.0.0.1 - - [27/Nov/2010:15:04:32 -0800] "GET /production/certificate_revocation_list/ca
HTTP/1.1" 200 589 "-" "-"
```

You can see two log entries, matching up with the Puppet agent downloading its signed certificate and the certificate revocation list maintained by the Puppet CA worker. Both entries contain HTTP Status 200 "OK" codes, indicating that the Puppet agent successfully transferred the certificate and revocation list from the Puppet CA.

You can also see that the access logs for the active Puppet CA worker does not contain any catalog requests. Check the access logs of the two load balanced Puppet master workers running on ports 18140 and 18141 in order to make sure catalog requests are being routed correctly to only those two systems:

```
# less puppetmaster_worker_access_18140.log
127.0.0.1 - - [27/Nov/2010:15:04:32 -0800] "GET
/production/catalog/mock.example.lan?facts_format=b64_zlib_yaml&facts=… HTTP/1.1" 200 942 "-
" "-"
```

Note that the catalog requests are still being directed by the front-end load balancer to the worker running on Port 18140, while certificate requests are being directed to the active Puppet CA on port 18142.

With this, you've configured the front-end HTTP load balancer to direct all certificate related requests to a single Puppet CA worker. This redirection ensures that the certificate revocation list and serial.txt files are maintained properly.

Synchronizing the Hot Standby Puppet CA Directory

Now that the certificate requests are being handled properly, the next step is to configure the hot standby Puppet CA worker. If the primary Puppet CA worker fails, another worker should quickly take over responsibility for responding to certificate requests. We will take advantage of the load balancer's ability to redirect requests in order to quickly fail over to the backup Puppet CA worker.

You first need to configure a periodic task to automatically synchronize the CA directory across the primary and secondary workers. Next, you'll configure the load balancer to use the secondary worker as a hot standby, automatically activated in the event the primary worker goes offline. Finally, you will test the new configuration and work through the exercise of testing the fail-over and fail-back to the primary Puppet CA worker.

In the following examples, we have configured both Puppet CA workers on the same system using two distinct certificate authority directories. Copy the existing certificate authority directory to the hot standby using rsync. This command could also be configured as a cron task, to keep the hot standby directory contents up to date:

```
# cadir=$(puppet master --configprint cadir)
```

This command sets an environment variable named $cadir set to the default value of the cadir configuration setting used by the primary CA worker.

```
# rsync -avxH --delete ${cadir}{,.standby}/
```

This rsync command synchronizes the primary CA directory into the standby CA directory, deleting any files existing in the destination and not in the source.

Puppet CA Hot Standby

Once the certificate data has been synchronized, you can test failover between the two virtual hosts on ports 18142 and 18143. In the previous section, we configured the virtual host running on port 18143 as a hot standby. We also configured /etc/puppet/rack/puppetmaster_18143/config.ru to use a unique CA directory named ca.standby.

We're going to use the iptables firewall to block traffic to the primary Puppet CA worker, effectively simulating a failure of the service. We expect the load balancer configuration to automatically redirect certificate requests to the hot standby.

```
$ sudo iptables -I INPUT -i lo -p tcp --dport 18142 -j REJECT --reject-with icmp-
host-prohibited
```

Once the primary Puppet CA worker is inaccessible, you can test that certificate requests are automatically redirected to the secondary worker listening on port 18143, using the curl command

```
$ curl --silent -o /dev/null -D /dev/stdout -q -k -H "Accept: s"
https://puppet:8140/production/certificate/ca
HTTP/1.1 200 OK
Date: Sat, 04 Dec 2010 23:37:35 GMT
Server: Apache/2.2.3 (CentOS)
X-Powered-By: Phusion Passenger (mod_rails/mod_rack) 2.2.11
Content-Length: 839
Status: 200
Content-Type: text/plain; charset=UTF-8
Connection: close
```

You can see the results of this curl in the logs:

```
$ tail -n2 /var/log/httpd/balancer_error.log
[Sat Dec 04 15:42:36 2010] [error] (113)No route to host: proxy: HTTP: attempt to connect to
127.0.0.1:18142 (127.0.0.1) failed
[Sat Dec 04 15:42:36 2010] [error] ap_proxy_connect_backend disabling worker for (127.0.0.1)
```

And:

```
$ tail -n1 /var/log/httpd/puppetmaster_worker_access_18143.log
127.0.0.1 - - [04/Dec/2010:15:42:36 -0800] "GET /production/certificate/ca HTTP/1.1" 200 839
"-" "curl/7.15.5 (x86_64-redhat-linux-gnu) libcurl/7.15.5 OpenSSL/0.9.8b zlib/1.2.3
libidn/0.6.5"
```

The first command we've executed is a standard curl HTTP request. Rather than display the contents of the request body, we display the HTTP Response headers on standard output. The HTTP header output provides an indication of the status of the response, with anything other than status 200 indicating an error.

After requesting the Puppet CA certificate, you can look at the error log file of the front-end load balancer to see how the request as handled. As expected, the iptables firewall rule prevented the load balancer from forwarding the request to the primary Puppet CA worker listening on port 18142. The load balancer properly failed over to the hot standby Puppet CA worker listening on port 18143 and forwarded the request to the virtual host.

Looking at the access logs in puppetmaster_worker_access_18143.log of the Puppet CA worker listening on port 18143, we can see the incoming request and resulting HTTP 200 OK status code for the response.

Now we want to make sure we can still provision new Puppet managed nodes while the hot standby certificate authority is currently active. With a different CA directory configured on the hot standby, the process of listing and signing certificates is slightly different, requiring the use of the puppet cert --cadir configuration option:

```
# puppet agent --certname test.example.lan --test --noop
info: Creating a new SSL key for test.example.lan
info: Creating a new SSL certificate request for test.example.lan
info: Certificate Request fingerprint (md5): A5:47:AE:F9:08:A8:5D:EF:5D:82:7E:3F:8C:8C:09:82
Exiting; no certificate found and waitforcert is disabled
```

The first time a Puppet agent is run, a new certificate request is generated and submitted to the Puppet master. Since the primary Puppet CA worker is offline, we expect to see the pending certificate request in the standby directory:

```
# puppet cert --cadir /var/lib/puppet/ssl/ca.standby --list
test.example.lan
```

In order to see the pending certificate-signing request in the standby directory, you need to provide the --cadir option, as we've done using the puppet cert command shown in Listing 4-25.

Listing 4-25. Signing a CSR on the standby Puppet CA

```
# puppet cert --cadir /var/lib/puppet/ssl/ca.standby --sign test.example.lan
notice: Signed certificate request for test.example.lan
notice: Removing file Puppet::SSL::CertificateRequest test.example.lan at
'/var/lib/puppet/ssl/ca.standby/requests/test.example.lan.pem'
```

Similar to listing the pending requests, you're able to sign a specific request waiting in the standby directory using puppet cert with the --cadir option.

```
# puppet agent --certname test.example.lan --test --noop
warning: peer certificate won't be verified in this SSL session
info: Caching certificate for test.example.lan
info: Caching catalog for test.example.lan
info: Applying configuration version '1291556503'
notice: /Stage[main]//Node[default]/Notify[Passenger]/message: is absent, should be Passenger
is setup and serving catalogs. (noop)
notice: Finished catalog run in 0.40 seconds
```

Finally, you can reconnect the Puppet agent and obtain the signed certificate using the same command we started with. The peer certificate warning in this output may be safely ignored.

Primary Puppet CA Fail Back

The failover to the secondary CA is now working properly, and new certificates can be signed. Let's test the process of re-activating the primary Puppet CA Worker. The load balancer will automatically start using the primary worker when it comes online again, so the process becomes a matter of synchronizing the secondary certificate authority back to the primary CA directory. You need to synchronize changes before re-activating the firewall rule to allow traffic back to the primary certificate authority.

Similar to the rsync command synchronizing the primary CA directory into the standby location, the rsync command shown in Listing 4-26 reverses the direction and synchronizes the standby CA directory into the primary location before re-enabling the primary CA using the host firewall.

Listing 4-26. How to rsync standby CA back to the primary CA

```
# rsync -avxH --delete /var/lib/puppet/ssl/ca{.standby,}/
building file list ... done
./
inventory.txt
serial
requests/
signed/
signed/test.example.lan.pem
sent 2103 bytes  received 104 bytes  4414.00 bytes/sec
total size is 5980  speedup is 2.71

# iptables -L INPUT -n -v --line-number
Chain INPUT (policy ACCEPT 0 packets, 0 bytes)
num   pkts bytes target      prot opt in     out     source               destination
1        0     0 REJECT      tcp  --  lo     *       0.0.0.0/0            0.0.0.0/0
tcp dpt:18142 reject-with icmp-host-prohibited
2     290K   59M RH-Firewall-1-INPUT  all  --  *      *       0.0.0.0/0            0.0.0.0/0

# iptables -D INPUT 1
```

The two iptables commands first list the rules associated with incoming traffic. We see that rule #1 is rejecting traffic destined for the port used by the primary CA worker. The second iptables command deletes rule #1 to allow traffic once again.

You performed three simple tasks to re-activate the primary Puppet CA Worker. First, you synchronized the CA directory from the standby in Listing 4-23. Notice that three files have changed since the hot standby worker has become active. These three files changed when you signed the certificate request for test.example.lan in Listing 4-22. Immediately after synchronizing the CA directory, you removed the iptables rule blocking access to the primary Puppet CA worker. The first iptables command lists rules in the INPUT chain by number and the second iptables command removes rule number one from the firewall policy.

▒ **Caution** When failing back to the primary Puppet CA worker, there will be short delay where certificate requests are still directed to the hot standby. This delay is determined by how frequently the load balancer polls failed worker nodes to find out if they're back online. In situations where a large number of certificate requests are being handled while the Puppet CA is being switched online, it is recommended to make the ca.standby directory read-only to the puppet user and group to prevent changes from occurring after synchronization.

An Alternative: Load Balancing with DNS Round Robin

Up until now, we've relied on an HTTP load balancer using Apache to scale. This configuration allows us to easily redirect and consolidate all certificate requests to a single Puppet CA worker. However, we could also use DNS round robin to achieve the same ends.

DNS round robin is commonly used to cluster a group of worker processes providing the same service. In this configuration, redirection to different workers is performed at the name resolution stage instead of using a reverse HTTP proxy. As a result, the Puppet master infrastructure is no longer able to make decisions about the redirection based on the client request. Furthermore, if a specific Puppet master worker is offline, the DNS system is not checking the state of the worker and as a result, a portion of the Puppet agent systems will receive timeout errors when they are directed to connect to the failed worker system. We recommend deploying HTTP load balancing whenever possible to scale Puppet because of these shortcomings in DNS round robin.

Like our HTTP load balancing, all certificate-related requests should be consolidated onto one worker system to mitigate problems with certificate serial numbers and revocation lists diverging among the Puppet CA systems. To this end, the Puppet agent supports the configuration of a different Puppet CA server from the Puppet master server the configuration catalog is obtained from. When configuring Puppet using round robin DNS, it is recommended to maintain a single Puppet CA worker in addition to the number of Puppet master workers required. The Puppet agent configuration should set the --ca_server configuration option to bypass the round robin DNS configuration and contact the appropriate Puppet CA worker directly.

Measuring Performance

Catalog retrieval time is the primary measure of how one or more Puppet masters are performing. Catalog compilation is a very I/O-, CPU- and memory-intensive process. All of the imported manifests must be located and read from the file system, and CPU and memory are used to parse and compile the catalog. In order to measure this process, you can use a simple `curl` script to periodically obtain a compiled catalog. If the command takes longer than is normal for the environment, there is a strong indication additional capacity should be added to the Puppet master infrastructure.

Using the un-encrypted Puppet master back-end workers configured when setting up the Apache load balancer, you can write a small script to measure the catalog compilation time of the node `test.example.com`.

To do this, you need to know the four components of a catalog request:

- The URI containing the environment, catalog, and node to obtain a catalog from

- The SSL authentication headers

- A list of facts and their values

- A header telling the Puppet master what encoding formats the client accepts

All of this information is available in the Apache access logs (see Listing 4-27). The list of facts is easily obtained by running the Puppet agent normally, then inspecting the HTTP access logs and copying the URL into a script.

Listing 4-27. Curl URL based on Apache access logs

```
# tail balancer_access.log
127.0.0.1 - - [05/Dec/2010:05:41:41 -0800] "GET \
/production/catalog/test.example.lan?facts_format=b64_zlib_yaml&facts=eNqdVVt… HTTP/1.1"
200 944 "-" "-"
```

The path following the `GET` verb contains `/production/catalog/test.example.lan`. This indicates a catalog request for the host `test.example.lan` from the production environment. The query portion of the URL contains two pieces of information: the format of the facts listing, and the listing of facts itself. These pieces of information are encoded in the `facts_format` and `facts` query parameters of the URL.

To construct the full URL, prefix the URL from Listing 4-28 with `http://127.0.0.1:18141`, the address of the Apache worker virtual host. The command the operator uses to measure catalog compilation time is:

Listing 4-28. Curl catalog request command

```
$ time curl -v -H "Accept: pson, yaml" \
   -H "X-Client-DN: /CN=test.example.com" \
   -H "X-Client-Verify: SUCCESS" \
'http://127.0.0.1:18141/production/catalog/test.example.com?facts=…&facts_format=b64_zlib_ya
ml
```

Placing this command in a script and executing it on the Puppet master worker nodes allows us to know when catalog compilation time grows beyond normal thresholds.

Splay Time

Related to catalog compilation time, Puppet agent processes sometimes present a thundering herd problem when all systems have their clocks synchronized and are configured to run from the `cron` daemon at a specific time. The catalog compilation process is quite processor–intensive, and if the

Puppet master receives too many requests in a short period of time, the systems may start to thrash and degrade in performance.

When running a Puppet agent out of cron, we recommend introducing a small random splay time to ensure that all of the Puppet agent nodes do not request their configuration catalog at exactly the same moment. The Example.com operator follows this recommendation and uses the Puppet agent wrapper script shown in Listing 4-29 when executing the Puppet agent out of cron.

Listing 4-29. Bash script to splay Puppet agents

```
#! /bin/bash
set -e
set -u
sleep $((RANDOM % 300))
exec puppet agent --no-daemonize --onetime
```

The sleep command in this shell script causes a delay between zero and five minutes. With hundreds of Puppet agent managed nodes, this random delay will ensure incoming requests to the Puppet Mater workers are spread out over a short window of time.

Summary

In this chapter, you've configured the Puppet master infrastructure in a number of ways. Specifically, you configured the Apache web server as a reverse HTTPS proxy to handle the SSL verification and authentication of incoming Puppet agent managed nodes. Once authenticated, the Apache system behaves as a HTTP load balancer, distributing requests automatically to some number of back-end Puppet master worker virtual hosts.

In addition, we showed you how to handle incoming certificate requests in a special manner, forwarding all certificate requests to a single Puppet CA worker process with a hot standby ready and waiting for redundancy. The consolidation of certificate requests to a single Puppet CA worker mitigates the overhead and problems associated with keeping the Puppet CA certificate revocation list, serial numbers, and index synchronized across workers.

In addition to HTTP load balancing, distributing incoming requests using DNS round robin is a viable alternative when using the --ca_server Puppet agent configuration option. Similar to the HTTP load-balancing configuration, the ca_server option allows the operator to consolidate certificate requests onto a single worker system and alleviates the issues managing and synchronizing the certificate authority database files.

Finally, you learned how to measure the catalog compilation time of the Puppet master workers and use splay time to avoid overwhelming the Puppet masters.

Resources

- Using Passenger - http://projects.puppetlabs.com/projects/1/wiki/Using_Passenger

- Apache Configuration Reference - http://httpd.apache.org/docs/2.2/

- Apache Mod Proxy Balancer - http://httpd.apache.org/docs/2.2/mod/mod_proxy_balancer.html

- DNS Round Robin - http://en.wikipedia.org/wiki/Round_robin_DNS

- Puppet REST API - http://docs.puppetlabs.com/guides/rest_api.html

CHAPTER 5

■■■

Externalizing Puppet Configuration

In Chapter 2 we talked about the ways that you could define your hosts or nodes to Puppet. We talked about specifying them in a variety of forms as node statements in your Puppet manifest files. We also mentioned that Puppet has the capability to store node information in external sources. This avoids the need to specify large numbers of nodes manually in your manifests files, a solution which is time-consuming and not scalable.

Puppet has two ways to store node information externally:

- External Node Classification
- LDAP server classification

The first capability is called External Node Classification (ENC). ENC is a script-based integration system that Puppet queries for node data. The script returns classes, inheritance, variables and environment configuration that Puppet can then use to define a node and configure your hosts.

■ **Tip** External node classifiers are also one of the means by which tools like the Puppet Dashboard and Foreman can be integrated into Puppet and provide node information, as you will see in Chapter 7.

The second capability allows you to query Lightweight Directory Access Protocol (LDAP) directories for node information. This integration is used less often than ENCs, but it is especially useful because you can specify an existing LDAP directory, for example your asset management database or an LDAP DNS back end, for your node data.

Using external node classification, either via an ENC or via LDAP, is the recommended way to scale your Puppet implementation to cater for large volumes of hosts. Most of the multi-thousand node sites using Puppet, for example Google and Zynga, make use of external node classification systems to allow them to deal with the large number of nodes. Rather than managing files containing hundreds, thousands or even tens of thousands of node statements, you can use this:

```
node mail.example.com { … }
node web.example.com { … }
node db.example.com { … }
…
```

This allows you to specify a single source of node information and make quick and easy changes to that information without needing to edit files.

In this chapter, we discuss both approaches to storing node information in external sources. First we look at creating an external node classifier, and we provide some simple examples of these for you to model your own on; then we demonstrate the use of the LDAP node classifier.

External Node Classification

Writing an ENC is very simple. An ENC is merely a script that takes a node name, for example `mail.example.com`, and then returns the node's configuration in the form of YAML data. YAML or Yet Another Markup Language (`http://www.yaml.org/`) is a serialization language used in a variety of programming languages. YAML is human-friendly, meaning it's structured and is designed to be easy for humans to read. It is often used as a configuration file format; for example, the database configuration file used in Ruby on Rails applications, database.yml, is a YAML file.

Let's look at some simple YAML examples to get an idea for how it works. YAML is expressed in a hash where structure is important. Let's start by specifying a list of items:

```
---
- foo
- bar
- baz
- qux
```

The start of a YAML document is identified with three dashes, "---". Every ENC needs to return these three dashes as the start of its output. We've then got a list of items preceded by dashes.

We can also express the concept of assigning a value to an item, for example:

```
---
foo: bar
```

Here we've added our three dashes and then expressed that the value of item "foo" is "bar." We can also express grouped collections of items (which we're going to use heavily in our ENCs):

```
---
foo:
 - bar
baz:
 - qux
```

We've again started with our three dashes and then specified the names of the lists we're creating: foo and baz. Inside each list are the list items, again preceded with a dash, but this time indented one space to indicate their membership of the list.

This indentation is very important. For the YAML to be valid, it must be structured correctly. This can sometimes be a real challenge but there are some tools you can use to structure suitable YAML. For example, VIM syntax highlighting will recognize YAML (if the file you're editing has a .yml or .yaml extension) or you can use the excellent Online YAML Parser to confirm the YAML you're generating is valid: `http://yaml-online-parser.appspot.com/`.

But before we generate our first YAML node, we need to configure Puppet to use an external node classifier instead of our file-based node configuration.

■ **Note** You can see a more complete example of structured YAML at http://www.yaml.org/start.html.

Configuring Nodes Using An External Node Classifier

To use external nodes, we first need to tell Puppet to use a classifier to configure our nodes rather than use node definitions. We do this by specifying the node_terminus option and the name and location of our classifier in the [master] (or [puppetmasterd] in pre-2.6.0 versions) section of the puppet.conf configuration file on our Puppet master. You can see this in Listing 5-1, where we've specified a classifier called puppet_node_classifier located in the /usr/bin directory.

Listing 5-1. The external_nodes configuration option

```
[master]
node_terminus = exec
external_nodes = /usr/bin/puppet_node_classifier
```

The node_terminus configuration option is used to configure Puppet for node sources other than the default flat file manifests. The exec option tells Puppet to use an external node classifier script.

A classifier can be written in any language, for example shell script, Ruby, Perl, Python, or a variety of other languages. The only requirement is that the language can output the appropriate YAML data. For example, you could also easily add a database back end to a classifier that queries a database for the relevant hostname and returns the associated classes and any variables.

Following are some example node classifiers written in different languages.

■ **Note** You can have nodes specified both in Puppet manifests and external node classifiers. For this to work correctly, though, your ENC must return an empty YAML hash.

An External Node Classifier in a Shell Script

In Listing 5-2, you can see a very simple node classifier, the puppet_node_classifier script we specified in Listing 5-1. This classifier is written in shell script.

Listing 5-2. Simple Node Classifier

```
#!/bin/sh
cat <<"END"
---
classes:
  - base
parameters:
  puppetserver: puppet.example.com
END
exit 0
```

The script in Listing 5-2 will return the same classes and variables each time it is called irrelevant of what hostname is passed to the script.

```
$ puppet_node_classifier web.example.com
```

Will return:

```
---
classes:
  - base
parameters:
  puppetserver: puppet.example.com
```

The `classes` block holds a list of the classes that belong to this node, and the `parameters` block contains a list of the variables that this node specifies. In this case, the node includes the base class and has a variable called **$puppetserver** with a value of **puppet.example.com**.

Puppet will use this data to construct a node definition as if we'd defined a **node** statement. That node statement would look like Listing 5-3.

Listing 5-3. Node definition from Listing 5-2's classifier

```
node web.example.com {
        $puppetserver = 'puppet.example.com'
        include base
}
```

This is the simplest ENC that we can devise. Let's look at some more complex variations of this script that can return different results depending on the particular node name being passed to the classifier, in the same way different nodes would be configured with different classes, definitions, and variables in your manifest files.

■ **Tip** Any parameters specified in your ENC will be available as top-scope variables.

A Ruby External Node Classifier

Let's look at another example of an ENC, this time specifying a list of hosts or returning an empty YAML hash if the host is not found. This ENC is written in Ruby, and you can see it in Listing 5-4.

Listing 5-4. Ruby node classifier

```
#!/usr/bin/env ruby

require 'yaml'

node = ARGV[0]
default = { 'classes' => []}

unless node =~ /(^\S+)\.(\S+\.\S+)$/
```

```
    print default.to_yaml
    exit 0
end

hostname = $1

base = { 'environment' => 'production',
         'parameters' => {
                      'puppetserver' => 'puppet.example.com'
         },
         'classes' => [ 'base' ],
       }

case hostname
  when /^web?\w+$/
     web = { 'classes' => 'apache'  }
     base['classes'] << web['classes']
     puts YAML.dump(base)
  when /^db?\w+$/
     db = { 'classes' => 'mysql'  }
     base['classes'] << db['classes']
     puts YAML.dump(base)
  when /^mail?\w+$/
     mail = { 'classes' => 'postfix'  }
     base['classes'] << mail['classes']
     puts YAML.dump(base)
  else
     print default.to_yaml
end

exit 0
```

Our simple ENC here captures the incoming node name and rejects and returns an empty hash (defined in the default variable) if it is not an appropriately formed fully-qualified domain name (FQDN).

We then set up some basic defaults, the puppetserver variable, our environment, and a base class. The ENC then takes the host name portion of the FQDN and checks it against a list of host names, for example matching it against web, web1, web123 and so on for database and mail hosts.

For example, if we passed the ENC a node name of web.example.com, it would return a YAML hash of:

```
---
parameters:
  puppetserver: puppet.example.com
classes:
 - base
 - apache
environment: production
```

Which would result in a node definition of:

```
node web.example.com {
  $puppetserver = puppet.example.com
  include base
  include apache
}
```

This would specify that this node belonged to the **production** environment.
If the ENC doesn't match any host names, then it will return an empty YAML hash.

A Perl External Node Classifier

In Listing 5-5, you can see another node classifier written in Perl.

Listing 5-5. Perl-based node classifier

```perl
#!/usr/bin/perl -w
use strict;
use YAML qw( Dump );

my $hostname = shift || die "No hostname passed";

$hostname =~ /^(\w+)\.(\w+)\.(\w{3})$/
    or die "Invalid hostname: $hostname";

my ( $host, $domain, $net ) = ( $1, $2, $3 );

my @classes = ( 'base', $domain );
my %parameters = (
    puppetserver    => "puppet.$domain.$net"
    );

print Dump( {
    classes      => \@classes,
    parameters   => \%parameters,
} );
```

In Listing 5-5, we've created a Perl node classifier that makes use of the Perl YAML module. The YAML module can be installed via CPAN or your distribution's package management system. For example, on Debian it is the `libyaml-perl` package, or on Fedora it is the `perl-YAML` package.

The classifier slices our hostname into sections; it assumes the input will be a fully qualified domain name and will fail if no hostname or an inappropriately structured hostname is passed. The classifier then uses those sections to classify the nodes and set parameters. If we called this node classifier with the hostname `web.example.com`, it would return a node classification of:

```
---
classes:
  - base
  - example
parameters:
  puppetserver: puppet.example.com
```

This would result in a node definition in Puppet structured like:

```
node 'web.example.com' {
        include base, example

        $puppetserver = "puppet.example.com"
}
```

▓ **Note** From Puppet 2.6.5 and later, you can also specify parameterized classes and resources in external node classifiers (see http://docs.puppetlabs.com/guides/external_nodes.html for more details).

Back-Ending a Node Classification

Lastly, as mentioned, we could also back-end our node classification script with a database, as you can see in Listing 5-6.

Listing 5-6. A database back-end node classifier

```perl
#!/usr/bin/perl -w
use strict;
use YAML qw( Dump );
use DBI;

my $hostname = shift || die "No hostname passed";

$hostname =~ /^(\w+)\.(\w+)\.(\w{3})$/
    or die "Invalid hostname: $hostname";

my ( $host, $domain, $net ) = ( $1, $2, $3 );

# MySQL Configuration
my $data_source = "dbi:mysql:database=puppet;host=localhost";
my $username = "puppet";
my $password = "password";

# Connect to the server
my $dbh = DBI->connect($data_source, $username, $password)
    or die $DBI::errstr;

# Build the query
my $sth = $dbh->prepare( qq{SELECT class FROM nodes WHERE node = '$hostname'})
    or die "Can't prepare statement: $DBI::errstr";

# Execute the query
my $rc = $sth->execute
    or die "Can't execute statement: $DBI::errstr";
```

```perl
# Set parameters
my %parameters = (
    puppet_server    => "puppet.$domain.$net"
    );

# Set classes
my @class;
while (my @row=$sth->fetchrow_array)
 { push(@class,@row) }

# Check for problems
die $sth->errstr if $sth->err;

# Disconnect from database
$dbh->disconnect;

# Print the YAML
print Dump( {
    classes       => \@class,
    parameters => \%parameters,
} );
```

This node classifier would connect to a MySQL database called puppet running on the local host. Using the hostname, the script receiving it would query the database and return a list of classes to assign to the node. The nodes and classes would be stored in a table. The next lines comprise a SQL statement to create a very simple table to do this:

```sql
CREATE TABLE `nodes` (
`node` varchar(80) NOT NULL,
`class` varchar(80) NOT NULL ) TYPE=MyISAM;
```

The classes, and whatever parameters we set (which you could also place in the database in another table), are then returned and outputted as the required YAML data.

■ **Tip** You can also access fact values in your node classifier scripts. Before the classifier is called, the `$vardir/yaml/facts/` directory is populated with a YAML file named for the node containing fact values, for example `/var/lib/puppet/yaml/facts/web.example.com.yaml`. This file can be queried for fact values.

All of these external node classifiers are very simple and could easily be expanded upon to provide more sophisticated functionality. It is important to remember that external nodes override node configuration in your manifest files. If you enable an external node classifier, any duplicate node definitions in your manifest files will not be processed and will in fact be ignored by Puppet.

■ **Note** In Puppet versions earlier than 0.23, external node scripts were structured differently. We're not going to cover these earlier scripts, but you can read about them at
`http://docs.puppetlabs.com/guides/external_nodes.html`.

Storing Node Configuration in LDAP

In addition to external node classifiers, Puppet also allows the storage of node information in LDAP directories. Many organizations already have a wide variety of information about their environments, such as DNS, user and group data, stored in LDAP directories. This allows organizations to leverage these already-existing assets stored in LDAP directories or to decouple their configuration from Puppet and centralize it. Additionally, it also allows LDAP-enabled applications to have access to your configuration data.

■ **Note** The use of LDAP nodes overrides node definitions in your manifest files and your ENC. If you use LDAP node definitions, you cannot define nodes in your manifest files or in an ENC.

Installing Ruby LDAP Libraries

The first step in using LDAP for your node configuration is to ensure the Ruby LDAP libraries are installed. First, check for the presence of the LDAP libraries:

```
# ruby -rldap -e "puts :installed"
```

If this command does not return `installed`, the libraries are not installed. You can either install them via your distribution's package management system or download them from the Ruby/LDAP site. For Red hat and derivatives, this is the **ruby-ldap** package. For Ubuntu/Debian, the package is `libldap-ruby1.8`.

If there isn't a package for your distribution, you can download the required libraries either in the form of an RPM or a source package from the Ruby/LDAP site. The Ruby/LDAP site is located at `http://ruby-ldap.sourceforge.net/`.

Check out the current Ruby LDAP source code:

```
$ svn checkout http://ruby-activeldap.googlecode.com/svn/ldap/trunk/ ruby-ldap-ro
```

Then, change into the resulting directory and then make and install the code:

```
$ cd ruby-ldap-ro
$ ruby extconf.rb
$ sudo make && make install
```

Setting Up the LDAP Server

Next, you need to set up your LDAP server. We're going to assume you've either already got one running or can set one up yourself. For an LDAP server, you can use OpenLDAP, Red Hat Directory Server (or

Fedora Directory Server), Sun's Directory Server, or one of a variety of other servers. We're going to use OpenLDAP for the purposes of demonstrating how to use LDAP node definitions.

■ **Tip** For some quick start instructions on setting up OpenLDAP, you can refer to
`http://www.openldap.org/doc/admin23/quickstart.html`.

Adding the Puppet Schema

Now we need to add the Puppet schema to our LDAP directory's configuration.

■ **Caution** You may need to tweak or translate the default LDAP schema for some directory servers, but it is suitable for OpenLDAP.

The Puppet schema document is available in the Puppet source package in the `ext/ldap/puppet.schema` file, or you can take it from the project's Git repository at `https://github.com/puppetlabs/puppet/blob/master/ext/ldap/puppet.schema`.

We need to add it to our schema directory and `slapd.conf` configuration file. For example, on an Ubuntu or Debian host, the schema directory is `/etc/ldap/schema`, and the `slapd.conf` configuration is located in the `/etc/ldap` directory. On Red Hat, the configuration file is located in /etc/openldap and the schemas are located in /etc/openldap/schema. Copy the **puppet.schema** file into the appropriate directory, for example on Ubuntu:

```
$ cp puppet/ext/ldap/puppet.schema /etc/ldap/schema
```

Now you can add an `include` statement to your `slapd.conf` configuration file; there should be a number of existing statements you can model:

```
include          /etc/ldap/schema/puppet.schema
```

Or you can add a schema to a running OpenLDAP server, like so:

```
$ ldapadd -x -H ldap://ldap.example.com/ -D "cn=config" -W -f puppet.ldif
```

To update OpenLDAP with the new schema, you may also now need to restart your server.

```
# /etc/init.d/slapd restart
```

Now that you've added the schema and configured the LDAP server, you need to tell Puppet to use an LDAP server as the source of its node configuration.

Configuring LDAP in Puppet

LDAP configuration is very simple. Let's look at the required configuration options from the [master] section of the puppet.conf configuration file in Listing 5-7.

Listing 5-7. LDAP configuration in Puppet

```
[master]
node_terminus = ldap
ldapserver = ldap.example.com
ldapbase = ou=Hosts,dc=example,dc=com
```

First, we set the `node_terminus` option to `ldap` to tell Puppet to look to an LDAP server as our node source. Next, we specify the hostname of our LDAP server, in this case `ldap.example.com`, in the `ldapserver` option. Lastly, in the `ldapbase` option, we specify the base search path. Puppet recommends that hosts be stored in an OU called `Hosts` under our main directory structure, but you can configure this to suit your environment.

If required, you can specify a user and password using the `ldapuser` and `ldappassword` options and override the default LDAP port of 389 with the `ldapport` option. There is some limited support for TLS or SSL, but only if your LDAP server does not require client-side certificates.

▧ **Tip** You can see a full list of the potential LDAP options at

`http://docs.puppetlabs.com/references/stable/configuration.html`.

After configuring Puppet to use LDAP nodes, you should restart your Puppet master daemon to ensure that the new configuration is updated.

Now you need to add your node configuration to the LDAP server. Let's take a quick look at the Puppet LDAP schema in Listing 5-9.

Listing 5-8. The LDAP schema

```
attributetype (  1.3.6.1.4.1.34380.1.1.3.10 NAME 'puppetClass'
        DESC 'Puppet Node Class'
        EQUALITY caseIgnoreIA5Match
        SYNTAX 1.3.6.1.4.1.1466.115.121.1.26 )

attributetype ( 1.3.6.1.4.1.34380.1.1.3.9 NAME 'parentNode'
        DESC 'Puppet Parent Node'
        EQUALITY caseIgnoreIA5Match
        SYNTAX 1.3.6.1.4.1.1466.115.121.1.26
        SINGLE-VALUE )

attributetype ( 1.3.6.1.4.1.34380.1.1.3.11 NAME 'environment'
        DESC 'Puppet Node Environment'
        EQUALITY caseIgnoreIA5Match
        SYNTAX 1.3.6.1.4.1.1466.115.121.1.26 )

attributetype ( 1.3.6.1.4.1.34380.1.1.3.12 NAME 'puppetVar'
        DESC 'A variable setting for puppet'
        EQUALITY caseIgnoreIA5Match
        SYNTAX 1.3.6.1.4.1.1466.115.121.1.26 )
```

```
objectclass ( 1.3.6.1.4.1.34380.1.1.1.2 NAME 'puppetClient' SUP top AUXILIARY
      DESC 'Puppet Client objectclass'
      MAY ( puppetclass $ parentnode $ environment $ puppetvar ))
```

The Puppet schema is made up of an object class, puppetClient, and four attributes: puppetclass, parentnode, environment and puppetvar. The object class puppetClient is assigned to each host that is a Puppet node. The puppetclass attribute contains all of the classes defined for that node. At this stage, you cannot add definitions, just classes. The parentnode attribute allows you to specify node inheritance, environment specifies the environment of the node, and puppetvar specifies any variables assigned to the node.

In addition, any attributes defined in your LDAP node entries are available as variables to Puppet. This works much like Facter facts (see Chapter 1); for example, if the host entry has the ipHost class, the ipHostNumber attribute of the class is available as the variable $ipHostNumber. You can also specify attributes with multiple values; these are created as arrays.

You can also define default nodes in the same manner as doing so in your manifest node definitions: creating a host in your directory called default. The classes assigned to this host will be applied to any node that does not match a node in the directory. If no default node exists and no matching node definition is found, Puppet will return an error.

You can now add your hosts, or the relevant object class and attributes to existing definitions for your hosts, in the LDAP directory. You can import your host definitions using LDIF files or manipulate your directory using your choice of tools such as phpldapadmin (http://phpldapadmin.sourceforge.net/wiki/index.php/Main_Page).

Listing 5-9 is an LDIF file containing examples of node definitions.

Listing 5-9. LDIF nodes

```
# LDIF Export for: ou=Hosts,dc=example,dc=com
dn: ou=Hosts,dc=example,dc=com
objectClass: organizationalUnit
objectClass: top
ou: Hosts

dn: cn=default,ou=Hosts,dc=example,dc=com
cn: default
description: Default
objectClass: device
objectClass: top
objectClass: puppetClient
puppetclass: base

dn: cn=basenode,ou=Hosts,dc=example,dc=com
cn: basenode
description: Basenode
objectClass: device
objectClass: top
objectClass: puppetClient
puppetclass: base

dn: cn=web,ou=Hosts,dc=example,dc=com
cn: web
description: Webserver
```

```
objectClass: device
objectClass: top
objectClass: puppetClient
parentnode: basenode
puppetclass: apache

dn: cn=web1.example.com, ou=Hosts,dc=example,dc=com
cn: web1
description: webserving host
objectclass: device
objectclass: top
objectclass: puppetClient
objectclass: ipHost
parentnode: web
ipHostNumber: 192.168.1.100
```

This listing includes a default node, a node called basenode, and a template node called web. Each node has particular classes assigned to it, and the web node has the basenode defined as its parent node and thus inherits its classes also. Lastly, we define a client node, called web1, which inherits the web node as a parent.

Summary

In this chapter we've explored how you can use both external node classification and the LDAP node terminus. Both of these allow you to scale to larger numbers of nodes without needing to maintain large numbers of nodes in your manifest files. In Chapter 7, we'll also look at how you can use Puppet Dashboard or the Foreman dashboard as an external node classifier.

Resources

The following links will take you to Puppet documentation related to external nodes:

- External nodes http://docs.puppetlabs.com/guides/external_nodes.html

- LDAP nodes http://projects.puppetlabs.com/projects/puppet/wiki/Ldap_Nodes

- Puppet configuration reference
http://docs.puppetlabs.com/references/stable/configuration.html

CHAPTER 6

███

Exporting and Storing Configuration

So far in the book, you've seen how Puppet models configuration on a single host. In many cases, however, you have configuration on multiple hosts that have a relationship; for example, your monitoring system needs to know about configuration on hosts being monitored. In this chapter we look at three features that exist in Puppet to help model resources on multiple hosts: virtual resources, exported resources, and stored configuration.

The first feature, virtual resources, is a method of managing resources where multiple configurations require a resource. For example, a user may be required on some hosts but not others. Virtual resources allow you to define a resource but be selective about where you instantiate that resource.

The second feature, exported resources, allows us to take resources defined on one host and use them on other hosts; for example, it allows us to tell a Puppet-managed load balancer about each of the workers available to it. Puppet collects and stores each of these resources when configuration runs occur, and then it provides these resources and their information to other hosts if they ask.

Lastly, stored configuration provides a mechanism to store these resources. Stored configurations allow Puppet to write resources into a SQL database. This database will then be queried by Puppet and required resources will be collected and included in the configuration catalog.

In this chapter you will learn how to use virtual and exported resources, including how to use the exported resource feature to collect specific resources from stored configuration. We cover a number of use cases, including the automatic management of SSH host keys, automated load balancer re-configuration, and automated monitoring with Nagios.

We demonstrate how to configure Puppet with a SQL server for stored configurations and how to prune old configuration data from the SQL database in order to prevent other systems from collecting stale resources. We also show you how to use message queuing to allow you to better scale your stored configuration environment and how to accommodate a multiple-Puppet-master environment, like we demonstrated in Chapter 5.

Virtual Resources

Virtual resources are closely related to the topic of exported resources. Because of the similarity, it's important to cover virtual resources first to provide a foundation for learning about exported resources.

Virtual resources are designed to address the situation where multiple classes require a single resource to be managed. This single resource doesn't clearly "belong" to any one class, and it is cumbersome to break each of these resources out into a unique class. Virtual resources also help solve the problem of duplicate resource declaration errors in Puppet.

To illustrate the problem, consider the Example.com operator. He would like the ability to declare user resources to manage the accounts for his colleagues, but each person should have their account managed on only some systems. For example, all developer accounts need to be managed on all development and testing systems, while being absent from the production systems. Conversely, the system administrator accounts need to be present on every system. Finally, there are service accounts, e.g., the apache and mysql users and groups required by multiple Puppet classes, such as the apache, mysql, and webapp classes. The webapp class requires the mysql and apache service accounts, but should not declare the resource itself since the mysql class will likely have a conflicting resource declaration.

Virtual resources provide the ability for the Example.com operator to define a large set of user resources in once place and selectively add a smaller subset of those users to the configuration catalog. The operator doesn't need to worry about duplicate resource declarations, because the resources are only declared once and then instantiated, or "realized," one or more times.

Declaring a virtual resource is easy, just add the @ character to the beginning of the resource declaration to make the resource virtual. You can then use one of two methods to realize your virtual resources:

- The "spaceship" syntax <| |>[1]

- The realize function

Declaring and Realizing a Virtual Resource

Let's see how the Example.com operator might declare and realize the user and service accounts in Listing 6-1.

Listing 6-1. Virtual user resources <modulepath>/accounts/virtual.pp

```
class accounts::virtual {
  @user { "mysql":
    ensure => present,
    uid => 27,
    gid => 27,
    home => "/var/lib/mysql",
    shell => "/bin/bash",
  }
  @user { "apache":
    ensure => present,
    uid => 48,
    gid => "apache",
    home => "/var/www",
    shell => "/sbin/nologin",
  }
}
```

Resources declared virtually will not be managed until they're realized. Simply declaring the accounts::virtual class makes these virtual resources available, but is not enough to manage the mysql and apache user accounts. Listing 6-2 shoes how the operator makes sure the mysql user account is present on the system.

---

[1] So named because the syntax looks like a spaceship.

Listing 6-2. Realizing a virtual resource using the spaceship operator

```
class webapp {
  include accounts::virtual
  package { "webapp": ensure => present }
  User <| title == "mysql" |>
}
```

In the last line of this webapp class, the operator uses the spaceship operator to find the user resource with the title of mysql. This syntax specifies a very specific resource to realize, however an error will not be thrown if there is no virtual user resource with the title mysql. The spaceship operator is analogous to a search function, where returning no results is perfectly valid. In situations where a specific resource is required, the realize function may be used to generate an error if the virtual resource is not found.

Applying the Realize Function

The realize function provides another method to make a virtual resource real. A specific resource identified by the type and title must be passed as an argument to the realize function. This requirement of a specific resource makes the realize function much less flexible than the collection syntax and spaceship operator. The realize function is more appropriate to use when an error should be thrown if the virtual resource has not been declared in the catalog. For example, the operator may want catalog compilation to fail if there is no mysql user resource, as you can see in Listing 6-3.

Listing 6-3. The realize() function

```
class webapp {
  realize(User["mysql"])
  package { "webapp":
    ensure => present,
  }
}
```

The configuration catalog resulting from the webapp class defined in Listing 6-3 is the same as the configuration catalog generated from the webapp class shown in listing 6-2. We've seen the operator realize a specific resource, the mysql user, but how does he handle the situation where he'd like to make a number of virtual resources real? Puppet provides a convenient way to solve this problem without forcing the operator to specify each and every resource by name.

Making Virtual Resources Real

When using the spaceship operator, any parameter may be used to collect resources. This feature allows a large number of relationships to be managed in a concise and clear style. For example, if there are multiple user accounts with a primary group of "apache," the operator may realize all of them using a single statement:

```
User <| gid == "apache" |>
```

So far you've seen how to realize collections of virtual resources using the spaceship operator and specific resources using the realize function. A key aspect of the Puppet model is specifying relationships between resources, and we haven't yet discussed how to establish a relationship to a realized virtual resource. Prior to Puppet 2.6.0, this was very difficult to configure, but new syntax added in version 2.6.0 makes this problem very easy to solve.

In Puppet 2.6.0, resource collections may also have a block associated with them to add additional parameters. When realizing virtual resources, the relationship metaparameters may be specified to ensure the resource is managed in the correct order. Look at Listing 6-4 to see how the Example.com operator ensures the mysql user account is always managed before the webapp package.

Listing 6-4. *Specifying parameters in a collection*

```
class webapp {
  User <| title == mysql |> { before => Package["webapp"] }
  package { "webapp":
    ensure => present,
  }
}
```

As you can see, appending a block containing parameters after the collection will add the parameter to all of the realized resources. This also works for collections that contain many resources, such as:

```
User <| gid == "apache" |> { before => Package["apache"] }
```

In addition to a block associated with a collection, Puppet version 2.6.0 and newer also supports a new relationship-chaining syntax. This syntax allows relationships to be declared without using the metaparameters before, require, subscribe and notify as we'll see in the next section.

Relationship-Chaining Syntax

A major new feature in Puppet 2.6.0, the relationship-chaining syntax allows you to replace the before, require, subscribe and notify parameters with arrow operators. These new operators allow relationships to be declared outside of the blocks where resources themselves are declared.

For example, two resources may be declared without any relation to each other, and their relationship established at a later point in time.

```
define apache::account($ensure=present) {
  user { "apache":
    ensure => $ensure,
    gid => 48
  }
  group { "apache":
    ensure => $ensure,
    gid => 48,
  }
  if ($ensure == present) {
    Group["apache"] -> User["apache"]
  } else {
    User["apache"] -> Group["apache"]
  }
}
```

In this code example, Puppet will manage the group before the user if the apache account is present. However, if the apache account is absent, then the user is managed before the group to prevent the operating system from complaining that a group cannot be removed when a user exists with the same gid number.

The complete list of syntax arrows are ->, <-, ~> and <~. The tilde arrows add notifications to the relationship just like the subscribe and notify parameters.

```
Group["apache"] -> User["apache"]
```

The apache group is before the apache user.

```
User["apache"] <- Group["apache"]
```

The apache user requires the apache group.

```
File["httpd.conf"] ~> Service["httpd"]
```

The httpd.conf file notifies the httpd service.

```
Service["httpd"] <~ File["httpd.conf"]
```

The httpd service subscribes to the httpd.conf file.

Additional information about the new relationship-chaining syntax in Puppet 2.6.0 is available online at: http://docs.puppetlabs.com/guides/language_tutorial.html.

In the next section, we expand on the concept of virtual resources and make resources available across nodes and configuration catalogs. Resources available for collection across nodes are called exported resources, though it's important to think of them in terms of the virtual resources feature they are designed to resemble.

Getting Started with Exported and Stored Configurations

Now that you're ready to look at exported resources and stored configuration using the groundwork we've introduced with virtual resources, let's start with a database server.

The Stored Configuration Database Server

The first step in using exported resources is to install and create the database your stored configuration will use. You can use a variety of database back-ends to store your configuration, including:

- MySQL
- PostgreSQL
- SQlite3, and
- Oracle

To allow Puppet to use these different database back ends, Puppet uses the Ruby Active Record object relational mapper (see the Ruby Active Record sidebar). Many people start with the SQLite3 database as a stored configuration back end because it's fast and easy to set up. Unfortunately, it relies on direct file access to write transactions, and this makes it difficult to scale for larger configurations. As a result, we recommend you use a more fully-featured database server. In this chapter, we demonstrate how to use MySQL as our stored configuration database server.

RUBY ACTIVE RECORD

The Ruby Active Record library is best known from the Ruby on Rails web application framework. Active Record is an Object Relational Mapper (ORM), which is an abstraction layer that allows a programming language to support a variety of database servers. The library provides the means to model relational data stored in SQL as objects and classes in Ruby without the need to write complicated, cross-database-compatible SQL statements. More information about Active Record is available at:
http://ar.rubyonrails.org/.

Your database server needs to be installed on a host that is accessible through the network by your Puppet master or Puppet masters. You can install the database server locally on your Puppet master, but we don't recommend this for performance and scalability reasons.

In the following sections we show you how to install the MySQL server on Enterprise Linux- and Debian/Ubuntu-based systems.

■ Note For other platforms, please consult the installation procedure for MySQL (or the database server of your choice) for additional information.

Installing Packages on Enterprise Linux-Based Systems

MySQL server packages are available from the vendor-provided media on most Enterprise Linux-based systems without the need to enable third-party repositories. Either the yum package manager or Puppet may be used to install MySQL. Unfortunately, the MySQL Ruby library package, mysql-ruby, is not available from the vendor package repositories and should be obtained from the Enhanced Packages for Enterprise Linux third party repository.

■ Note The Enhanced Packages for Enterprise Linux package repository contains many third-party packages not included in the main Enterprise Linux distribution. These packages are compiled and maintained to cleanly interoperate with Enterprise Linux releases. Additional information about the EPEL repository is available online at http://fedoraproject.org/wiki/EPEL/FAQ.

To install MySQL on Red Hat Enterprise Linux using Puppet, add this line of code:

```
# yum install mysql-server
```

You also need to ensure taht the Ruby MySQL bindings are present on each Puppet master system:

```
# yum install ruby-mysql
```

With the MySQL server RPM packages and Ruby client libraries installed, the next step is to use RubyGems to install the Rails framework.

Installing Packages on Debian and Ubuntu

The first step to configure stored configurations is to install and configure a SQL server. On Debian and Ubuntu systems, this task is easily accomplished by installing the mysql-server package:

```
# aptitude install mysql-server
```

In addition to the MySQL server packages, the client libraries allowing Ruby programs to connect to a MySQL server need to be installed. On Debian and Ubuntu, these client libraries are contained in the libmysql-ruby1.8 and libmysql-ruby packages.

```
# aptitude install libmysql-ruby1.8 libmysql-ruby
```

Once the MySQL server packages and Ruby client libraries are present on the system, you can move on to installing the Ruby on Rails framework.

Installing Rails Using Gems

Exported resources and stored configurations in Puppet take advantage of the Ruby on Rails framework to model and store Puppet resources in a relational database supported by the Active Record library. Installing the Rails framework is straightforward if you are working with a recent version of Ruby and the rubygems package.

In this section, we will install Ruby on Rails using the gem system command, which is well supported on Enterprise Linux- and Debian-based systems. Indeed, any system with the gem command will support this installation process.

First, install Rails for Puppet versions 0.25.x, 2.6.x and later, as you can see in Listing 6-5.

Listing 6-5. Installing Ruby on Rails using RubyGems

```
# gem install rails -v 2.3.5 --no-ri --no-rdoc
Successfully installed rails-2.3.5
1 gem installed
```

There is a problem with Puppet and ActiveRecord versions prior to version 2.3.5, so you need to update the ActiveRecord library to at least this version:

```
# gem install activerecord -v 2.3.5 --no-ri --no-rdoc
Successfully installed activerecord-2.3.5
1 gem installed
```

Once Rails and ActiveRecord have been installed, you can verify that the proper versions are present using the gem list command.

```
# gem list
*** LOCAL GEMS ***
actionmailer (2.3.5)
actionpack (2.3.5)
```

```
activerecord (2.3.5)
activeresource (2.3.5)
activesupport (2.3.5)
rails (2.3.5)
rake (0.8.7)
```

Notice that activerecord and activesupport are both available at version 2.3.5. With these libraries installed, you're ready to proceed with the Puppet settings to enable stored configurations.

Configuring Puppet Master for Stored Configuration

In the previous sections you installed Ruby on Rails, ActiveRecord, and the MySQL Ruby libraries for the platform the Puppet master is executing on. You're now ready to configure the Puppet master to connect to the database and store configuration information. This configuration is done in the puppet.conf file located in the configuration directory, /etc/puppet by default.

Before configuring the Puppet master we need to make sure a database has been created for use with Puppet. Any database name will suffice; in this example, the operator uses the default name of "puppet" accompanied by a MySQL account named "puppet" with a password of "teppup."

First, connect to the MySQL command line interface:

```
# mysql -u root -p
Welcome to the MySQL monitor. Commands end with ; or \g.
Your MySQL connection id is 36
Server version: 5.0.51a-24+lenny4 (Debian)

Type 'help;' or '\h' for help. Type '\c' to clear the buffer.

mysql>
```

Once connected, create a new database named "puppet":

```
mysql> create database puppet;
Query OK, 1 row affected (0.00 sec)
```

Finally, create a MySQL account named "puppet" to access this new database. Notice the password is set to "teppup." The username and password should be changed to something more secure and reflected in puppet.conf.

```
grant all privileges on puppet.* to puppet@localhost identified by 'teppup';
Query OK, 1 rows affected (0.05 sec)
```

With the database and account created in MySQL, you're ready to configure /etc/puppet/puppet.conf. The lines in Listing 6-6 need to be inserted in the [master] section of the configuration file.

Listing 6-6. puppet.conf MySQL stored configuration settings

```
# vim /etc/puppet/puppet.conf
[master]
  storeconfigs = true
  dbadapter = mysql
```

```
dbname = puppet
dbuser = puppet
dbpassword = teppup
dbserver = localhost
dbsocket = /var/run/mysqld/mysqld.sock
```

If you chose to change the name of the database, the account, or the account password, please make sure to reflect those changes in the puppet.conf settings.

The database tables will not be created until the Puppet master compiles a catalog. We can easily test the configuration of Stored Configs using a standalone Puppet master and agent. After the agent runs, we can expect the tables and configuration information to be visible in the mysql console.

▨ **Note** When using a load balancer configuration as we demonstrated in Chapter 5, each Puppet master worker process must be configured to connect to the same SQL server instance.

```
# puppet master --verbose --no-daemonize --masterport 8141
notice: Starting Puppet master version 2.6.4
```

This command starts the standalone Puppet master with the new Stored Configuration settings on an alternate port number, 8141, using the masterport option. Next, we connect a single Puppet agent to this server in order to trigger the table creation in the "puppet" database:

```
# puppet agent --test --masterport 8141
info: Caching catalog for debian.example.com
info: Applying configuration version '1293480381'
notice: Finished catalog run in 0.01 seconds
```

The Puppet Agent runs without trouble. Looking back at the output of the Puppet master, we should see the following information noting the establishment of a database connection to the MySQL server:

```
info: Connecting to mysql database: puppet
info: Expiring the node cache of debian.example.com
info: Not using expired node for debian.example.com from cache; expired at Mon Dec 27 15:05:21
-0500 2010
info: Caching node for debian.example.com
notice: Compiled catalog for debian.example.com in environment production in 0.03 seconds
```

Once a Puppet agent has connected to a Puppet master with Stored Configurations enabled, the database tables should be created automatically. The automatic creation of the database tables may be verified using the mysql command line utility, as shown in Listing 6-7.

Listing 6-7. Verifying stored configuration tables

```
# mysql -u puppet -p \
  -D puppet \
  -e 'select name,last_compile from hosts;' \
```

```
  --batch
name    last_compile
mail.example.com     2010-12-14 15:06:21
```

This command may appear slightly complicated, so let's work through each of the options. The -u option specifies the MySQL account to use when connecting to the MySQL server. The -p option prompts for a password, and the -D option specifies the database to connect to. These three options may be different for you if you chose to change any of the default names or passwords when setting up the MySQL database. The -e option tells the mysql command to execute once and exit after doing so. The select command prints the name and last_compile field from all rows in the hosts table. Finally, the --batch option tells the mysql command to output the information in a simplified format.

The results of the mysql command show the host named "mail" is successfully storing configuration information in the MySQL database.

Adding a MySQL Table Index

With the MySQL tables created in the puppet database, we have the option to add an index improving the access time of storing and retrieving configuration information. This index is optional, but we recommend it for sites with more than one hundred Puppet-managed hosts.

First, connect to the puppet database using the puppet MySQL account:

```
# mysql -u puppet -p -D puppet
Reading table information for completion of table and column names
You can turn off this feature to get a quicker startup with -A

Welcome to the MySQL monitor. Commands end with ; or \g.
Your MySQL connection id is 54
Server version: 5.0.51a-24+lenny4 (Debian)

Type 'help;' or '\h' for help. Type '\c' to clear the buffer.

mysql>
```

Next, add the index for fields frequently accessed by Stored Configurations, as shown in Listing 6-8.

Listing 6-8. Adding an index on the resources table

```
mysql> create index exported_restype_title on resources (exported, restype, title(50));
Query OK, 5 rows affected (0.09 sec)
Records: 5  Duplicates: 0  Warnings: 0
```

This command creates an index on the exported, restype and title fields in the resources table.

■ **Note** Up-to-date information regarding the tuning of database settings and indices is available on the Puppet community wiki. Stored configurations are being increasingly used at large sites, and improvements to performance and settings are an evolving and ongoing process. For more information, please see:
http://projects.puppetlabs.com/projects/1/wiki/Using_Stored_Configuration.

Using Exported Resources

With stored configurations enabled in the Puppet master, we can now export resources from a node's catalog. These exported resources may then be collected on another node, allowing nodes to exchange configuration information dynamically and automatically. In this section we'll examine a number of common use cases for exported resources.

The first example will export the public SSH host identification key from each Puppet-managed node and store the resources centrally in the stored configuration database. Every node may then collect all of the public host keys from all other nodes. This configuration increases security and eliminates the "unknown host" warning commonly shown when logging in via SSH for the first time.

The second example we provide uses exported resources to dynamically re-configure a load balancer when additional Puppet master worker processes come online.

Finally, you'll see how to dynamically and automatically reconfigure the Nagios monitoring system to check the availability to new Puppet managed systems.

Automated SSH Public Host Key Management

When new systems are brought online in a large network, the known_hosts files of all other systems become stale and out of date, causing "unknown host" warnings when logging in using SSH. Puppet provides a simple and elegant solution to this problem using stored configurations and exported resources. When new systems are brought online, Puppet updates the known_hosts file on all other systems by adding the public host key of the new system. This automated management of the known_hosts file also increases security, by reducing the likelihood of a "man-in-the-middle" attack remaining unnoticed.

We learned in this chapter any resource may be declared virtually using the @ symbol before the resource declaration. A similar syntax, @@, is used when resources should be declared virtually and exported to all other nodes using stored configurations. The use of @@ allows any node's catalog to collect the resource. Listing 6-9 shows how this looks for SSH public keys.

Listing 6-9. *Exporting ssh key resources*

```
class ssh::hostkeys {
  @@sshkey { "${fqdn}_dsa":
    host_aliases => [ "$fqdn", "$hostname", "$ipaddress" ],
    type         => dsa,
    key          => $sshdsakey,
  }
  @@sshkey { "${fqdn}_rsa":
    host_aliases => [ "$fqdn", "$hostname", "$ipaddress" ],
    type         => rsa,
    key          => $sshrsakey,
  }
}
```

This Puppet code snippet looks a little strange compared to what we've worked with so far.

The class ssh::hostkeys should be included in the catalog of all nodes in the network for their SSH public host keys to be exported and collectible. All of the resources and parameters are set to variables coming from Facter fact values. In Listing 6-10, two sshkey resources have been declared as virtual resources and exported to the central stored configuration database, as indicated by the @@ symbols. The titles of each resource contain the suffixes _dsa or _rsa, preventing these two resources from conflicting with each other. To make sure each resource has a unique title for the entire network, the title also contains the fully qualified domain name of the node exporting the public host keys.

The host_aliases parameter provides additional names and addresses the node may be reached by. This information is important to prevent the "unknown host" warnings when connecting to the node from another system. In this example, we're providing the fully qualified domain name, short hostname, and IP address of the system. Each of these values comes from facter and is automatically provided.

They type and key parameters provide the public key information itself. The values of $sshdsakey and $sshrsakey also come from Facter and are automatically available on each host.

Exporting these two sshkey resources is not sufficient to configure the known_hosts file on each node. We must also collect all exported sshkey resources for Puppet to fully manage and keep updated the known_hosts file shown in Listing 6-10.

Listing 6-10. Collecting exported sshkey resources

```
class ssh::knownhosts {
  Sshkey <<| |>> { ensure => present }
}
```

The ssh::knownhosts class should be included in the catalog for all nodes where Puppet should manage the SSH known_hosts file. Notice that we've used double angle braces to collect resources from the stored configuration database. This is similar to collecting virtual resources, however virtual resources only use a *single* pair of angle braces. We're also specifying that the ensure parameter should take on the value "present" when collecting the exported sshkey resources.

■ **Note** The ability to specify additional parameters when a resource is collected is new in Puppet 2.6.x and later. It will not work with Puppet 0.25.x and earlier.

With the two classes configured and added to the node classification for every host in the network, the operator verifies host keys are collected on every node in the network.

First, our operator runs the Puppet agent on the mail.example.com host. Since this is the first host to run the Puppet agent, he expects only two SSH keys to be collected: the keys exported by the mail host itself, as you can see in Listing 6-11.

Listing 6-11. The first Puppet agent on mail.example.com

```
# puppet agent --test
info: Caching catalog for mail.example.com
info: Applying configuration version '1293584061'
notice: /Stage[main]//Node[default]/Sshkey[mail.example.com_dsa]/ensure: created
notice: /Stage[main]//Node[default]/Sshkey[mail.example.com_rsa]/ensure: created
notice: Finished catalog run in 0.02 seconds
```

Note the two sshkey resources being collected from the stored configuration database, the ssh dsa and rsa public key exported from the mail.example.com host.

In Listing 6-12, the operator runs Puppet on the web server, expecting the public keys for both the web host and the mail host to be collected.

Listing 6-12. The second Puppet agent run on web.example.com

```
# puppet agent --test
info: Caching catalog for web.example.com
info: Applying configuration version '1293584061'
notice: /Stage[main]//Node[default]/Sshkey[mail.example.com_rsa]/ensure: created
notice: /Stage[main]//Node[default]/Sshkey[mail.example.com_dsa]/ensure: created
notice: /Stage[main]//Node[default]/Sshkey[web.example.com_rsa]/ensure: created
notice: /Stage[main]//Node[default]/Sshkey[web.example.com_dsa]/ensure: created
notice: Finished catalog run in 0.43 seconds
```

The Puppet agent on web.example.com manages a total of four ssh host key resources, as shown in Listing 6-12. The rsa and dsa keys from both the mail host and the web host are now being exported and stored in the configuration database.

Finally, running the Puppet agent once more on the mail.example.com host should result in the two public keys exported by the web host being collected and managed. Listing 6-13 shows how the operator verifies this.

Listing 6-13. The third Puppet agent run on mail.example.com

```
# puppet agent --test
info: Caching catalog for mail.example.com
info: Applying configuration version '1293584061'
notice: /Stage[main]//Node[default]/Sshkey[web.example.com_rsa]/ensure: created
notice: /Stage[main]//Node[default]/Sshkey[web.example.com_dsa]/ensure: created
info: FileBucket adding /etc/ssh/ssh_known_hosts as {md5}815e87b6880446e4eb20a8d0e7298658
notice: Hello World!
notice: /Stage[main]//Node[default]/Notify[hello]/message: defined 'message' as 'Hello World!'
notice: Finished catalog run in 0.04 seconds
```

As expected, the two SSH public key resources exported by the web host are correctly being collected on the mail host. By exporting and collecting two sshkey resources, the staff of Example.com can rely on all hosts automatically knowing the identity of all other hosts, even as new hosts are added to the network. So long as Puppet runs frequently, every system will have a known_hosts file containing the public key of every other system in the network.

In the next example, you'll see how this feature also allows the automatic addition of worker nodes to a load balancer pool.

Exporting Load Balancer Worker Resources

In the previous example, SSH public key resources were exported and stored in the configuration database so that every host in the network is able to collect the public identification keys of every other host in the network. Along the same lines, but on a much smaller scale, you can also export resources to a single node on the network, such as a load balancer.

In this example, HTTP worker nodes will export configuration resources that only the load balancer will collect. This combination eliminates the need to manually reconfigure the load balancer every time a new worker node is added to the network.

Each load balancer worker will export a defined resource type representing the load balancer configuration. Let's see how the Example.com operator configures this system now. The load balancer software being used in this example is Apache. The Example.com operator models the configuration of a

HTTP worker using a file fragment placed into the directory /etc/httpd/conf.d.members/. Let's first take a look at the defined resource type, shown in Listing 6-14.

Listing 6-14. Load balancer worker-defined resource type

```
define balancermember($url) {
  file { "/etc/httpd/conf.d.members/worker_${name}.conf":
    ensure => file,
    owner => 0,
    group => 0,
    mode => "0644",
    content => "  BalancerMember $url \n",
  }
}
```

This configuration file fragment contains a single line, the URL to a member of the load balancer pool. Using a defined resource type is recommended since all resources declared within will be exported when the defined type itself is exported.

The load balancer configuration is similar to the Apache configuration presented in the Scaling Puppet chapter. Without using exported resources, the Example.com operator might define his load balancer configuration statically, as shown in Listing 6-15.

Listing 6-15. Load balancer front-end configuration

```
<Proxy balancer://puppetmaster>
  BalancerMember http://puppetmaster1.example.com:18140
  BalancerMember http://puppetmaster2.example.com:18140
  BalancerMember http://puppetmaster3.example.com:18140
</Proxy>
```

In this example, three Puppet master workers have been statically defined. If the Example.com operator would like to add additional capacity, he would have to add a fourth line to this Apache configuration block. Exported resources allow him to save this manual step and automatically add the configuration once a new worker node comes online and is configured by Puppet. To accomplish this, the Example.com operator replaces all of the BalancerMember statements with an Include statement to read in all of the file fragments. In the Puppet manifest, these configuration statements are modeled using the balancermember defined type, shown in Listing 6-16.

Listing 6-16. Including exported file fragments in the load balancer configuration

```
<Proxy balancer://puppetmaster>
  Include /etc/httpd/conf.d.members/*.conf
</Proxy>
```

The Example.com operator no longer needs to manually add each line once he configures Apache to include all files in the conf.d.members directory. Instead, he configures Puppet to manage the individual file fragments using exported resources.

The Puppet configuration to export each load balancer member is very similar to what we saw with the SSH host key example. The Puppet configuration is very simple. Each worker node needs to export a single balancermember resource for itself:

```
class worker {
  @@balancermember { "${fqdn}":
    url => "http://${fqdn}:18140",
  }
}
```

Notice that the Example.com operator uses the fully qualified domain name as the title of the resource. In doing so, he is guaranteed there will be no duplicate resource declarations because each worker node should have a unique value for their fqdn fact. Declaring the defined resource in this manner exports two resources into the stored configuration database, the balancermember resource and the contained file resource shown in Listing 6-14. Neither of these resources will be collected on the worker nodes themselves.

The last step in automating the configuration is for the Example.com operator to collect all of the exported resources on the load balancer node itself, as you can see in Listing 6-17.

Listing 6-17. Collecting exported load balancer workers

```
class loadbalancer_members {
  Balancermember <<| |>> { notify => Service["apache"] }
}
```

The operator uses the double angle brace syntax to collect all balancermember resources from the stored configuration database. In addition, he's using a parameter block to notify the Apache service of any changes puppet makes to the balancermember resources. Just like with virtual resources, a parameter block may be specified to add additional parameters to collected resources. This syntax is new in Puppet 2.6.x; previous versions of Puppet could not create relationships to collected resources.

In this example, we've seen a simplified version of the file fragment pattern using Apache's Include configuration statement. Web server worker nodes can easily model their configuration in Puppet using a defined resource type. Using a defined resource type, the Example.com operator exports load balancer resources to automatically reconfigure the front-end load balancer as new members come online.

In the next section, you'll see how exported resources are ideal for automatically reconfiguring a central Nagios monitoring system as new hosts are added to the network.

Automating Nagios Service Checks

So far, you've seen how exported resources enable Puppet to automatically reconfigure the Example.com systems as new machines are brought online. You've seen how to automate the management of SSH known hosts keys to improve security, and how to automatically reconfigure Apache as additional capacity is added into a load balancer pool.

In this final example of exported resources, you'll see how the Example.com operator configures Puppet to automatically monitor new systems as they're brought online. The problem of monitoring service availability is something all sites share. Puppet helps solve this problem quickly and easily, and reduces the amount of time and effort required to manage the monitoring system itself.

This example specifically focuses on Nagios. Puppet has native types and providers for Nagios built into the software. The concepts in this section, however, apply to any software requiring a central system to be reconfigured when new hosts come online and need to be monitored.

In Nagios, the system performing the service checks is called the monitor system. The Nagios service running on the monitor system looks to the configuration files in /etc/nagios to sort out which target systems need to be monitored. The Example.com operator wants Puppet to automatically reconfigure the monitor system when a new target system comes online.

To accomplish this goal, the Example.com operator first configures two classes in Puppet. The first class, named nagios::monitor, manages the Nagios service and collects the service check resources exported by the nagios::target class. Let's take a look at these two classes now (see Listing 6-18).

Listing 6-18. /etc/puppet/modules/nagios/manifests/monitor.pp

```
# Manage the Nagios monitoring service
class nagios::monitor {

  # Manage the packages
  package { [ "nagios", "nagios-plugins" ]: ensure => installed }

  # Manage the Nagios monitoring service
  service { "nagios":
    ensure    => running,
    hasstatus => true,
    enable    => true,
    subscribe => [ Package["nagios"], Package["nagios-plugins"] ],
  }

  # collect resources and populate /etc/nagios/nagios_*.cfg
  Nagios_host    <<||>> { notify => Service["nagios"] }
  Nagios_service <<||>> { notify => Service["nagios"] }
}
```

As you can see, the Example.com operator has configured Puppet to manage the Nagios packages and service. The class nagios::monitor should be included in the catalog for the monitor node. In addition to the packages and the service, two additional resource types are collected from the stored configuration database, all nagios_host and nagios_service resources. When collecting these host and service resources, the operator adds the notify metaparameter to ensure that the Nagios monitoring service automatically reloads its configuration if any new nodes have exported their information to the stored configuration database.

▓ **Note** Additional information about the nagios_host and nagios_service Puppet types are available online. There are a number of additional resource types related to Nagios management in addition to these two basic service checks. If you need to make Nagios aware of the interdependencies between hosts to reduce the number of notifications generated during a service outage, or manage custom Nagios service checks and commands, please see the comprehensive and up-to-date Puppet type reference at http://docs.puppetlabs.com/references/stable/type.html.

Let's see how the Example.com operator implements the nagios::monitor class in the Puppet configuration. With the nagios::monitor class added to the monitor node's classification in site.pp, the Example.com operator runs the Puppet agent on node monitor1, as you can see in Listing 6-19.

Listing 6-19. The first Puppet agent run to configure Nagios

```
# puppet agent --test
info: Caching catalog for monitor1
info: Applying configuration version '1294374100'
notice: /Stage[main]/Nagios::Monitor/Package[nagios]/ensure: created
info: /Stage[main]/Nagios::Monitor/Package[nagios]: Scheduling refresh of Service[nagios]
notice: /Stage[main]/Nagios::Monitor/Package[nagios-plugins]/ensure: created
info: /Stage[main]/Nagios::Monitor/Package[nagios-plugins]: Scheduling refresh of
Service[nagios]
notice: /Stage[main]/Nagios::Monitor/Service[nagios]/ensure: ensure changed 'stopped' to
'running'
notice: /Stage[main]/Nagios::Monitor/Service[nagios]: Triggered 'refresh' from 2 events
notice: Finished catalog run in 14.96 seconds
```

Notice that the first Puppet agent configuration run on monitor1 does not mention anything about managing Nagios_host or Nagios_service resources. This is because no nodes have yet been classified with the nagios::target class, and as a result there are no exported host or service resources in the stored configuration database.

The Example.com operator configures Puppet to export Nagios service and host resources using the class nagios::target. As you can see in Listing 6-20, the class contains only exported resources. The resources will not be managed on any nodes until they are collected like the operator is doing in Listing 6-18.

Listing 6-20. /etc/puppet/modules/manifests/target.pp

```
# This class exports nagios host and service check resources
class nagios::export::target {

  @@nagios_host { "$fqdn":
    ensure  => present,
    alias   => $hostname,
    address => $ipaddress,
    use     => "generic-host",
  }

  @@nagios_service { "check_ping_${hostname}":
    check_command       => "check_ping!100.0,20%!500.0,60%",
    use                 => "generic-service",
    host_name           => "$fqdn",
    notification_period => "24x7",
    service_description => "${hostname}_check_ping"
  }

}
```

In Listing 6-20, the Example.com operator has configured two exported resources, one of which provides the monitor node with information about the target host itself. This resource defines a Nagios host in /etc/nagios/*.cfg on the nodes collecting these resources. The title of the nagios_host resource is set to the value of the $fqdn fact. Using the fully qualified domain name as the resource title ensures there will be no duplicate resources in the stored configuration database. In addition, the operator has added an alias for the target host using the short hostname in the $hostname fact. Finally, the address of the target node is set to the $ipaddress variable coming from Facter.

Once a resource describing the target host is exported, the operator also exports a basic service check for the host. As we see, this service check is performing a basic ICMP ping command to the target node. The host_name parameter of the resource is also provided from Facter via the $fqdn fact. The check_command looks a bit confusing, and rightly so, as this parameter is directly using the Nagios configuration file syntax. Reading the check_ping line left to right, we interpret it to mean that Nagios will issue a warning when the ping takes longer than 100 milliseconds or experiences 20% packet loss. Nagios will also issue a critical alert if the ping command takes longer than 500 milliseconds to complete or experiences more than 60% packet loss. The notification period is also set to be 24 hours a day, 7 days a week, which is a default notification period provided by the default Nagios configuration. Finally, the operator has configured a descriptive label for the service using the short name of the host set by Facter.

Let's see how the monitor1 node is configured automatically when a target node is classified with this nagios::target class. First, the Example.com operator runs the Puppet agent on a new system named target1 (Listing 6-21).

Listing 6-21. Puppet agent on target1 exporting Nagios checks

```
# puppet agent --test
info: Caching catalog for target1
info: Applying configuration version '1294374100'
notice: Finished catalog run in 0.02 seconds
```

It appears the puppet agent run on target1 didn't actually manage any resources. This is true; the resources exported in the nagios::target class are actually being exported to the stored configuration database rather than being managed on the node. They are not being collected on the node target1, which is why the output of Listing 6-21 does not mention them.

We expect the Puppet agent on the node monitor1 to collect the resources exported by node target1. Let's see the results in Listing 6-22.

Listing 6-22. Puppet agent collecting resources in monitor1

```
# puppet agent --test
info: Caching catalog for monitor1
info: Applying configuration version '1294374100'
notice: /Stage[main]/Nagios::Monitor/Nagios_service[check_ping_puppet]/ensure: created
info: /Stage[main]/Nagios::Monitor/Nagios_service[check_ping_puppet]: Scheduling refresh of
Service[nagios]
notice: /Stage[main]/Nagios::Monitor/Nagios_host[target1.example.com]/ensure: created
info: /Stage[main]/Nagios::Monitor/Nagios_host[target1.example.com]: Scheduling refresh of
Service[nagios]
notice: /Stage[main]/Nagios::Monitor/Service[nagios]: Triggered 'refresh' from 2 events
notice: monitor
notice: /Stage[main]//Node[monitord]/Notify[monitor]/message: defined 'message' as 'monitor'
notice: Finished catalog run in 0.87 seconds
```

As we expect, running the Puppet agent on monitor1 after target1 has checked in causes the resources to be collected from the stored configuration database. Looking back to the nagios::monitor class in Listing 6-18, we also see the operator has added the notify parameter to ensure that the Nagios service automatically reloads the new configuration information after all of the resources are collected.

When the Example.com operator brings new systems online, he needs only to ensure they have the nagios::target class included in their catalog, and Puppet will automatically take care of reconfiguring the central Nagios monitoring system. In addition, if the operator would like more than one system to monitor all of these nodes, he only needs to include the nagios::monitor class in the catalog of additional monitors and they'll automatically collect all of the host and service resources from the stored configuration database.

In the next section, we'll cover methods to scale stored configuration to support a large number of nodes and reduce the amount of time each Puppet agent requires to submit a copy of its configuration to the Puppet master.

Scaling Stored Configurations

Puppet stored configurations require the Puppet agent to upload the configuration catalog after each catalog run. This process introduces a potential bottleneck when many Puppet agents are running concurrently. In this section, we cover enabling thin stored configurations, an option added in Puppet 0.25.x to reduce the amount of information stored in the SQL database.

We also cover the Puppet queue daemon and queue service for stored configurations, which enables Puppet agents to operate asynchronously with regard to database updates.

Thin Stored Configurations

The default behavior of stored configurations is to store a complete copy of every catalog in the SQL database. If only a small number of resources are being exported and collected, there may be too much overhead associated with storing the complete catalog. Thin stored configurations were added in Puppet 0.25.0 to address this problem. With thin stored configurations, only exported resources, node facts, and tags are stored in the SQL database. This limited set of information greatly reduces the number of synchronous database updates required for each Puppet agent run.

Thin stored configurations are very easy to set up. The option is located in puppet.conf on each Puppet master system. See how the Example.com operator enables thin stored configurations for his network in Listing 6-23.

Listing 6-23. Enabling thin stored configurations in puppet.conf

```
# /etc/puppet/puppet.conf
[master]
  storeconfigs = true
  thin_storeconfigs = true
  dbadapter = mysql
  dbname = puppet
  dbuser = puppet
  dbpassword = teppup
  dbserver = localhost
  dbsocket = /var/run/mysqld/mysqld.sock
```

Only the line thin_storeconfigs = true needs to be added into the master section of puppet.conf. The Puppet master should then be restarted to reflect this change.

Alternatively, the --thin_storeconfigs=true command line argument may be passed to the puppet master application. No client-side configuration settings are required to enable thin stored configurations.

Queue Support for Stored Configurations

Queue support is intended to take much of the load related to stored configurations off the Puppet master systems themselves. To accomplish this task, all database updates are moved to a separate process, named puppetqd in 0.25.x and puppet queue starting with version 2.6.0.

Puppet queue uses the ActiveMQ middleware service to handle message passing and queuing. In this section, you'll see how the Example.com operator sets up ActiveMQ on one system and uses the stomp Ruby gem to connect all of the Puppet master systems to the message bus.

■ **Note** Apache ActiveMQ is a message broker middleware service designed to handle asynchronous and synchronous message passing. ActiveMQ is written in Java and requires a Java runtime on any system providing the ActiveMQ service. More information about Apache ActiveMQ is available online at

http://activemq.apache.org/.

The first step while setting up setting up queue support for stored configurations is to install ActiveMQ. Active MQ requires a Java runtime, available for most Unix platforms at http://www.oracle.com/technetwork/java/. The information presented here uses Java 6 update 16. Please refer to the Apache ActiveMQ documentation for the recommended version of Java for the version of ActiveMQ you're installing.

Once Java and ActiveMQ are installed, the Stomp protocol must be enabled in the ActiveMQ configuration, and then the ActiveMQ service will be started. We'll see how the operator configures and starts ActiveMQ on Debian and Enterprise Linux based systems in the following two sections. With ActiveMQ up and running, we'll also see how the operator configures the Puppet Master and Puppet Queue applications to connect to the message bus using the Stomp ruby library.

Installing ActiveMQ on Enterprise Linux-Based Systems

For an Enterprise Linux-based system, the Example.com operator first installs the Java 6 runtime from Oracle. Official packages for Java are not available in most online package repositories due to restrictions in the distribution terms of the license. The operator has chosen to download the RPM to the local system as a result, as shown in Listing 6-24.

Listing 6-24. *Installing Java on Enterprise Linux*

```
# rpm -Uvh jdk-6u16-linux-amd64.rpm
Preparing...                ########################################### [100%]
   1:jdk                     ########################################### [100%]
```

Once Java is installed and available, the next step is to install the ActiveMQ packages. These packages are available online at http://puppetlabs.com/downloads/mcollective/. We create a new directory and download them in Listing 6-25.

Listing 6-25. Installing ActiveMQ on Enterprise Linux

```
# mkdir /tmp/activemq
# cd /tmp/activemq
# wget http://puppetlabs.com/downloads/mcollective/tanukiwrapper-3.2.3-1jpp.x86_64.rpm
# wget http://puppetlabs.com/downloads/mcollective/activemq-5.4.0-2.el5.noarch.rpm
# rpm -Uvh *.rpm
Preparing...                ########################################### [100%]
   1:tanukiwrapper           ########################################### [ 50%]
   2:activemq                ########################################### [100%]
```

As you can see in Listing 6-25, the Example.com operator creates a temporary directory named /tmp/activemq and downloads two packages required for ActiveMQ into this directory. Using the rpm command installs both packages. For a production environment we recommend staging these packages in a local YUM repository to simplify and automate management of these packages using Puppet.

Once Java and Apache ActiveMQ are installed, we're ready to proceed with the configuration of the stomp protocol. The stomp protocol is supported but not enabled by default in ActiveMQ. Before connecting the Puppet queue process to the message bus, stomp support must be enabled in the ActiveMQ configuration as we can see from Listing 6-26.

Listing 6-26. Enabling the stomp connector in /etc/activemq/activemq.xml

```
diff --git a/activemq.xml b/activemq.xml
index 5ac00dd..7051a14 100755
--- a/activemq.xml
+++ b/activemq.xml
@@ -119,6 +119,8 @@
        -->
        <transportConnectors>
            <transportConnector name="openwire" uri="tcp://0.0.0.0:61616"/>
+           <!-- Enable Stomp for Puppet Queue -->
+           <transportConnector name="stomp" uri="stomp://127.0.0.1:61613"/>
        </transportConnectors>

    </broker>
```

The Example.com operator has added a single line specifying the address and port ActiveMQ should bind to and listen for stomp messages on. This line should be added to the transportConnectors section of the /etc/activemq/activemq.xml file.

Once ActiveMQ has been configured to handle stomp messages, the service needs to be started (Listing 6-27).

Listing 6-27. Starting the ActiveMQ service on Enterprise Linux

```
# /etc/init.d/activemq start
Starting ActiveMQ Broker...

# /etc/init.d/activemq status
ActiveMQ Broker is running (2635).
```

```
# tail /var/log/activemq/activemq.log
… Listening for connections at: stomp://puppet.example.com:61613
```

The Example.com operator uses the ActiveMQ init script to start the service. Since ActiveMQ is a Java service, the operator verifies that the service is actually up and running by calling the status method of the init script. If there is a problem with the configuration file, the service may fail to start up properly and would not give an indication of the problem in the start command. Finally, checking the log files to make sure ActiveMQ is listening for stomp messages on port 6163 is a sensible final verification that things are working as expected. If there is a problem starting the server, a listing of the problem will be present in the file /var/log/activemq.log.

Installing ActiveMQ on Debian-Based Systems

The Java JDK is easy to install on Debian-based systems by adding the "non-free" Apt repositories for Java to the /etc/apt/sources.list configuration file:

```
deb http://debian.osuosl.org/debian/ lenny main non-free
deb-src http://debian.osuosl.org/debian/ lenny main non-free
deb http://security.debian.org/ lenny/updates main non-free
deb-src http://security.debian.org/ lenny/updates main non-free
deb http://volatile.debian.org/debian-volatile lenny/volatile main non-free
deb-src http://volatile.debian.org/debian-volatile lenny/volatile main non-free
```

▒ **Note** By default, all of the software installed on a Debian system is completely free, open source software. While ActiveMQ is distributed under an open source license, the Sun Java runtime is not. In an effort to accommodate non-free software like Java in a free software project, the Debian maintainers have created the "non-free" and "contrib" repositories. These additional package repositories provide a good compromise between the conflicting goals of commercial and free open source software. More information about the non-free and contrib repositories is available online at http://www.debian.org/social_contract.

Once this additional repository is enabled, the operator uses the aptitude executable to install the Java Development Kit:

```
# aptitude update
# aptitude install sun-java6-jdk sudo aptitude install sun-java6-bin
```

With Java installed, the operator downloads the ActiveMQ release archive and starts the service. ActiveMQ archives are available online at http://activemq.apache.org/download.html. ActiveMQ packages are not available in Debian Lenny, so the operator installs the service into /var/lib/activemq/opt/activemq.

First, he creates the activemq service account so the service doesn't run as the root user:

```
# puppet resource group activemq ensure=present
notice: /Group[activemq]/ensure: created
```

```
# puppet resource user activemq ensure=present \
  gid=activemq managehome=true \
  home=/var/lib/activemq \
  shell=/bin/bash \
  comment=ActiveMQ
```

With the user and group in place, the operator unpacks the archive and moves it into the activemq home directory. These commands create the directory /var/lib/activemq/opt/activemq. In addition, the operator makes sure to give ownership to the activemq user.

```
# tar xzf apache-activemq-5.4.2-bin.tar.gz
# mkdir ~activemq/opt/
# mv apache-activemq-5.4.2 ~activemq/opt/activemq
# chown -R activemq:activemq ~activemq/opt/
```

Before starting the message service, the operator must generate a default configuration and make a small change to enable the stomp messaging service. Using the setup command, they write a default configuration file into the home directory of the service account.

```
# sudo -H -u activemq ./bin/activemq setup ~activemq/.activemqrc
INFO: Creating configuration file: /var/lib/activemq/.activemqrc
```

Once the configuration file has been created, a single line must be added to the activemq.xml configuration file. As you can see in Listing 6-28, a stomp URI line is inserted in the transportConnectors section.

Listing 6-28. Debian activemq.xml stomp configuration

```
# diff -U2 ~activemq/opt/activemq/conf/activemq.xml{.orig,}
--- activemq.xml.orig    2011-01-13 22:30:46.000000000 -0800
+++ activemq.xml         2011-01-13 22:31:36.000000000 -0800
@@ -122,4 +122,5 @@
        <transportConnectors>
            <transportConnector name="openwire" uri="tcp://0.0.0.0:61616"/>
+           <transportConnector name="stomp" uri="stomp://127.0.0.1:61613"/>
        </transportConnectors>
```

Once the XML configuration file has been updated to work with stomp, the operator is ready to start the service (Listing 6-29).

Listing 6-29. Starting the ActiveMQ service

```
# sudo -H -u activemq ./bin/activemq start
INFO: Loading '/var/lib/activemq/.activemqrc'
INFO: Using java '/usr/bin/java'
INFO: Starting - inspect logfiles specified in logging.properties and log4j.properties to get
details
INFO: pidfile created : '/var/lib/activemq/opt/activemq/data/activemq.pid' (pid '3476')
```

The sudo command in Listing 6-29 ensures the ActiveMQ service is running under the unprivileged activemq account, with the home directory environment variable reset to /var/lib/activemq using the -H flag.

Puppet Master Queue Configuration

With ActiveMQ up and running, we now need to connect the Puppet queue daemon process to the message bus to handle queued messages and write them to the database. The first step in this process is to install the stomp gem. This Ruby library provides a stomp protocol interface for Ruby applications (Listing 6-30).

Listing 6-30. Installing the stomp gem for Puppet queue

```
# gem install stomp
Successfully installed stomp-1.1.6
1 gem installed
Installing ri documentation for stomp-1.1.6...
Installing RDoc documentation for stomp-1.1.6…
```

After the installation of the stomp gem, a slight change to /etc/puppet/puppet.conf is needed to configure the Puppet master to hand off configuration information to ActiveMQ rather than performing the database writes itself. In the [main] section of the puppet.conf file, the puppet queue application will be configured to read from ActiveMQ and write to the database, offloading the work from the master (shown in Listing 6-31).

Listing 6-31. /etc/puppet/puppet.conf with queue support enabled

```
# vim /etc/puppet/puppet.conf
[main]
  dbadapter = mysql
  queue_type = stomp
  queue_source = stomp://localhost:61613
  dbname = puppet
  dbuser = puppet
  dbpassword = teppup
  dbserver = localhost
  dbsocket = /var/run/mysqld/mysqld.sock

[master]
  storeconfigs = true
  thin_storeconfigs = true
  async_storeconfigs = true
```

Note that the operator has changed the configuration slightly from Listing 6-7 and 6-23, where he had initially configured stored configurations. When queue support is enabled, the puppet queue daemon will pick up the settings in the [main] section to read data from the ActiveMQ stomp interface and write the information to the SQL database. In addition, the Puppet master application will use the settings in [main] and the settings in [master] to read from the SQL database and write to the ActiveMQ queue.

With these settings in place, let's see how the operator tests out the new queue system. First, he starts the Puppet master as he normally would:

```
# puppet master --no-daemonize --verbose
```

Then, he does a normal Puppet agent run. He hasn't yet started the Puppet queue application, so we expect any configuration updates to be queued in the ActiveMQ system until the Puppet queue application is running and drains the queue.

```
# puppet agent --test
info: Caching catalog for puppet.example.com
info: Applying configuration version '1294903443'
notice: Finished catalog run in 0.02 seconds
```

Everything looks good so far. The Puppet Agent is able to communicate with the master and obtain a configuration catalog, but exported resources won't be written to the SQL database until the Puppet queue application is started in Listing 6-32.

Listing 6-32. *Starting the Puppet queue application*

```
# puppet queue --no-daemonize --verbose
notice: Starting puppetqd 2.6.4
info: Loaded queued catalog in 0.03 seconds
info: Connecting to mysql database: /var/run/mysqld/mysqld.sock
notice: Processing queued catalog for puppet.example.lan in 2.67 seconds
```

Once the operator starts the Puppet queue daemon, it immediately connects to the ActiveMQ stomp port specified in the puppet.conf [main] section and drains the queued configuration update. As additional Puppet agents retrieve catalogs, the Puppet master will place configuration updates in the queue which the Puppet queue daemon will drain and write to the SQL database. It is important to remember the Puppet master still reads directly from the database, so the Puppet queue daemon isn't required to be running for catalogs to be compiled.

In this section, we've seen how the Example.com operator configures the ActiveMQ messaging service to queue up expensive database updates. The Puppet queue daemon is then responsible for asynchronously handling each of these configuration updates and writing to the SQL database. This combination greatly reduces the performance impact of many Puppet agent systems checking in with the Puppet master. In the next section, we'll see how the operator periodically prunes the SQL database when a node with exported resources and stored configurations is retired.

Expiring Stale Resources

A potential pitfall of using stored configurations is the situation where nodes retired from service still have configuration resources stored in the configuration database. Without periodically pruning the configuration database, these stale resources will linger indefinitely, tainting the configurations of remaining nodes. The Example.com operator incorporates a small utility to remove nodes from the configuration database when they take them offline.

Pruning a single node is quite straightforward using the puppetstoredconfigclean.rb script in the ext directory of the Puppet source code. If this script is not installed on your system, it may be downloaded from https://github.com/puppetlabs/puppet/tree/2.6.4/ext.

```
$ wget https://github.com/puppetlabs/puppet/tree/2.6.4/ext/puppetstoredconfigclean.rb
```

To clean out a node from the configuration database, simply give its short hostname as an argument to the script. In Listing 6-33, the operator removes the stored configurations for the nodes mail01dev, mail02dev, and mail03dev.

Listing 6-33. Removing Retired Nodes from the Configuration Database

```
# ruby puppetstoredconfigclean.rb mail0{1,2,3}dev
Killing mail01dev...done.
Killing mail02dev...done.
Killing mail03dev...done.
```

After running the stored configuration cleaning script, any resources exported by these nodes will no longer be collected in any Puppet manifest.

▪ **Note** In future releases, a Puppet command will be available to remove this configuration rather than requiring an external script.

Summary

Exported resources and stored configuration are two very powerful features in Puppet. Using the central stored configuration database, each Puppet master system is capable of exporting and collecting resources as new hosts are brought online.

In this chapter, you've learned about the basics of virtual resources and how to export resources from one catalog and collect them in another. You saw three examples of how we might use exported resources:

- SSH public host keys that are easily stored centrally and distributed

- Adding load balancer members to an Apache configuration

- Exported resources to allow Nagios to automatically add new systems

You also saw how to scale stored configuration using ActiveMQ message queues, and the Puppet Queuing daemon. And finally, you learned how to prune expired hosts and resources from your stored configuration database.

Resources

- Virtual Resources http://docs.puppetlabs.com/guides/virtual_resources.html

- Exported Resources
  http://docs.puppetlabs.com/guides/exported_resources.html

- Using Stored Configuration
  http://projects.puppetlabs.com/projects/1/wiki/Using_Stored_Configuration

■ ■ ■

## CHAPTER 7

Puppet Consoles: Puppet Dashboard and The Foreman

Until recently, you needed to manage Puppet via its manifest files and from the command line. As Puppet has matured, a small ecosystem of tools has emerged, including two console products: Puppet Dashboard and The Foreman.

Both console products are relatively new. The company that supports Puppet development, Puppet Labs, created Puppet Dashboard. Israeli developer Ohad Levy in turn wrote The Foreman. Both are Ruby on Rails applications and both are undergoing regular development.

Each tool suits a slightly different sort of environment. Puppet Dashboard can be used as an External Node Classifier (ENC) as well as a reporting tool, and is moving towards being an integration interface for a variety of new Puppet functions including audit and inventory capabilities. The Foreman has a stronger focus on provisioning and data center management and already includes some inventory capabilities.

In this chapter, we show you how to install and configure both consoles and demonstrate some of their features and capabilities. We show you how to use both consoles:

- As ENCs (we learned about ENCs in Chapter 5)

- To display data about the status and state of your hosts

- To display and analyze Puppet reports

- To make use of additional capabilities to provision and manage Puppet and your hosts

Later, in Chapter 8, you'll learn more about Puppet's integration with other tools.

■ **Note** Both consoles are being rapidly developed and extended. We recommend you keep an eye on both of them for future developments to help determine what tools suit you best.

Puppet Dashboard

Puppet Dashboard is a Ruby on Rails application designed to display information about your Puppet masters and agents. It allows you to view graphs and reporting data aggregated from one or more Puppet masters. It also makes inventory data (your host's Facts and other information) from your Puppet agents available on one or more Puppet masters. Lastly, it can be used as an ENC to configure your Puppet nodes and specify the classes and parameters available on those nodes.

We're going to take you through installing the Dashboard, making use of its features, integrating with Puppet masters, and maintaining the Dashboard, including backups and management of data.

Let's start by installing the Dashboard.

Installing Puppet Dashboard

Installing the Puppet Dashboard requires some basic prerequisites, typical of a Ruby on Rails application. These include Ruby 1.8.x (Dashboard doesn't yet work with 1.9.x) and a MySQL database to store data in. Currently Dashboard only supports MySQL as a database back end. There are plans to support additional back ends in later releases.

We're going to take you through installing Version 1.0.4 of Dashboard on both Red Hat and Ubuntu, including how to install the required prerequisites.

Installing the Red Hat Prerequisites

First, we need to add the Extra Packages for Enterprise Linux (EPEL) package repository (which we first saw in Chapter 1).

1. Add the epel-release RPM Package Manager (as of this writing, this is the current RPM – you should go to the EPEL website to find the latest version):

```
$ sudo rpm -Uvh http://download.fedora.redhat.com/pub/epel/5/i386/↵
epel-release-5.4.noarch.rpm
```

2. Install any of the required packages you haven't already added:

```
$ sudo yum install -y mysql mysql-devel mysql-server ruby ruby-devel ruby-irb ruby-mysql↵
ruby-rdoc ruby-ri
```

3. Start MySQL and configure it to start at boot. Use the service command to start the service:

```
$ sudo service mysqld start
```

4. Then use the chkconfig command to configure MySQL to start when the host boots:

```
$ sudo chkconfig mysqld on
```

5. We also need to install the RubyGems package manager. Unfortunately, the RubyGems package manager provided with Red Hat (and CentOS) 5.x releases isn't suitable. We need to manually install an appropriate version. To do this, we download the RubyGems source and install it. This will download, unpack and install the gem command and required libraries.

```
$ cd /tmp
$ wget http://production.cf.rubygems.org/rubygems/rubygems-1.3.5.tgz
$ tar -xzf rubygems-1.3.5.tgz
$ cd rubygems-1.3.5
$ sudo ruby setup.rb
```

6.   Once you've installed RubyGems, you need to install the rake gem.

```
$ sudo gem install rake
```

That's it, you're done installing the Red Hat prerequisites.

Installing the Ubuntu Prerequisites

On Ubuntu 10.04 and later, you need to install several packages.

1.   Start with the following:

```
$ sudo apt-get install -y build-essential irb libmysql-ruby libmysqlclient-dev⏎
  libopenssl-ruby libreadline-ruby mysql-server rake rdoc ri ruby ruby-dev
```

2.   Install the RubyGems package manager. Unfortunately, the RubyGems
      package manager provided with Ubuntu 10.04 and earlier is not a recent
      enough version to support the required RubyGems. We need to manually
      install an appropriate version. To do this we download the RubyGems source
      and install it. This will download, unpack and install the gem command and
      required libraries:

```
$ cd /tmp
$ wget http://production.cf.rubygems.org/rubygems/rubygems-1.3.7.tgz
$ tar -xzf rubygems-1.3.7.tgz
$ cd rubygems-1.3.7
$ sudo ruby setup.rb
```

3.   Use the update-alternatives command to add the newly installed RubyGems
      version as an alternative command.

```
$ sudo update-alternatives --install /usr/bin/gem gem /usr/bin/gem1.8 1
```

Now that we have all the prerequisites, we can install the Dashboard itself.

Installing the Dashboard Package

The Dashboard is available in package form as RPMs (Red Hat, et al) and DEBs (Debian and Ubuntu, et
al) from the Puppet Labs package repositories. For RPMs this is http://yum.puppetlabs.com, and for
DEBs this is http://apt.puppetlabs.com. Puppet Dashboard can also be installed from source, via tarball
available from the Puppet Labs download site (http://www.puppetlabs.com/downloads/) or by cloning
the GitHub repository at https://github.com/puppetlabs/puppet-dashboard.

RPM Packages via Yum

To install the Dashboard from an RPM, you need to add the Puppet Labs Yum repository to your
Dashboard host.

1.   Create an entry:

```
$ sudo vi /etc/yum.repos.d/puppetlabs.repo
```

The entry should be:

```
[puppetlabs]
name=Puppet Labs Packages
baseurl=http://yum.puppetlabs.com/base/
enabled=1
gpgcheck=1
gpgkey=http://yum.puppetlabs.com/RPM-GPG-KEY-puppetlabs
```

2. Run the Yum package manager:

```
$ sudo yum update
```

This will update the Yum package repository data.

3. Run the Yum package manager again to install the Dashboard itself:

```
$ sudo yum install puppet-dashboard
```

The Dashboard package will be installed and the Dashboard site itself will be installed into the /usr/share/puppet-dashboard directory.

DEB Packages via APT

To install the Debian or Ubuntu DEB packages, you need to add details of the Puppet Labs APT repository to your Dashboard host.

1. Edit the /etc/apt/sources.list file by adding the following lines:

```
deb http://apt.puppetlabs.com/ubuntu lucid main
deb-src http://apt.puppetlabs.com/ubuntu lucid main
```

2. Add the Puppet Labs GPG key to validate the downloaded packages, like so:

```
$ sudo gpg --recv-key 4BD6EC30
$ sudo gpg -a --export 4BD6EC30 > /tmp/key
$ sudo apt-key add /tmp/key
```

3. Then, run an update to refresh APT:

```
$ sudo apt-get update
```

4. Finally, install the Puppet Dashboard package:

```
$ sudo apt-get install puppet-dashboard
```

The Dashboard package will be installed and the Dashboard site will be installed in the /usr/share/puppet-dashboard directory.

▓ **Note** You can also download the relevant RPM or DEB package directly from the repository sites and install it via the appropriate command line tool.

Installing from Source

We don't recommend installing the Dashboard from source because packages are much easier to manage and update, but it is possible. You can download a tarball from the Puppet Labs Download page:

```
$ wget http://www.puppetlabs.com/downloads/dashboard/puppet-dashboard-1.0.4.tgz
```

You can then unpack the tarball in an appropriate directory, for example:

```
$ cd /var/www/html
$ sudo tar -xzf puppet-dashboard-1.0.4.tgz
```

Alternately, you can clone the current Dashboard source code from GitHub. You will need to have installed Git to clone the required repository:

```
$ git clone https://github.com/puppetlabs/puppet-dashboard.git
```

You can then change into the resulting directory:

```
$ cd puppet-dashboard
```

And continue installing the Dashboard.

▓ **Caution** Development versions of Puppet Dashboard may be unstable and could potentially have bugs and issues. We recommend you use the packages, or even the tarball, to install the Dashboard.

Configuring the Dashboard

Once you have installed Puppet Dashboard, you need to create a database to hold the Dashboard's data, configure that database in the Dashboard and populate that database with the appropriate tables. This is a three-step process:

1. Edit the YAML configuration file (database.yml) to specify the database

2. Create the database "Dashboard" with the Ruby rake command based on the edited configuration file

3. Populate the database

We start by editing the /usr/share/puppet-dashboard/config/database.yml file, which specifies our database configuration.

▓ **Note** We assume you've installed the Dashboard via a package. If you have not, then be sure to use the appropriate directory where you installed the Dashboard.

The database.yml file is a YAML configuration file and any settings we specify in the file need to be valid YAML.

Ruby on Rails applications use the concept of environments (production, development, etc.) to allow you to specify multiple databases and configurations for different purposes in a single application. For our purposes, we're just going to create a single environment for a production Dashboard instance, as you can see in Listing 7-1.

***Listing 7-1.** The database.yml configuration file*

```
production:
  database: dashboard
  username: dashboard
  password: password
  encoding: utf8
  adapter: mysql
```

The database.yml file contains a series of database configurations for the different Rails environments. Inside each environment block we need to specify the name of the database we're using, the username and password used to connect to that database, as well as the encoding and database type. In this case, we're going to leave all of the default settings except the password. Select an appropriate password and save the file.

We're now going to use the Ruby rake command to automatically create a database based on the configuration in the database.yml file. To do this we need to change to the root of the Dashboard. Assuming we've used the package installation, that would be /usr/share/puppet-dashboard:

```
$ cd /usr/share/puppet-dashboard
```

Now run a rake command, like so:

```
$ sudo rake RAILS_ENV=production db:create
```

This will create a database called "dashboard," with a user of dashboard secured with the password you specified in the database.yml configuration file.

▨ **Tip** The RAILS_ENV=production environment variable tells Ruby on Rails that we're working in the production environment. Every time you run a rake command you need to specify the RAILS_ENV environment variable with the appropriate environment.

You could also manually create the database using the MySQL command line interface, for example:

```
$ sudo mysql -p
mysql> CREATE DATABASE dashboard CHARACTER SET utf8; CREATE USER 'dashboard'@'localhost' ↵
 IDENTIFIED BY 'password'; GRANT ALL PRIVILEGES ON dashboard.* TO 'dashboard'@'localhost';
```

After you've created the database, you then need to populate this database with the appropriate tables. To do this, use another rake command. First make sure you're in the root of the Puppet Dashboard application, then run the required rake task.

```
$ cd /usr/share/puppet-dashboard
$ sudo rake RAILS_ENV=production db:migrate
```

Running Puppet Dashboard

Once you have the Dashboard database configured, you can run it. Puppet Dashboard is a Ruby on Rails application that can be run in a number of different ways, such as using the internal Webrick server or via integration with a server like Passenger (which we talked about in Chapter 4). Webrick is a good way to quickly get started with the Dashboard, but it doesn't scale very well and performs poorly when you have a large number of Puppet agents reporting to the Dashboard. We recommend using a server like Passenger to run the Dashboard, it is a better performing and scalable solution than the internal Webrick server.

In the next two sections, we're going to show you how to use either the Webrick server or Passenger to run the Dashboard.

Running Puppet Dashboard with Webrick

Running with the built-in Webrick web server is very simple; indeed, the init scripts provided with the Dashboard packages do exactly this. However, there are some important limitations to consider with Webrick. It's quite slow and can't easily handle multiple simultaneous requests.

To run the Webrick server, change into the root of the Dashboard application: /usr/share/puppet-dashboard and run:

```
$ sudo ./script/server -e production
```

This will run the Webrick server on port 3000. You can now browse to your host, for example http://dashboard.example.com:3000 and view the Dashboard.

Or you can run the init script that comes with the Puppet Dashboard package like so:

```
$ sudo /etc/init.d/puppet-dashboard start
```

Running Puppet Dashboard with Passenger

Passenger is rather more sophisticated and far better performing than Webrick, and it can be combined with Apache or Nginx. We're going to show you integration with Apache, but we'll provide you some resources where you can read about how to integrate with Nginx too. The main advantage of Passenger is that it is drastically faster and more scalable than Webrick as an engine for running the Dashboard.

Running Passenger, however, is somewhat more complex than using Webrick. It requires a web server, which Passenger integrates with as a module, and then some further configuration on the Dashboard side. We're going to take you through the steps required to:

- Install any prerequisite packages including Apache and Passenger

- Configure an Apache virtual host to run Passenger and the Dashboard

▧ **Note** Passenger integration is also called `mod_rails`, and is similar in implementation to other embedded Apache modules like `mod_php`. We also talked about Passenger in Chapter 4 when we looked at how to scale Puppet with it.

Installing Prerequisite Packages

Our first step is to install the required prerequisite packages. This includes Apache, the MySQL Ruby bindings and Passenger itself.

Red Hat

On Red Hat and related distributions, this involves installing the following packages (we've assumed you've still got the EPEL repository enabled):

```
$ sudo yum install ruby ruby-libs ruby-devel httpd httpd-devel
```

Unfortunately, Passenger is not yet available for Red Hat as a package due to some packaging issues. We can however install Passenger from a gem, for example:

```
$ sudo gem install passenger
```

Once we've installed the Ruby Gem we need to use the `passenger-install-apache2-module` script to create the required Apache Passenger module.

```
$ sudo passenger-install-apache2-module
```

Follow the provided instructions to create and install the Apache Passenger module.

Ubuntu and Debian

On Ubuntu and Debian, the required packages are:

```
$ sudo apt-get install apache2 libapache2-mod-passenger rails librack-ruby libmysql-ruby
```

You might have already installed some of these packages, either to run Puppet or earlier in this chapter when you were setting up the Dashboard.

▧ **Note** Passenger is only sometimes available as a package on operating systems other than Red Hat or Ubuntu. Often, the easiest method of installing Passenger is via Ruby Gems, with `gem install passenger`.

Configure an Apache Virtual Host

Next, you need to configure an Apache virtual host for our Dashboard implementation, which will include enabling the required Passenger module. The Puppet Dashboard provides an example of this virtual host, which you can see in Listing 7-2. We will put the file in our Apache configuration directory, for example /etc/httpd/conf.d or /etc/apache2/conf.d, on Red Hat and Debian/Ubuntu flavored hosts, respectively.

Listing 7-2. Apache Virtual Host for Passenger

```
LoadModule passenger_module /var/lib/gems/1.8/gems/passenger-
2.2.11/ext/apache2/mod_passenger.so
PassengerRoot /var/lib/gems/1.8/gems/passenger-2.2.11
PassengerRuby /usr/bin/ruby

PassengerHighPerformance on
PassengerMaxPoolSize 12
PassengerPoolIdleTime 1500
PassengerStatThrottleRate 120
RailsAutoDetect On

<VirtualHost *:80>
        ServerName dashboard.example.com
        DocumentRoot /usr/share/puppet-dashboard/public/
        <Directory /usr/share/puppet-dashboard/public/>
                Options None
                AllowOverride AuthConfig
                Order allow,deny
                allow from all
        </Directory>
  ErrorLog /var/log/apache2/dashboard.example.com_error.log
  LogLevel warn
  CustomLog /var/log/apache2/dashboard.example.com_access.log combined
  ServerSignature On
</VirtualHost>
```

The virtual host file first loads the mod_passenger module, in this case customized for a Debian or Ubuntu environment. If we'd installed Passenger via a gem those lines might look more like this:

```
    LoadModule passenger_module /usr/lib/ruby/gems/1.8/gems↵
/passenger-2.2.9/ext/apache2/mod_passenger.so
    PassengerRoot /usr/lib/ruby/gems/1.8/gems/passenger-2.2.9
    PassengerRuby /usr/bin/ruby
```

The next options control Passenger-specific options. You can read about each in more detail at http://www.modrails.com/documentation/Users%20guide%20Apache.html#_configuring_phusion_ passenger.

Last is a very simple virtual host definition that specifies the location of the Dashboard application. The important options to note are DocumentRoot and Directory. For Passenger to serve out a Ruby on Rails application, these need to be set to the public directory underneath the root of the Rails application, in our case /usr/share/puppet-dashboard/public.

We can now reload Apache and browse to the URL and see the Dashboard, for example on Red Hat:

```
$ sudo service httpd restart
```

You can see the home page of the Dashboard in Figure 7-1.

167

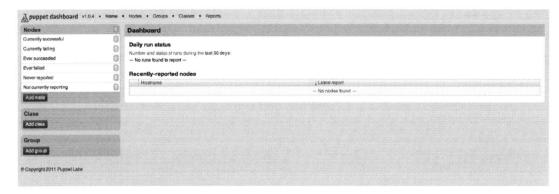

Figure 7-1. The Dashboard home page

■ **Tip** If you'd prefer to use the Nginx server rather than Apache, you can see some instructions at `http://wiki.rubyonrails.org/deployment/nginx-passenger`. Other deployment options include Unicorn (`http://unicorn.bogomips.org/`) and Thin (`http://wiki.rubyonrails.org/deployment/nginx-thin`).

With Puppet Dashboard installed we can now use it, starting with looking a how to integrate our Puppet masters and agents into the Dashboard.

DASHBOARD SECURITY

One of the limitations of the current Dashboard tool is its lack of authentication, authorization and encryption. Currently Dashboard does not provide any of these, though they are on the product's roadmap. The best way to protect your Dashboard from unauthorized access is to:

Configure a combination of host- and network-based firewalls to limit access to the Dashboard from appropriate network segments

HTTP Basic authentication, for example using Apache. If you do specify HTTP basic authentication, remember that ANY connection – including report aggregation and external nodes – will need to be authenticated. This means including the HTTP Basic username and password in any supplied URL, for example setting the `reporturl` option in the `puppet.conf` file to `http://username:password@dashboard.example.com`.

Integrating Puppet Dashboard

Now that you've installed the Dashboard, you can integrate Puppet and start to make use of some of its capabilities. We're going to demonstrate:

- Importing Puppet reports

- Live aggregation of Puppet reports

- Displaying reports

- Using the Dashboard for external node classification

Finally, we'll look at logging, database and data management, including backing up your Dashboard data.

But the first capability we're going to use is the Dashboard's ability to display Puppet reports and reporting statistics. We can do this in two ways: by importing existing reports using a Rake task, usually scheduled via a cron job, or by configuring Puppet to send its reports directly to the Dashboard.

▨ **Note** If desired, you can both import your existing historical data into the Dashboard with the Rake task, and ensure regular updates by configuring Puppet to send reports to the Dashboard.

Importing Existing Reports

Let's first see how we can incorporate existing reports from Puppet. The Dashboard comes with a Rake task to perform this action. Change into the root directory, /usr/share/puppet-dashboard, of the Dashboard application. Then, run the reports:import task.

```
$ sudo rake RAILS_ENV=production reports:import
```

By default, the task will look in /var/puppet/lib/reports for any reports to be imported. If your reports aren't located here then you can specify a location on the command line:

```
$ sudo rake RAILS_ENV=production reports:import REPORT_DIR=/path/to/your/reports
```

You can run this command multiple times, for example via a cron job. Any reports that have already been imported will be skipped. You should see lists of nodes appear in your Dashboard as reports for each are added. You can see some initial nodes in Figure 7-2.

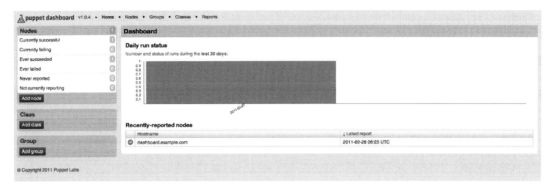

Figure 7-2. Initial nodes in the Dashboard

■ **Tip** You can see a full list of all reports on the Dashboard by clicking the Reports link in the top menu bar.

Live Report Aggregation

In addition to manual report importation, you can also configure Puppet to send your reports to the Dashboard. There are two methods to do this, depending on what version of Puppet you have running. For both methods you need to make changes on both the Puppet master and clients.

■ **Note** Many of the changes we're going to describe relate to reports and reporting capability we will talk about in Chapter 9.

Puppet 2.6.0 and later

For versions 2.6.0 and later, you need to enable reporting on our clients (if you haven't already) by setting the report option in the [agent] section of the puppet.conf file, like so:

```
[agent]
report = true
```

On the master you need to enable a new type of report called http, which sends report data over an HTTP connection, and specify a location to send our HTTP report, reporturl. You don't have to specify a URL, in which case it will default to the local host on port 3000. To do this you need to update the [master] section of the Puppet's master's puppet.conf file.

```
[master]
reports = http
```

```
reporturl = http://dashboard.example.com:80/reports
```

You then need to restart the Puppet master to update its configuration. Now, when Puppet clients connect, they will send a report to the URL you specified; Puppet Dashboard will receive and then process the report.

Puppet 0.25.x and earlier

For versions 0.25.x and earlier, you need to use a report processor provided with the Dashboard product rather than the in-built HTTP report type (which is not available in these earlier releases). You first need to enable reporting on our Puppet clients by setting the report option in the [puppetd] section of the puppet.conf file to true.

```
[puppetd]
report = true
```

Then on the Puppet master, find the value of your libdir, the location of the Puppet libraries:

```
$ puppetmasterd --configprint libdir
```

By default this will be something like /var/lib/puppet/lib. Create a directory under this path:

```
$ sudo mkdir -p /var/lib/puppet/lib/puppet/reports
```

Then copy the Puppet report processor into this directory from your Dashboard installation.

```
$ sudo cp /usr/share/puppet-dashboard/ext/puppet/puppet_dashboard.rb↵
 /var/lib/puppet/lib/reports
```

This special report processor assumes that your Dashboard instance is on the local host at port 3000. If this is not the case, you can edit the puppet_dashboard.rb file to change the target of the report. Change the following options at the top of the file:

```
HOST = 'localhost'
PORT = 3000
```

Update your puppet.conf file on the Puppet master in the [puppetmasterd] section:

```
[puppetmasterd]
reports = puppet_dashboard
```

And lastly, restart the Puppet master daemon.

Viewing Reports

Now that you've got Puppet adding its reports to the Dashboard, you can examine them and view the results. Click on a particular node to see details of its recent configuration runs, and you should see a screen similar to Figure 7-3.

171

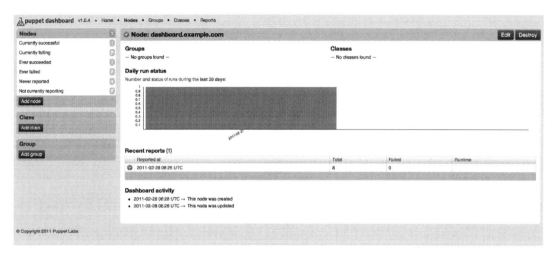

Figure 7-3. The node detail screen

The screen shows a list of recent runs, the total resources applied, any resources that failed, and the total runtime of the run in seconds.

Drilling down into an individual run will show log output, specifically that related to any failed resources. Also more resource metrics and timings on individual resource types will be displayed. You can see an example of this screen in Figure 7-4.

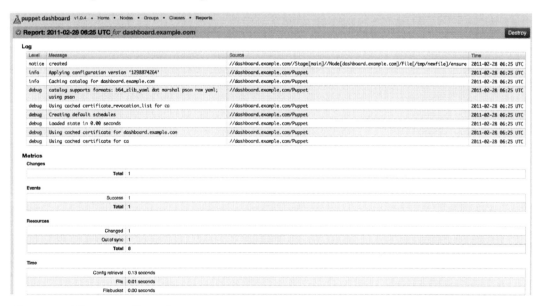

Figure 7-4. A Puppet configuration run

External Node Classification

In addition to its ability to display reports and data, the Dashboard can also act as an external classifier. We discussed external node classification (ENC) and why it's useful to simplify and organize large number of nodes in Chapter 5. This can become even easier with a web interface like the Dashboard that configures these nodes, classes and parameters.

To enable the Dashboard's external node classification capability, you need to configure Puppet to use an ENC. On Puppet 2.6.x and later, this means adding an ENC to your master's `puppet.conf` configuration file:

```
[master]
node_terminus = exec
external_nodes = /usr/share/puppet-dashboard/bin/external_node
```

■ **Note** On Puppet 0.25.x and earlier versions, this section is called [`puppetmasterd`] rather than [`master`].

The external_node ENC assumes that your Dashboard is located on the local host at port 3000. If this isn't the case, you can edit it to suit your environment. Open this file and find the line:

```
DASHBOARD_URL="http://dashboard:3000"
```

Modify the line to reflect where your Dashboard is located. You will then need to restart the Puppet master to update your ENC configuration. Or, if you don't want to edit the file, you can specify a local environment variable on the Puppet master, `PUPPET_DASHBOARD_URL`, that contains this information.

Inside the Dashboard you can now create three kinds of configuration: nodes, classes and groups. A node is the normal Puppet node and contains the node's hostname and a description of the node. Remember that the node's hostname needs to match the real node so that when Puppet queries the Dashboard, the right host is returned. You can also add any parameters (which are the same as Puppet variables) and any classes or groups that the node is assigned to. You can see the Add Node page in Figure 7-5.

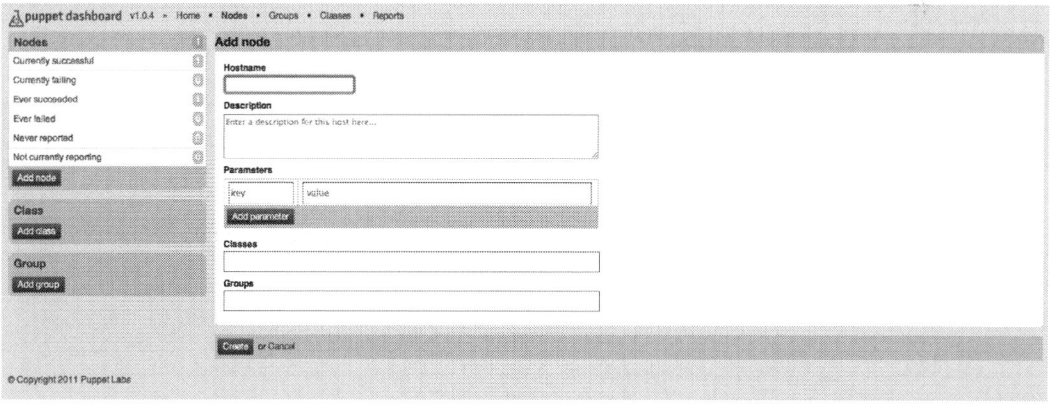

Figure 7-5. Adding a node

You can also create one or more classes that can be assigned to nodes or groups by clicking the Add Class link. These are simply class names – this doesn't directly create a Puppet class, it just lists those classes that should be applied to a particular node. You will still need to write the required Puppet manifests on your master.

Lastly, you can create Groups as you can see in Figure 7-6.

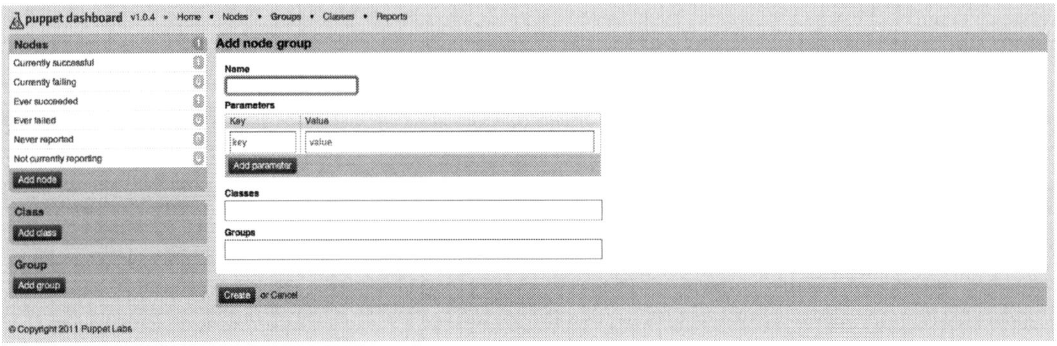

Figure 7-6. Adding Groups

Groups don't directly have a representation in Puppet manifests, but are rather a way of grouping your nodes on the Dashboard itself. Once you've created a Group (in which you can also add parameters and additional classes, which will be cumulatively applied to any node that is a member of the Group), you can then add nodes to it. Clicking on the newly created group in the left hand will display a screen showing all of the nodes assigned to that Group, as you can see in Figure 7-7.

Figure 7-7. The Group summary screen

▓ **Note** You can add classes, parameters and groups to existing nodes by clicking on the node and then on the Edit button. You can also delete nodes, classes and groups by clicking on the dramatically-named Destroy button.

With your node configuration in place on the Dashboard, when the Puppet master runs and uses the external node classifier to query for node data it will contact the Dashboard. The Dashboard's API will return the required data, class and parameter information to populate the required node.

▓ **Tip** You can see more detail on this process in Chapter 5.

Logging, Database Backup and Performance

With the Dashboard there are also a few simple management and maintenance tasks you need to know about.

First, like all Rails applications, Puppet Dashboard logs information and errors produced to logs contained in the `/usr/share/puppet-dashboard/logs` directory. These logs are useful to find diagnostic and informational data about the running of the Dashboard. Each Rails environment, production, development, etc., produces a separate log file named for the environment being logged. For example, check the `production.log` file for log data for your Rails production instance, or check `development.log` for development instance data.

These log files can accumulate and grow in size, and you should be sure sure to regularly prune them. The Dashboard comes with a Rake task to do this for you that you can manually schedule (or better yet, configure Puppet to run it as a cron job for you). To use the Rake task, change into the root of the Rails application, usually `/usr/share/puppet-dashboard`, and run:

```
$ sudo rake log:clear
```

▓ **Tip** You can also use `logrotate`, or a similar tool, to prune log files as part of your regular log management.

Second, like most database-driven applications, performance of the Puppet Dashboard can sometimes be improved by running optimization techniques over its MySQL database. Again, the Dashboard contains a Rake task that can perform this optimization for you. From the root of the application, run:

```
$ sudo rake RAILS_ENV=production db:raw:optimize
```

Third, you should back up your Dashboard's database. The best way to do this is to use the appropriate database backup tool used in your environment. If you don't have a tool, then you can use another in-built Rake task to create a dump of the database, which you can then back up:

```
$ sudo rake RAILS_ENV=production db:raw:dump
```

This will create a SQL dump of the Dashboard database in a file called `production.sql` in the current directory. You can override this file name an location using the following command line:

```
$ sudo rake RAILS_ENV=production FILE=/path/to/backup/file.sql db:raw:dump
```

Conveniently, there is also a Rake task to restore the database:

```
$ sudo rake RAILS_ENV=production FILE=production.sql db:raw:restore
```

▨ **Note** Lots of Rake tasks? You can see a full list of the available tasks by running `rake -T` in the root directory of the Dashboard application.

Lastly, you can purge older reports from your Dashboard database using another Rake task, reports:prune. For example, to prune reports 3 months old or older, you would use:

```
$ sudo rake RAILS_ENV=production reports:prune upto=3 unit=mon
```

You can run the `rake reports:prune` task without any options to get a full list of the task's options.

▨ **Note** The Dashboard is a relatively new product – it's growing and changing all the time. Keep an eye on new releases for new features and capabilities.

The Foreman

The other entry in the Puppet GUI ecosystem is The Foreman, or simply Foreman (http://theforeman.org/). Foreman is an integrated data center lifecycle management tool that provides provisioning, configuration management and reporting. Like Puppet Dashboard, Foreman is a Ruby on Rails application.

Foreman, unlike the Dashboard, has much more of a focus on provisioning and managing data center capabilities, for example integration with bootstrapping tools, PXE boot servers, DHCP servers and provisioning tools.

Here, we focus on getting started with Foreman so you learn how to:

- Install Foreman
- Configuring Foreman
- Integrate Foreman with Puppet

Installing Foreman

Installing Foreman requires some prerequisites. First, you need to install Puppet, a version later than 0.24.4. You can see how to do this in Chapter 1 of the book. You also need to install some additional packages. On Red Hat and related distributions, you need to install the following packages:

```
$ sudo yum install rubygems rubygem-rake rubygem-rack rubygem-sqlite3-ruby
```

Alternatively, on Ubuntu and Debian-based hosts, you will need:

```
$ sudo apt-get install rubygems rake librack-ruby libsqlite3-ruby
```

Both of these package installations might also prompt you to install additional dependencies, depending on your distribution and its version.

Once you have the required prerequisites, you can install Foreman itself. Levy has packaged Foreman for both RPM- and DEB-based distributions.

Installing Foreman via RPM

The easiest way to install Foreman via RPM is to add the Foreman Yum repository to your environment. To do this, create a Yum repository entry for the Foreman repository, in /etc/yum.repos.d/foreman.repo:

```
[foreman]
name=Foreman Repo
baseurl=http://yum.theforeman.org/stable
gpgcheck=0
enabled=1
```

Then run:

```
$ sudo yum install foreman
```

You will also need to have the EPEL repository enabled, which you can see from the instructions specified in Chapter 1 or via http://fedoraproject.org/wiki/EPEL/FAQ#howtouse. Foreman will load several additional packages from the EPEL repository.

▪ **Note** You can also install Foreman from source if you wish, though we recommend for manageability that you stick with packages. You can find the Foreman source at git://github.com/ohadlevy/foreman.git, or grab a daily snapshot of the Foreman development code at http://theforeman.org/foreman-nightly.tar.bz2.

Installing via DEB

Foreman is also available as an Ubuntu/Debian package. To make use of the current packages, add the following line to your /etc/apt/sources.list file:

```
deb http://deb.theforeman.org/ stable main
```

You then need to download the Foreman GPG key, add it to APT and update like so:

```
$ wget http://deb.theforeman.org/foreman.asc
$ sudo apt-key add foreman.asc
$ sudo apt-get update
```

Now Foreman should be available to install as a package. It is available in three versions:

- Foreman with Sqlite3 – foreman-sqlite3
- Foreman with PostgreSQL – foreman-pgsql
- Foreman with MySQL – foreman-mysql

We're going to install the MySQL version:

```
$ apt-get install foreman-mysql
```

▪ **Tip** Levy has also made available a Puppet module that can be configured to install Foreman and take care of much of the installation process for you. You can find the module at http://github.com/ohadlevy/puppet-foreman.

Configuring Foreman

The primary configuration we have to perform for Foreman is to its database back end. Foreman supports a variety of databases including MySQL, Sqlite3, PostgreSQL and Oracle. It also supports sharing a database with Puppet's stored configuration capability (see Chapter 6). We're going to choose a MySQL database, so we need to install the required packages.

Configuring Foreman on Red Hat

On Red Hat-based hosts you first need to install the required packages:

```
$ sudo yum install -y mysql mysql-devel mysql-server ruby-mysql
```

Next, you will need to manage MySQL. To do this, start MySQL and configure it to start at boot. Use the service command to start the service:

```
$ sudo service mysqld start
```

Then use the chkconfig command to configure to MySQL to start when the host boots:

```
$ sudo chkconfig mysqld on
```

Configuring Foreman on Ubuntu and Debian

On Ubuntu and Debian based hosts, you need to install the required packages:

```
$ sudo apt-get install -y libmysql-ruby libmysqlclient-dev mysql-server
```

Managing Foreman's Database

On both Red Hat and Ubuntu/Debian machines, you need to:

1. Create a database for Foreman, and secure it with a user and password.

```
$ sudo mysql -p
mysql> CREATE DATABASE foreman CHARACTER SET utf8; CREATE USER 'foreman'@'localhost'↵
 IDENTIFIED BY 'password'; GRANT ALL PRIVILEGES ON foreman.* TO 'foreman'@'localhost';
```

2. Edit the database.yml file and specify the database details you just used.

```
production:
  database: foreman
  username: foreman
  password: password
  encoding: utf8
  adapter: mysql
```

▪ **Note** Alternately, you can modify the database.yml file to use the same database as your stored configuration database in Puppet. See Chapter 6 for more details on stored configuration.

---

3. Run a Rake task to populate your database with the appropriate tables:

```
$ sudo RAILS_ENV=production rake db:migrate
```

Importing Data from Puppet

You can also import existing data from Puppet. If you are using stored configuration with Puppet and you are sharing the database with Foreman, you can run:

```
$ sudo RAILS_ENV=production rake puppet:migrate:populate_hosts
```

If you're not using stored configuration and your Puppet master is located on the same host as Foreman, then you should run the following Rake task:

```
$ sudo RAILS_ENV=production rake puppet:import:hosts_and_facts
```

You should regularly run this task via cron to keep your nodes and facts up-to-date.

If your Puppet master is not on the same host as Foreman, you can choose between two approaches. The first uses the same import Rake task but requires that you transfer (or mount) your Puppet facts YAML output files (usually located in the /var/lib/puppet/yaml/facts directory) from the master to the Foreman host:

```
$ sudo rake RAILS_ENV=production puppet:import:hosts_and_facts dir=/path/to/yaml/files
```

The second approach uses Foreman's ability to receive Fact data from Puppet. Foreman comes with a script you can install onto your Puppet masters and run with cron:

```
$ wget --no-check-certificate https://github.com/ohadlevy/puppet-foreman/raw↵
/master/foreman/files/push_facts.rb
```

You will need to update this line of the script to point to the location of your Foreman installation:
`url=http://foreman`

▓ **Tip** For more information on importing data to Foreman to Puppet, see:

`http://theforeman.org/projects/foreman/wiki/Puppet_Facts.`

Starting Foreman

Like Puppet Dashboard, Foreman is a Rails application and can run using a variety of servers, including the in-built Webrick server and an external server such as Apache running Passenger.

To run Foreman with Webrick, change into the root of the Foreman application, usually `/usr/share/foreman`, and run:

`$ sudo ./script/server -e production`

Or, you can run the supplied init script to achieve the same result:

`$ sudo service foreman start`

This will start Foreman on the local host running on port 3000. You can then place Apache or another proxy in front of it if required.

Running Foreman using Apache and Passenger is a more performant and scalable solution. Levy has included some examples of how to configure Foreman for use with Apache and Passenger, including making the Puppet module we discussed earlier capable of automatically configuring Foreman and Passenger (`https://github.com/ohadlevy/puppet-foreman`).

Once Foreman is running, you should see the home page displayed in Figure 7-8.

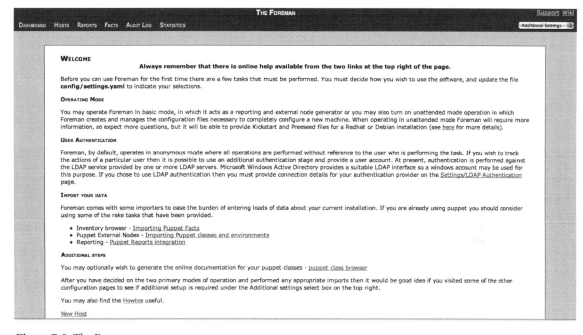

Figure 7-8. The Foreman

Integrating Foreman's Capabilities

Foreman has a lot of features that you can use to manage your environment, including recently-added capabilities to manage DNS and DHCP for provisioned hosts. We're going to cover the highlights of its functionality, focusing on its integration with Puppet, including:

- Using Foreman as an External Node Classifier

- Displaying reports in Foreman

- Displaying nodes in Foreman

- Using Foreman to trigger Puppet runs

You can read more about the overall functionality at http://theforeman.org/projects/foreman/wiki/Features.

Using Foreman as an ENC

Like Puppet Dashboard, Foreman can be used as an ENC. To do that, click on the Hosts tab to display the list of hosts currently in Foreman, as shown in Figure 7-9.

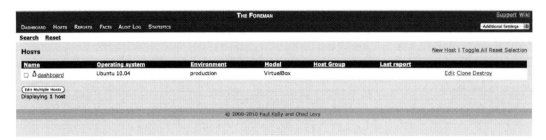

Figure 7-9. *Foreman's Hosts display*

You can add hosts to Foreman by clicking the New Host link, shown in Figure 7-10.

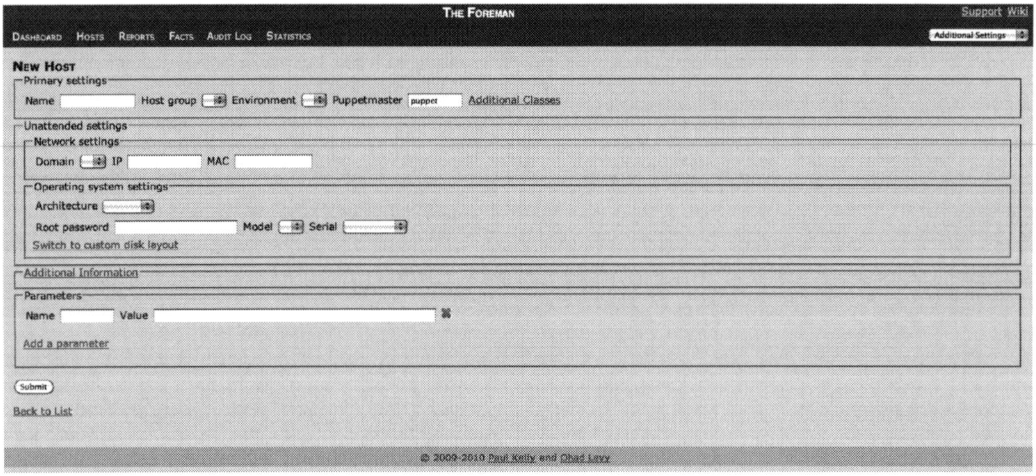

Figure 7-10. *Adding a new host to Foreman*

Populate the environment, the required classes and any proposed parameters, and click Submit to add the new host. You can also define global and per domain parameters in the Settings tab. If you define more than one parameter with the same name, Foreman has a hierarchical override structure with parameters processed in order of global, domain, and host, with the last one processed setting the value.

In addition to this manual configuration, Foreman can also import some information from your existing Puppet information so you can pre-seed your external node classifier. To import all the classes contained in your Puppet modules, run the following Rake task:

```
$ sudo RAILS_ENV=production rake puppet:import:puppet_classes
```

This task will include all classes in modules specified in your modulepath.

Once you have defined your hosts, you need to specify Foreman as the ENC for your Puppet instance. To do this, update the puppet.conf configuration file on the Puppet master:

```
[master]
node_terminus = exec
external_nodes = /usr/share/theforeman/extras/puppet/foreman/files/external_node.rb
```

■ **Note** On Puppet 0.25.x and earlier the section is called [puppetmasterd].

The external_node.rb script is an ENC that is provided with Foreman. It assumes your Foreman instance is running on a host named foreman on port 3000. Adjust this line to point it at your actual Foreman instance:

```
foreman_url=http://foreman:3000
```

■ **Tip** You can click on the YAML link in an individual host definition to see what the ENC output would be for that host. This is a good way of confirming your host is accurately configured.

Displaying Reports in Foreman

Foreman has the capability to import and display your Puppet reports. Foreman uses a custom report on your Puppet master to send reports. To use this custom report, you need to ensure all clients have reporting enabled by setting the report option on each client:

```
[agent]
report = true
```

You then need to add your Foreman report to the master and configure it to send the report to the right location. The Foreman custom report is contained in /usr/share/foreman/extras/puppet/foreman /files/foreman-report.rb.

Inside this file, find the line:

```
$foreman_url=http://foreman:3000
```

Ensure that this line points to the correct Foreman host and port for our environment. Then, copy this report into the Puppet reports directory on each of your Puppet masters; for example, on Red Hat it would look like this:

```
$ sudo cp /usr/share/foreman/extras/puppet/foreman/files/foreman-report.rb↵
 /usr/lib/ruby/1.8/puppet/reports/foreman.rb
```

Next, enable this report in the Puppet master's puppet.conf file:

```
reports = log, foreman
```

Restart the Puppet master and reports should begin to flow to Foreman. You can review these reports via the Reports tab that you can see in Figure 7-11.

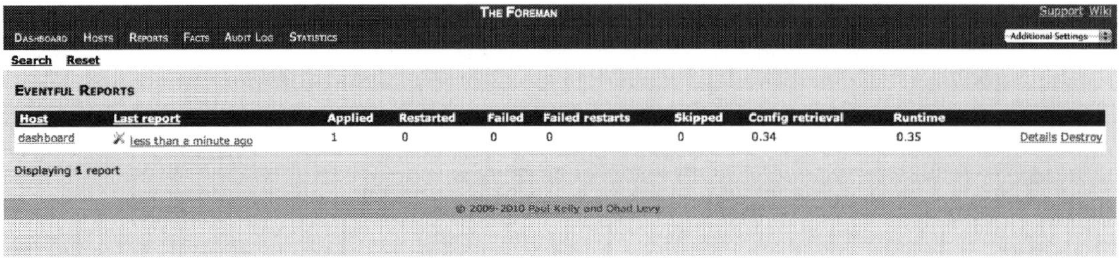

Figure 7-11. Displaying reports in Foreman

If you have reports you'd like to purge from Foreman, both to improve performance and to remove aged data, you can run another Rake task to expire reports. You can remove reports via date and via their status. To expire all reports older than a particular period, use the following Rake task from the root directory of the Foreman application:

```
$ sudo RAILS_ENV="production" rake reports:expire days=7
```

This removes all reports older than 7 days.

We can also remove all reports, except those with errors or failed resources, for example:

```
$ sudo RAILS_ENV="production" rake reports:expire days=10 status=0
```

This task would remove all reports older than 10 days which were successful and contain no errors or failed resources.

Displaying Nodes Information in Foreman

In addition to acting as an ENC, you can also use Foreman to display data about your Puppet nodes. Foreman can take this data from two sources: your existing stored configuration database, or via a manual import of Puppet data.

If you're using the same database for Puppet's stored configuration as for Foreman, then this data will automatically be populated into Foreman and you can see it via the Facts tab, as shown in Figure 7-12, or using the individual Fact links for each host. If you are not using the stored configuration database, then you can use the tasks we described in the Configuring Foreman section to keep your Puppet data up to date.

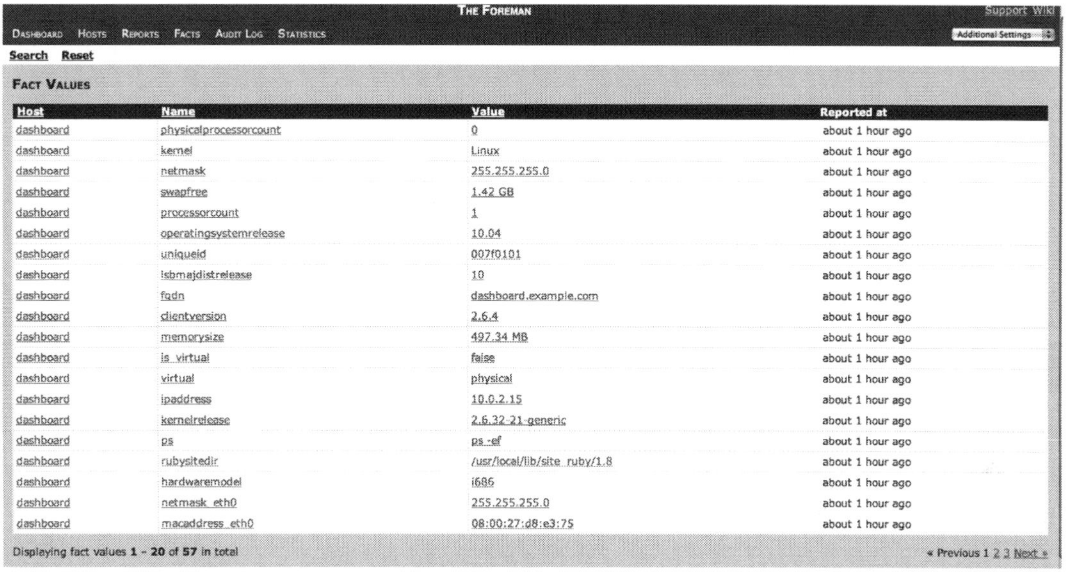
THE FOREMAN

DASHBOARD HOSTS REPORTS FACTS AUDIT LOG STATISTICS

Search Reset

FACT VALUES

Host	Name	Value	Reported at
dashboard	physicalprocessorcount	0	about 1 hour ago
dashboard	kernel	Linux	about 1 hour ago
dashboard	netmask	255.255.255.0	about 1 hour ago
dashboard	swapfree	1.42 GB	about 1 hour ago
dashboard	processorcount	1	about 1 hour ago
dashboard	operatingsystemrelease	10.04	about 1 hour ago
dashboard	uniqueid	007f0101	about 1 hour ago
dashboard	lsbmajdistrelease	10	about 1 hour ago
dashboard	fqdn	dashboard.example.com	about 1 hour ago
dashboard	clientversion	2.6.4	about 1 hour ago
dashboard	memorysize	497.34 MB	about 1 hour ago
dashboard	is_virtual	false	about 1 hour ago
dashboard	virtual	physical	about 1 hour ago
dashboard	ipaddress	10.0.2.15	about 1 hour ago
dashboard	kernelrelease	2.6.32-21-generic	about 1 hour ago
dashboard	ps	ps -ef	about 1 hour ago
dashboard	rubysitedir	/usr/local/lib/site_ruby/1.8	about 1 hour ago
dashboard	hardwaremodel	i686	about 1 hour ago
dashboard	netmask_eth0	255.255.255.0	about 1 hour ago
dashboard	macaddress_eth0	08:00:27:d8:e3:75	about 1 hour ago

Displaying fact values 1 - 20 of 57 in total « Previous 1 2 3 Next »

Figure 7-12. Displaying Facts in Foreman

You can also use the Search functions to find a specific Fact value.

▒ **Note** The Foreman also has a REST API that you can interact with. It uses JSON and provides access to most of its capabilities via a web services interface. You can see full details on the API and how to interact with it at `http://theforeman.org/projects/foreman/wiki/API`.

Using Foreman to trigger Puppet

Lastly, you can also use Foreman to trigger Puppet runs using the `puppet kick` (formerly `puppetrun`) command Foreman will execute the `puppet kick` command from the host running Foreman and trigger a Puppet run on a host. To use the capability you need to have Puppet installed on the Foreman host (which you should have in place anyway), and it will look for the puppetrun binary in `/usr/bin`. You also need the following enabled in the Foreman settings file, `config/settings.yml`:

```
:puppetrun: true
```

And we also need to allow Foreman to do some sudo magic to be able to use the `puppetrun` command and access your certificates. Add something like the following to your `sudoers` file on the Foreman host:

```
Defaults:foreman !requiretty foreman_user ALL = NOPASSWD: /usr/bin/puppetrun
```

Each client host you wish to trigger a Puppet run on needs to have `listen` enabled, for example:

```
[agent]
listen = true
```

> ■ **Note** We cover Puppet run/kick in Chapter 8.

You will also need to allow the connection in the /etc/puppet/auth.conf, for example (replacing foreman.example.com with the hostname of your Foreman host):

```
path /run method save allow foreman.example.com
```

You'll also need to ensure port 8139 is open between the Foreman host and your Puppet clients.

With all this enabled, you should now see a new option in the Hosts display called Run Puppet. Click on this to perform a Puppet run.

> ■ **Tip** The Foreman supports both authentication and encryption. You can read about how to integrate it with an LDAP directory at http://theforeman.org/projects/foreman/wiki/LDAP_Authentication. You can also see how to force The Foreman to use SSL for all connections at http://theforeman.org/projects/foreman /wiki/Force_SSL.

Summary

In this chapter, we've explored how you can use both the Puppet Dashboard and The Foreman as web-based front ends to your Puppet environment. We examined how to install, configure, use, and manage each tool, and we looked at their respective capabilities. Both offer powerful additional visualization and management capabilities that you'll find useful in managing your environment, and enable you to provide graphing to your team.

Resources

The following links will take you to documentation related to the Puppet Dashboard, The Foreman and related topics:

- The Puppet Dashboard http://www.puppetlabs.com/puppet/related-projects/dashboard/

- The Foreman http://theforeman.org/projects/foreman

- The Foreman mailing list http://groups.google.com/group/foreman-users

- The Foreman IRC channel #theforeman on Freenode

- The Foreman Forums http://theforeman.org/projects/foreman/boards

- External nodes http://docs.puppetlabs.com/guides/external_nodes.html

- Puppet configuration reference http://docs.puppetlabs.com/references
  /stable/configuration.html

CHAPTER 8

■■■

Tools and Integration

Puppet, by itself, provides a large number of features and functionality. As you've learned so far in this book, Puppet enables you to manage the configuration state of a wide variety of resources. Files, users, groups, software packages and running services are prime examples. Configuration management is an extremely complex and multi-faceted problem, however, and as result we cannot expect Puppet alone to address every problem. In this chapter, we cover a number of additional tools that work extremely well with Puppet. These tools address many of the problems Puppet alone does not address.

The first problem is concerned with de-duplicating effort. The Puppet Forge provides a central place for members of the Puppet community to publish and download re-usable modules. The Puppet Module tool works with the Forge, providing a convenient command line interface, much like the yum and apt-get packaging commands provide. This chapter demonstrates how to download, install, and use modules from the forge.

In addition, you'll learn how puppet-module can be used to generate a skeleton module structure and package modules. Even if the modules will never be published outside of your organization, these features provide a way to track module versions and distribute them to other groups internally.

While not an external tool, the Ruby DSL in Puppet 2.6 provides an alternative to declaring configuration resources using the Puppet language. The declarative nature of the Puppet language is a great way to express configuration state, but you may run across a configuration that is awkward or impossible to express using the Puppet language itself. In these situations, Puppet allows you to declare classes and resources using the Ruby programming language, providing additional functionality. You'll see how the Example.com developer uses the Ruby DSL to transform data external to Puppet into resources and their parameter values in the configuration catalog. One example of a problem that's difficult to solve with the Puppet language is the management of login accounts. As people join and leave Example.com, the developer would have to add and remove resource declarations in the Puppet manifests. A more ideal solution would be if Puppet could automatically declare resources based on information from an outside data source like LDAP. The Ruby DSL is ideally suited to the task of iterating over an arbitrary amount of external data, then declaring resources using the data.

As Puppet configurations change, testing the change is always a good idea before pushing to the production infrastructure. Puppet is designed to model the desired state of a system, which is closely related to how that system behaves. With the idea of desired behavior in mind, the natural language specifications of Cucumber inspired Nikolay Sturm to develop cucumber-puppet. Cucumber-puppet allows you to describe the desired behavior of Puppet infrastructure and test the configuration model stored in the catalog.

Puppet Forge and Module Tool

The Puppet Forge, located at `http://forge.puppetlabs.com/`, provides an online repository of Puppet modules. This service provides the means to publish and locate modules for commonly managed services like iptables, apache, and NTP. In addition, there are modules targeted for specific use cases, such as Hadoop.

If you find yourself needing to quickly deploy a complex infrastructure like Hadoop, the Puppet Forge will save you much time and effort. Modules on the Forge provide a reference configuration that may be easily modified if necessary. The Forge strives to become to Puppet what CPAN is to Perl hackers. Puppet modules may be manually downloaded from the Forge using a standard web browser, but the process is made much easier through the use of the Puppet Module tool, called puppet-module.

The puppet-module command provides an interface to the Forge API. This command line interface allows you to create skeleton Puppet Modules for your own work, search the forge for existing modules, and install them into your configuration. In this section, we cover the process of downloading an already-existing module and publishing a new module to the forge.

Installing the Puppet Module Tool

Unlike Puppet, which is distributed in many package repositories for various operating systems, the Puppet Module Tool is primarily distributed through the RubyGems package repository. This has the advantage of making installation straightforward and easy on all platforms with RubyGems installed. Listing 8-1 shows how the Example.com operator installs the Puppet Module tool.

Listing 8-1. *Installing Puppet Module using Gems*

```
$ gem install puppet-module
****************************************************************************

    Thank you for installing puppet-module from Puppet Labs!

    * Usage instructions: read "README.markdown" or run `puppet-module usage`
    * Changelog: read "CHANGES.markdown" or run `puppet-module changelog`
    * Puppet Forge: visit http://forge.puppetlabs.com/

****************************************************************************
Successfully installed puppet-module-0.3.2
1 gem installed
Installing ri documentation for puppet-module-0.3.2...
Installing RDoc documentation for puppet-module-0.3.2...

# puppet-module version
0.3.2
```

The operator first installs puppet-module using the gem command, then he checks to make sure the command is executable and at the correct version.

▓ **Note** The Puppet Module tool project page and source code are hosted on GitHub at `https://github.com/puppetlabs/puppet-module-tool`. An alternative to installing the software using RubyGems is to clone a copy of the source and use the install.rb script included in the source. This also gives you the ability to easily modify and contribute to the project.

Searching and Installing a Module from the Forge

The first step to download and install a Puppet module is to search for the name of a module providing the configuration you're looking for. A common service managed on many systems is the iptables host-based firewall. Whether you need to configure Apache, MySQL, or some other network-based service, the host-based firewall will need to be managed to grant access to the service. Before setting out to write his own Puppet module to accomplish this task, in Listing 8-2 the operator uses the puppet-module search command to see if one has been published to the Forge already.

Listing 8-2. Searching for modules using puppet-module

```
$ puppet-module search iptables
=====================================
Searching http://forge.puppetlabs.com
-------------------------------------
1 found.
--------
bobsh/iptables (1.2.0)
```

The operator notices there is already a module to manage the iptables firewall, published by bobsh (Ken Barber). To automatically download and install the module, the operator uses the install action in Listing 8-3. The module will be installed into the current working directory, so it's a good idea to change directories to somewhere located in the Puppet module search path.

Listing 8-3. Installing a module using puppet-module

```
$ cd /etc/puppet/modules

$ puppet-module install bobsh/iptables
Installed "bobsh-iptables-1.2.0" into directory: bobsh-iptables

$ tree bobsh-iptables/
bobsh-iptables/
|-- COPYING
|-- Modulefile
|-- README.rst
|-- REVISION
|-- Rakefile
|-- lib
|   `-- puppet
|       |-- test
|       |   `-- iptables.rb
|       `-- type
|           `-- iptables.rb
|-- metadata.json
`-- tests
    |-- 010_basic.pp
    |-- 020_icmp_types.pp
    |-- 021_icmp_any.pp
    |-- 030_multiple_sources.pp
    |-- 040_state_types.pp
```

```
`-- 050_sport_and_dport.pp
```

```
5 directories, 14 files
```

The operator first uses the `puppet-module install` command to download and unpack the iptables module. Once installed, the module contents indicate that the documentation is in the README.rst file. Examples are also located in the bobsh-iptables/tests/ directory. These examples provide a quick way to get started using the new `iptables` type provided by the module.

Now that the operator has a module installed from the Forge, let's see how he uses the module in his Puppet manifests.

Using a Module

The iptables module provides a new Puppet type named `iptables`. We'll see how the Example.com operator writes a simple manifest to use this newly installed `iptables` type.

First, the Example.com operator generates a new module named `site-firewall` using the puppet-module tool. The process he uses is shown in Listing 8-4. He picks the name "site" because this module is specific to his deployment and will not be distributed outside of Example.com. In this situation, the puppet-module tool provides a quick and convenient way to generate the skeleton directory structure of the module.

***Listing 8-4.** Generating a skeleton module with puppet-module*

```
# cd ~
# puppet-module generate site-firewall
==================================================================
Generating module at ~/site-firewall
------------------------------------------------------------------
site-firewall
site-firewall/files
site-firewall/files/README.markdown
site-firewall/templates
site-firewall/templates/README.markdown
site-firewall/manifests
site-firewall/manifests/init.pp
site-firewall/manifests/README.markdown
site-firewall/spec
site-firewall/spec/spec.opts
site-firewall/spec/unit
site-firewall/spec/unit/puppet
site-firewall/spec/unit/puppet/provider
site-firewall/spec/unit/puppet/provider/README.markdown
site-firewall/spec/unit/puppet/type
site-firewall/spec/unit/puppet/type/README.markdown
site-firewall/spec/README.markdown
site-firewall/spec/spec_helper.rb
site-firewall/tests
site-firewall/tests/init.pp
site-firewall/lib
site-firewall/lib/puppet
site-firewall/lib/puppet/facter
```

```
site-firewall/lib/puppet/facter/README.markdown
site-firewall/lib/puppet/parser
site-firewall/lib/puppet/parser/functions
site-firewall/lib/puppet/parser/functions/README.markdown
site-firewall/lib/puppet/provider
site-firewall/lib/puppet/provider/README.markdown
site-firewall/lib/puppet/type
site-firewall/lib/puppet/type/README.markdown
site-firewall/Modulefile
site-firewall/metadata.json
site-firewall/README
```

As we can see in Listing 8-4, the generate action creates quite a bit of boilerplate for the operator to fill in and use as a guide. This saves quite a bit of work over the manual method of creating the module directory structure. The puppet-module tool prefixes each module with the author of the class, so the module is actually named "firewall." Once the skeleton directory structure is created, Listing 8-5 shows how the operator adds a few iptables resources to the firewall class in init.pp. In your configuration, it is a good idea to commit the boilerplate code to version control at this point if you wish to do so. This will allow you to easily track changes you make to the generated code.

Listing 8-5. Adding resources to the firewall class

```
$ vim site-firewall/manifests/init.pp
Add the following resources:

$ diff --git a/manifests/init.pp b/manifests/init.pp
index ec7243a..bee3943 100644
--- a/manifests/init.pp
+++ b/manifests/init.pp
@@ -13,5 +13,19 @@
 # [Remember: No empty lines between comments and class definition]
 class firewall {

+  Iptables {
+    source      => "0.0.0.0",
+    destination => "0.0.0.0",
+  }
+
+  iptables { "100 Puppet Prod":
+    dport => "8140",
+  }
+  iptables { "101 Puppet Test":
+    dport => "8141",
+  }
+  iptables { "101 Puppet Dev":
+    dport => "8142",
+  }

 }
```

The diff output in Listing 8-5 indicates that a number of iptables resources have been added to the firewall class in the init.pp file. Once these resources have been declared, the operator packages the generated module and places it in the module search path with the two commands shown in Listing 8-6. If the module is directly copied into the module path without being built, Puppet will fail to load the module since the metadata has not been automatically generated. The workflow for developing modules generated by puppet-module is to develop them outside of the module search path, then build and install them using puppet-module.

Listing 8-6. Placing a custom module into the Puppet module path

```
$ puppet-module build
==========================================
Building /root/site-firewall for release
------------------------------------------
Done. Built: pkg/site-firewall-0.0.1.tar.gz

$ mv pkg/site-firewall-0.0.1 /etc/puppet/modules/firewall
```

The first command builds the module package and fills in the metadata for the module. The second command moves the built module into the puppet-module search path. We're now ready to try out the module and make sure the search path is working correctly. The operator uses puppet apply -e, shown in Listing 8-7, to evaluate a single class declaration.

Listing 8-7. Using the iptables module by loading the firewall class

```
$ puppet apply -e 'include firewall' --noop
notice: /Iptables[100 Puppet Prod]: rules would have changed... (noop) in 0.00 seconds

$ puppet apply -e 'include firewall'
Saving firewall rules to /etc/sysconfig/iptables:          [  OK  ]
notice: /Iptables[100 Puppet Prod]: rules have changed... in 0.39 seconds
```

Finally, in Listing 8-8, the operator verifies the rules are properly being managed using the iptables command.

Listing 8-8. Verifying that the iptables rules are being managed by Puppet

```
$ iptables -L INPUT -n
Chain INPUT (policy ACCEPT)
target     prot opt source              destination
ACCEPT     tcp  --  0.0.0.0             0.0.0.0              tcp dpt:8140 /* 100 Puppet↵
 Prod */
ACCEPT     tcp  --  0.0.0.0             0.0.0.0              tcp dpt:8142 /* 101 Puppet Dev */
ACCEPT     tcp  --  0.0.0.0             0.0.0.0              tcp dpt:8141 /* 101 Puppet↵
 Test */
```

Using the iptables command, we're able to see Puppet is correctly using the iptables module to manage the host-based firewall. In the next section we'll learn how the operator uses the puppet-module tool to build his own Puppet modules.

Creating a Module with the Puppet-Module Tool

The Puppet Forge is an excellent resource to download and re-use Puppet modules from the community. Modules you develop may also easily be published to the Forge. There are a number of benefits to publishing modules. First, people who use your modules may add functionality and help fix bugs, saving you time and effort. In addition, providing re-usable modules allows the Puppet community to focus on developing new functionality that could directly benefit you. Publishing your own modules also allows other Puppet users to save time and effort.

In this section, we'll see how the operator develops and publishes a small module to manage the NTP service on Debian and Redhat systems. It is important to keep in mind that modules published to the forge may be used on a wide variety of platforms. We'll learn how the operator uses conditionals in the Puppet manifests to clearly indicate when a particular platform is or is not supported.

Managing Modules with Git

As we learned in the previous section, the puppet-module generate command is useful for generating a skeleton module structure. This module structure is not directly usable by Puppet, and must first be built into a module package using the build action. To get started, the Example.com operator generates the skeleton structure and adds the tree to a Git repository to track changes and history, as shown in Listing 8-9.

Listing 8-9. Using puppet-module generate and git add

```
$ cd ~/src/modules/
$ puppet-module generate operator-ntp
=====================================================
Generating module at /root/src/modules/operator-ntp
-----------------------------------------------------
...
$ cd operator-ntp

$ git init
Initialized empty Git repository in .git/

$ git add .

$ git commit -a -m 'Initial commit'
Created initial commit fb7d7b2: Initial commit
 17 files changed, 223 insertions(+), 0 deletions(-)
 create mode 100644 Modulefile
 create mode 100644 README
 create mode 100644 files/README.markdown
 create mode 100644 lib/puppet/facter/README.markdown
 create mode 100644 lib/puppet/parser/functions/README.markdown
 create mode 100644 lib/puppet/provider/README.markdown
 create mode 100644 lib/puppet/type/README.markdown
 create mode 100644 manifests/README.markdown
 create mode 100644 manifests/init.pp
 create mode 100644 metadata.json
```

```
create mode 100644 spec/README.markdown
create mode 100644 spec/spec.opts
create mode 100644 spec/spec_helper.rb
create mode 100644 spec/unit/puppet/provider/README.markdown
create mode 100644 spec/unit/puppet/type/README.markdown
create mode 100644 templates/README.markdown
create mode 100644 tests/init.pp
```

With the newly generated NTP module, the operator uses the `git init`, `add` and `commit` actions to track the history of changes to the module. The module source code may then be published to the Internet using `http://github.com/`. Many module authors in the Puppet community publish their source code to github. Storing the module inside of a Git repository also allows the operator to track changes, tag releases, and quickly test out topic branches for new functionality.

Managing Platform-Specific Resources

The next step is to add functionality for a specific platform to the module. This module is designed to manage the NTP service and bind to a configurable set of upstream NTP servers. First, the operator adds support for Debian based systems. In Listing 8-10, he uses the new parameterized class feature of Puppet 2.6 to allow people using the module to specify the list of servers to synchronize against.

Listing 8-10. Debian-specific functionality in the NTP module

```
$ vim manifests/init.pp
# Class: ntp
#
#   This module manages the ntp service.
#
#   Tested platforms:
#    - Debian 6.0 Squeeze
#
# Parameters:
#
#   $servers = [ "0.debian.pool.ntp.org iburst",
#                "1.debian.pool.ntp.org iburst",
#                "2.debian.pool.ntp.org iburst",
#                "3.debian.pool.ntp.org iburst", ]
#
# Actions:
#
#  Installs, configures, and manages the ntp service.
#
# Requires:
#
# Sample Usage:
#
#   class { "ntp": servers => [ 'time.apple.com' ] }
#
# [Remember: No empty lines between comments and class definition]
class ntp($servers=[ "0.debian.pool.ntp.org iburst",
```

```
                    "1.debian.pool.ntp.org iburst",
                    "2.debian.pool.ntp.org iburst",
                    "3.debian.pool.ntp.org iburst",],
        $ensure="running",
        $autoupdate=false
) {

  if ! ($ensure in [ "running", "stopped" ]) {
    fail("ensure parameter must be running or stopped")
  }

  if $autoupdate == true {
    $package_ensure = latest
  } elsif $autoupdate == false {
    $package_ensure = present
  } else {
    fail("autoupdate parameter must be true or false")
  }

  case $operatingsystem {
    debian, ubuntu: {
      $supported  = true
      $pkg_name   = [ "ntp" ]
      $svc_name   = "ntp"
      $config     = "/etc/ntp.conf"
      $config_tpl = "ntp.conf.debian.erb"
    }
    default: {
      $supported = false
      notify { "${module_name}_unsupported":
        message => "The ${module_name} module is not supported on ${operatingsystem}",
      }
    }
  }

  if ($supported == true) {

    package { $pkg_name:
      ensure => $package_ensure,
    }

    file { $config:
      ensure => file,
      owner  => 0,
      group  => 0,
      mode   => 0644,
      content => template("${module_name}/${config_tpl}"),
      require => Package[$pkg_name],
    }
```

```
    service { "ntp":
      ensure     => $ensure,
      name       => $svc_name,
      hasstatus  => true,
      hasrestart => true,
      subscribe  => [ Package[$pkg_name], File[$config] ],
    }

  }

}
```

Building and Testing a Puppet Module

Once the main NTP class has been filled in, the operator builds the module using the puppet-module build command. The process shown in Listing 8-11 fills in the metadata for the module and creates a module usable by Puppet. He then moves this module into the module search path at /etc/puppet/modules/ntp to test the module. When building the module, make sure you are in the top level of the module directory structure containing the Modulefile file.

Listing 8-11. Using the puppet-module build and install commands

```
$ puppet-module build
=======================================================
Building /root/src/modules/operator-ntp for release
-------------------------------------------------------
Done. Built: pkg/operator-ntp-0.0.1.tar.gz

$ cd /etc/puppet/modules
$ puppet-module install ~/src/modules/operator-ntp/pkg/operator-ntp-0.0.1.tar.gz
$ ln -s operator-ntp ntp
```

The operator first builds a new module package using the puppet-module build command. Once built, the operator changes directories to /etc/puppet/modules to install the module. The Puppet autoloader will not find the module unless it is in the "ntp" directory, because the main class is named ntp. To address this problem, the operator simply creates a symbolic link from NTP to the forge module name. This will allow future versions to easily replace the existing version.

A NOTE ABOUT MODULE NAMES

If Puppet cannot find a module with a name exactly matching the module being created, the following errors may be encountered. While building the NTP module, puppet-module creates a module named operator-ntp. This module should be renamed when installing the module to ensure the autoloader properly loads the class.

```
# puppet apply --verbose -e 'class { ntp: ensure => stopped }'
Puppet::Parser::AST::Resource failed with error ArgumentError: Invalid resource type
class at line 1 on node debian.puppetlabs.vm

# puppet apply --verbose -e 'include ntp'
info: Could not find class ntp for debian.puppetlabs.vm
Could not find class ntp at line 1 on node debian.puppetlabs.vm
```

Both of these errors may be corrected by symbolically linking /etc/puppet/modules/ntp to /etc/puppet/modules/operator-ntp after installing the module with puppet-module install.

It's now time to test out the newly developed module. To make sure the autoloader properly finds the NTP module, in Listing 8-12 the operator executes a simple puppet apply command evaluating a single class declaration.

Listing 8-12. Testing a new Puppet module with puppet apply on Debian

```
$ puppet apply --verbose -e 'class { ntp: ensure => running}'
info: Applying configuration version '1298492452'
notice: /Stage[main]/Ntp/Package[ntp]/ensure: ensure changed 'purged' to 'present'
info: /Stage[main]/Ntp/Package[ntp]: Scheduling refresh of Service[ntp]
info: FileBucket got a duplicate file /etc/ntp.conf ({md5}3e250ecaf470e1d3a2b68edd5de46bfd)
info: /Stage[main]/Ntp/File[/etc/ntp.conf]: Filebucketed /etc/ntp.conf to puppet with sum↵
 3e250ecaf470e1d3a2b68edd5de46bfd
notice: /Stage[main]/Ntp/File[/etc/ntp.conf]/content: content changed↵
 '{md5}3e250ecaf470e1d3a2b68edd5de46bfd' to '{md5}6e3461437c627101cf53e634abc62400'
info: /Stage[main]/Ntp/File[/etc/ntp.conf]: Scheduling refresh of Service[ntp]
notice: /Stage[main]/Ntp/Service[ntp]: Triggered 'refresh' from 2 events

$ puppet apply --verbose -e 'class { ntp: ensure => running }'
info: Applying configuration version '1298492574'
```

Here, the operator uses puppet apply -e to evaluate a single statement from the command line. The operator makes sure the class is idempotent by running Puppet a second time with the same command. Finally, to make sure the service can be easily stopped, he changes the ensure parameter. Once the module has been tested on a Debian system, the operator makes sure the module can properly stop the service, as shown in Listing 8-13.

Listing 8-13. Testing to ensure that the NTP service can be stopped

```
$ puppet apply --verbose -e 'class { ntp: ensure => stopped }'
info: Applying configuration version '1298492670'
notice: /Stage[main]/Ntp/Service[ntp]/ensure: ensure changed 'running' to 'stopped'

$ puppet apply --verbose -e 'class { ntp: ensure => stopped }'
info: Applying configuration version '1298492677'
```

These two commands leave the package installed and configured, but stop the service. The operator has verified that his new module works well on a Debian-based system. The last step before publishing his module to the Forge is to add Enterprise Linux support for the module. By using conditionals and variables for the package, file and service resources, he's able to easily modify the existing class to support Enterprise Linux.

Adding Enterprise Linux Support to the NTP Module

Once the NTP module has been tested on Debian-based systems, the operator needs to make sure the module also works well on Enterprise Linux systems. First, the operator exercises the logic preventing the module from running on unsupported operating systems. On an Enterprise Linux system, as shown in Listing 8-14, he installs the module as normal.

Listing 8-14. Installing the NTP module on Enterprise Linux

```
$ facter operatingsystem
CentOS

$ puppet-module install ~/src/modules/operator-ntp/pkg/operator-ntp-0.0.1.tar.gz
Installed "operator-ntp-0.0.1" into directory: operator-ntp

$ ln -s operator-ntp ntp
$ cd ~
```

Once installed on the Enterprise Linux system, the operator uses the same commands he used on the Debian system to test the newly-developed NTP module, shown in Listing 8-15.

Listing 8-15. Initial test of the NTP module on Enterprise Linux

```
# puppet apply --verbose -e 'class { ntp: ensure => running }'
info: Applying configuration version '1298493317'
notice: The ntp module is not supported on CentOS
notice: /Stage[main]/Ntp/Notify[ntp_unsupported]/message: defined 'message' as 'The ntp module
is not supported on CentOS'
```

The operator expects to receive this message because Enterprise Linux support has not yet been developed. Let's see how he modifies the module to support both Debian and Enterprise Linux systems. In Listing 8-16, he installs the NTP package to obtain a template of the NTP configuration file and copies it into the templates directory of the module. Then, he checks the service name to see if it matches the Debian service name or not.

Listing 8-16. Obtaining the NTP service name and configuration for Enterprise Linux

```
$ yum install ntp
…
Installed:
  ntp.x86_64 0:4.2.2p1-9.el5.centos.2.1

$ cd ~/src/modules/operator-ntp/
$ cp /etc/ntp.conf ./templates/ntp.conf.el.erb
$ git add ./templates/ntp.conf.el.erb
$ chkconfig --list | grep ntp
ntpd            0:off   1:off   2:off   3:off   4:off   5:off   6:off
```

The operator notices the name of the service on Enterprise Linux-based systems is "ntpd," which differs slightly from the "ntp" on Debian-based systems. Luckily, Puppet handles these minor differences with ease. Let's see how, in Listing 8-17, he modifies the NTP class to handle this difference and manage the NTP service.

Listing 8-17. Extending the NTP class to support Enterprise Linux and Debian

```
$ git diff
diff --git a/Modulefile b/Modulefile
index 180cb31..cd60026 100644
--- a/Modulefile
+++ b/Modulefile
@@ -1,10 +1,10 @@
 name     'operator-ntp'
-version '0.0.1'
+version '0.0.2'
 source 'UNKNOWN'
 author 'Example.com Operator'
 license 'UNKNOWN'
-summary 'UNKNOWN'
-description 'UNKNOWN'
+summary 'NTP Module'
+description 'NTP Module for Debian, Ubuntu, CentOS, RHEL, OEL'
 project_page 'UNKNOWN'

 ## Add dependencies, if any:
diff --git a/manifests/init.pp b/manifests/init.pp
index 622b216..ee655f7 100644
--- a/manifests/init.pp
+++ b/manifests/init.pp
@@ -30,10 +30,7 @@
 #   }
 #
 # [Remember: No empty lines between comments and class definition]
-class ntp($servers=[ "0.debian.pool.ntp.org iburst",
-                     "1.debian.pool.ntp.org iburst",
-                     "2.debian.pool.ntp.org iburst",
-                     "3.debian.pool.ntp.org iburst",],
```

```
+class ntp($servers="UNSET",
+            $ensure="running",
+            $autoupdate=false
 ) {
@@ -57,6 +54,28 @@ class ntp($servers=[ "0.debian.pool.ntp.org iburst",
        $svc_name   = "ntp"
        $config     = "/etc/ntp.conf"
        $config_tpl = "ntp.conf.debian.erb"
+       if ($servers == "UNSET") {
+         $servers_real = [ "0.debian.pool.ntp.org iburst",
+                           "1.debian.pool.ntp.org iburst",
+                           "2.debian.pool.ntp.org iburst",
+                           "3.debian.pool.ntp.org iburst", ]
+       } else {
+         $servers_real = $servers
+       }
+     }
+     centos, redhat, oel: {
+       $supported  = true
+       $pkg_name   = [ "ntp" ]
+       $svc_name   = "ntpd"
+       $config     = "/etc/ntp.conf"
+       $config_tpl = "ntp.conf.el.erb"
+       if ($servers == "UNSET") {
+         $servers_real = [ "0.centos.pool.ntp.org",
+                           "1.centos.pool.ntp.org",
+                           "2.centos.pool.ntp.org", ]
+       } else {
+         $servers_real = $servers
+       }
+     }
     default: {
       $supported = false
diff --git a/templates/ntp.conf.debian.erb b/templates/ntp.conf.debian.erb
index e4275de..f51414f 100644
--- a/templates/ntp.conf.debian.erb
+++ b/templates/ntp.conf.debian.erb
@@ -20,7 +20,7 @@ filegen clockstats file clockstats type day enable
 # pool: <http://www.pool.ntp.org/join.html>

 # Managed by puppet class { "ntp": servers => [ ... ] }
-<% servers.each do |server| -%>
+<% servers_real.each do |server| -%>
 server <%= server %>
 <% end -%>

diff --git a/templates/ntp.conf.el.erb b/templates/ntp.conf.el.erb
index cfb4c8c..db2aa9c 100644
--- a/templates/ntp.conf.el.erb
+++ b/templates/ntp.conf.el.erb
@@ -14,9 +14,11 @@ restrict -6 ::1
```

```
 # Use public servers from the pool.ntp.org project.
 # Please consider joining the pool (http://www.pool.ntp.org/join.html).
-server 0.centos.pool.ntp.org
-server 1.centos.pool.ntp.org
-server 2.centos.pool.ntp.org
+
+# Managed by puppet class { "ntp": servers => [ ... ] }
+<% servers_real.each do |server| -%>
+server <%= server %>
+<% end -%>

 #broadcast 192.168.1.255 key 42              # broadcast server
 #broadcastclient                      # broadcast client
```

The operator has made a number of small edits to the NTP module, as shown in the difference between the Debian-only module and the newly-added Enterprise Linux support. These changes justify a new build of the module with a new version number. Working through the difference, let's review the changes made:

- Increment the version in the Modulefile. This allows overwriting the already-installed module.

- Add a description and summary for the Modulefile. These will show up on the Forge when published.

- Add a case selection for the CentOS, RedHat, and OEL operating systems.

- Add a conditional to set different default upstream servers from the Debian or CentOS pool if the user does not specify their own list of servers.

These changes modify the variables used by the Package, File and Service resources declared in the bottom section of the NTP class. Once these changes are made, the operator builds a new version of the package. He then installs the package on both the Enterprise Linux and Debian systems, using the commands shown in Listing 8-18.

Listing 8-18. Building and installing version 0.0.2 of the NTP module

```
$ cd ~/src/modules/operator-ntp
$ puppet-module build
=========================================================
Building ~/src/modules/operator-ntp for release
---------------------------------------------------------
Done. Built: pkg/operator-ntp-0.0.2.tar.gz

$ cd /etc/puppet/modules
$ puppet-module install ~/src/modules/operator-ntp/pkg/operator-ntp-0.0.2.tar.gz
======================================
Existing module 'operator-ntp' found
--------------------------------------
Overwrite module installed at ./operator-ntp? [y/N]: y
Installed "operator-ntp-0.0.2" into directory: operator-ntp
```

Releasing the NTP Module to the Forge

After installing version 0.0.2 of the NTP module on both the Enterprise Linux and Debian systems, a final test shown in Listing 8-19 verifies that the module is ready for publication.

Listing 8-19. Final test of NTP module on Debian and Enterprise Linux

```
debian # puppet apply --verbose -e 'class { ntp: ensure => running, autoupdate => true }'
info: Applying configuration version '1298498306'
notice: /Stage[main]/Ntp/Package[ntp]/ensure: ensure changed 'purged' to 'latest'
info: /Stage[main]/Ntp/Package[ntp]: Scheduling refresh of Service[ntp]
info: FileBucket got a duplicate file /etc/ntp.conf ({md5}3e250ecaf470e1d3a2b68edd5de46bfd)
info: /Stage[main]/Ntp/File[/etc/ntp.conf]: Filebucketed /etc/ntp.conf to puppet with sum↵
3e250ecaf470e1d3a2b68edd5de46bfd
notice: /Stage[main]/Ntp/File[/etc/ntp.conf]/content: content changed↵
'{md5}3e250ecaf470e1d3a2b68edd5de46bfd' to '{md5}6e3461437c627101cf53e634abc62400'
info: /Stage[main]/Ntp/File[/etc/ntp.conf]: Scheduling refresh of Service[ntp]
notice: /Stage[main]/Ntp/Service[ntp]: Triggered 'refresh' from 2 events
debian # puppet apply --verbose -e 'class { ntp: ensure => running, autoupdate => true }'
info: Applying configuration version '1298498352'

centos # puppet apply --verbose -e 'class { ntp: ensure => running, autoupdate => true }'
info: Applying configuration version '1298499949'
notice: /Stage[main]/Ntp/Package[ntp]/ensure: created
info: /Stage[main]/Ntp/Package[ntp]: Scheduling refresh of Service[ntp]
info: FileBucket got a duplicate file /etc/ntp.conf ({md5}5baec8bdbf90f877a05f88ba99e63685)
info: /Stage[main]/Ntp/File[/etc/ntp.conf]: Filebucketed /etc/ntp.conf to puppet with sum↵
5baec8bdbf90f877a05f88ba99e63685
notice: /Stage[main]/Ntp/File[/etc/ntp.conf]/content: content changed↵
'{md5}5baec8bdbf90f877a05f88ba99e63685' to '{md5}35ea00fd40740faf3fd6d1708db6ad65'
info: /Stage[main]/Ntp/File[/etc/ntp.conf]: Scheduling refresh of Service[ntp]
notice: /Stage[main]/Ntp/Service[ntp]/ensure: ensure changed 'stopped' to 'running'
notice: /Stage[main]/Ntp/Service[ntp]: Triggered 'refresh' from 2 events
```

As we can see, the NTP service is being properly managed and brought online for both Enterprise Linux and Debian systems. The operator commits this change to the Git repository using the commands in Listing 8-20 before publishing the module to the Forge.

Listing 8-20. Final commit before publishing to the Forge

```
$ cd ~/src/modules/operator-ntp
$ git add *
$ git commit -m 'Add Enterprise Linux support'
$ git tag 0.0.2
```

The operator is able to track when this version of the NTP module was released to the Forge by using the git tag action. Finally, he's ready to publish the package created by the puppet-module build command. Doing so requires registration at http://forge.puppetlabs.com/. For up-to-date information about how to publish a module, please log into the Forge and use the "Add a Module" link located at: http://forge.puppetlabs.com/modules/new.

You've just seen how the Example.com operator uses the puppet-module tool to install a module from the Puppet Forge. The iptables module allowed the operator to quickly manage host-based firewall rules without writing his own module from scratch. In addition, we saw how the operator quickly generated a skeleton module structure, and added a few resources to the NTP class to manage time synchronization. In the next section you'll see how the Ruby DSL allows the Example.com developer to leverage Ruby to declare resources and classes in the configuration catalog.

Puppet Ruby DSL

The Ruby DSL included in Puppet 2.6 provides the full power of the Ruby language directly in Puppet Modules. Within a single module, manifest files may be written in either of the Puppet or Ruby languages. These manifest files may be intermixed in the same catalog compilation. The file extension determines the language used; manifests with a "pp" or "rb" extension indicate a Puppet or Ruby manifest, respectively. For most problems and configurations, the simple language of Puppet manifests are more than adequate. However, in the situation where a dynamic data set is accessed through the ENC API, the Ruby DSL is an ideal solution to the problem of declaring resources from the data. Ruby's ability to iterate over Hashes and Arrays with the each method provides a convenient way to declare a large number of resources. This solution would be difficult to implement using the Puppet language, which lacks loops and iterators.

The Ruby DSL in Puppet is currently a subset of the Puppet DSL. As such, there are a number of limitations when using the Ruby DSL. Specifically, the run-stages feature of Puppet 2.6 is not supported when declaring classes from Ruby. However, declaring a class using the Puppet DSL does allow association with a stage. In this situation, the Ruby DSL may be used to define a class that is then declared in the Puppet DSL.

In addition, the Ruby DSL in Puppet 2.6.4 cannot easily declare resources and variables in top scope. To work around this issue, we recommended that you use an External Node Classifier or a Puppet syntax site.pp to define variables at top scope. The Ruby DSL works particularly well when declaring resources inside of a class.

In this section we'll see how the Example.com developer uses the Ruby DSL to manage an arbitrary number of resources by reading data from an external location. The Puppet Ruby DSL is a subset of the full Puppet DSL, so not every feature of Puppet is supported. For example, the Ruby DSL does not work well with the new Run Stages feature of Puppet 2.6. In these situations, the resources should be declared using the Puppet DSL rather than Ruby.

The Problem: Resources from Data

It can be difficult to pull in data external to Puppet, but it is required for configuration management. R.I. Pienaar wrote the extlookup function to address this concern, but it too has problems if the number of resources to declare is not known in advance. For example, most Puppet deployments have an accounts module to manage system and login accounts on systems managed by Puppet. As people join and leave the company, the number of account resources change. Ideally, the data related to a person could be defined in once place and the configuration automatically updates itself to reflect this change. Without the Ruby DSL, Puppet manifests need to be edited to declare or remove account resources.

Puppet 2.6 also supports a new data type in the form of a hash table. Let's see how the Example.com developer uses a hash of hashes set by an external node classifier to declare an arbitrary number of account resources using the Ruby DSL.

Declaring Resources from Data

To get started with the Ruby DSL, the Example.com developer decides to write a very simple module using Ruby rather than Puppet syntax. The goal of this module it to modify the message of the day file. The /etc/motd file will contain a parameter set by an External Node Classifier script. Once he's comfortable with this configuration, he plans to extend the ENC script to contain a hash of user accounts. With the account information coming from the ENC, he can iterate over each entry, managing the appropriate resources with Puppet. First, let's take a look at the output of this basic ENC script in Listing 8-21.

Listing 8-21. *Basic ENC script output for the Ruby DSL*

```
$ cd /etc/puppet
$ ./resources_enc.rb
---
parameters:
  enc_location: Florida
classes:
    -  motd_location
```

This simple ENC script declares the motd_location class the developer will write using the Ruby DSL. It also sets a single parameter, named enc_location, to the string "Florida." The ENC script the developer is using for this simple test is shown in Listing 8-22.

Listing 8-22. *Basic ENC script for Ruby DSL*

```
#!/usr/bin/env ruby
#

# Load the YAML library in ruby. Provide the to_yaml method for all
# Ruby objects.
require 'yaml'

# The output hash. Must contain the "parameters" and "classes" key.
# See: http://docs.puppetlabs.com/guides/external_nodes.html
@out = Hash.new

# Output Array of classes, Hash of Parameters
@out["classes"]    = Array.new
@out["parameters"] = Hash.new

# Add the motd_location class to the catalogs
@out["classes"] << "motd_location"
# Add a location parameter
@out["parameters"]["enc_location"] = "Florida"

# Output the YAML node classification to standard output.
puts @out.to_yaml
# Must exit with a status of zero for classification to succeed.
exit(0)
```

A Small Puppet Module Using the Ruby DSL

Finally, in Listing 8-23 the developer creates a small basic module using the Ruby DSL rather than the Puppet DSL. This module manages the file resource for the message of the day. This is implemented as a standard Puppet module except the init.pp file is replaced with an init.rb file in the manifests directory. The module looks like:

Listing 8-23. *motd_location Ruby DSL module*

```
# cd /etc/puppet/modules
# tree motd_location
motd_location
••• manifests
    ••• init.rb
```

Notice instead of the init.pp file, the developer has named the file init.rb to indicate the Ruby DSL is being used. The basic motd_location class is defined in this file and looks like Listing 8-24.

Listing 8-24. *motd_location Ruby DSL*

```
# <modulepath>/motd_location/manifests/init.rb
# Message of the Day class implemented in the Ruby DSL

hostclass :motd_location do

  # Lookup the enc_location parameter set by the ENC
  # Assign it to the location variable in Ruby
  location = scope.lookupvar("enc_location")

  # Set a Ruby String variable to represent the contents
  # of the message of the day file
  motd_content = "This system is in: #{location}\n"

  # Declare a file resource using Ruby syntax
  # This is equivalent to the Puppet Syntax:
  # file { motd:
  #   ensure  => "file",
  #   path    => "/etc/motd",
  #   content => $motd_content,
  #   owner   => 0,
  #   group   => 0,
  #   mode    => 0644,
  # }
  file("motd",
    :ensure  => "file",
    :path    => "/etc/motd",
    :content => motd_content,
    :owner   => 0,
    :group   => 0,
```

```
    :mode      => 0644)
```

End

The hostclass method is equivalent to the Puppet class motd_location { ... } syntax and defines the new class. This motd_location class carries out three actions:

- Assigns a local ruby variable named location

- Assigns a local ruby variable named motd_content

- Declares a file resource in the configuration catalog

Using the scope.lookupvar method, the developer obtains the value of the enc_location string set by the ENC. When accessing parameters set by the ENC, by Facter, or in the node definitions of site.pp, scope.lookupvar should be used to obtain the value. Assigning the value to a local variable also has the benefit of bringing the value into the local scope.

To define the contents of /etc/motd, the developer assigns another string variable, substituting the value of the location variable. In Ruby the #{} statement performs substring substitution and replaces the value of the variable contained inside the curly braces.

Finally, the Puppet file resource is declared using a similar syntax to the Puppet syntax. The file method is called, specifying the title of the resource as the first argument. In addition, a list of the properties of the file is also specified. This file method declares a file resource and is equivalent to file { motd: ... } in Puppet syntax.

Testing the Ruby DSL

With this module and node classification configured, the developer is ready to test the Ruby DSL as shown in Listing 8-25.

Listing 8-25. Testing the Ruby DSL with the motd_location class

```
$ puppet apply --noop /etc/puppet/manifests/site.pp
--- /etc/motd    2011-02-24 01:20:12.000000000 -0500
+++ /tmp/puppet-file20110224-19081-ekisu3-0    2011-02-24 01:41:41.000000000 -0500
@@ -0,0 +1 @@
+This system is in: Florida
notice: /Stage[main]/Motd_location/File[motd]/content: is↵
 {md5}d41d8cd98f00b204e9800998ecf8427e, should be {md5}3f9e49a378a930da4e06760635fcb810 (noop)
```

As we can see from the output of Puppet, the /etc/motd file would have a single line added containing the value of the enc_location parameter. This parameter was set by the ENC and declared in the motd_location module using the Ruby DSL.

Account Information from an ENC

With a basic module in place, the developer decides to extend the ENC script. The extended ENC script provides all of the information about the accounts to manage. This information will be provided and stored in a Hash data type, which is also new in Puppet 2.6. Once the data is defined, a new module named accounts_ruby will declare resources from the data. To accomplish this, the developer will iterate over all of the information set by the ENC and declare user resources similar to the file resource declared in the motd_location module.

If the developer used the Puppet DSL instead of the Ruby DSL this task would be particularly difficult. The Puppet language does not have loops and cannot easily iterate over a set of data. Let's see how the developer solves this problem in Listing 8-26. First, the extended ENC script produces output containing the account information:

Listing 8-26. ENC script with account information

```
$ /etc/puppet/resources_enc.rb
--
parameters:
  enc_location: Florida
  account_resources:
    alice:
      groups:
      - sudo
      - sudo_nopw
      - devel
      comment: Alice
      gid: 601
      uid: 601
      shell: /bin/bash
      password: "!!"
      home: /home/alice
    bob:
      groups:
      - sudo
      - sudo_nopw
      - ops
      comment: Bob
      gid: 602
      uid: 602
      shell: /bin/zsh
      password: "!!"
      home: /home/bob
classes:
- motd_location
- accounts_ruby
```

The output of the ENC script in Listing 8-26 now contains considerably more information. Notice a second class named accounts_ruby has been added. In addition, a new parameter named account_resources contains a Hash key for each user account to be created. The value of the key is itself a Hash containing each parameter of the account resource. The ENC script producing this node classification is shown in Listing 8-27.

Listing 8-27. ENC script for Ruby DSL accounts module

```
$ cat /etc/puppet/resources_enc.rb
#!/usr/bin/env ruby
#
```

```
# Load the YAML library in ruby. Provide the to_yaml method for all
# Ruby objects.
require 'yaml'

# The output hash. Must contain the "parameters" and "classes" key.
# See: http://docs.puppetlabs.com/guides/external_nodes.html
@out = Hash.new

# Output Array of classes, Hash of Parameters
@out["classes"]    = Array.new
@out["parameters"] = Hash.new

# Add the motd_location class to the catalogs
@out["classes"] << "motd_location"
# And, add the accounts_ruby class to the catalog
@out["classes"] << "accounts_ruby"

# Add a location parameter
@out["parameters"]["enc_location"] = "Florida"

# Store account information dynamically in the account_resources
# parameter. These values could come from LDAP, SQL, etc...
@out["parameters"]['account_resources'] = Hash.new

@out["parameters"]['account_resources']["alice"] = {
  "comment"  => "Alice",
  "home"     => "/home/alice",
  "uid"      => 601,
  "gid"      => 601,
  "groups"   => [ "sudo", "sudo_nopw", "devel" ],
  "shell"    => "/bin/bash",
  "password" => "!!",
}

@out["parameters"]['account_resources']["bob"] = {
  "comment"  => "Bob",
  "home"     => "/home/bob",
  "uid"      => 602,
  "gid"      => 602,
  "groups"   => [ "sudo", "sudo_nopw", "ops" ],
  "shell"    => "/bin/zsh",
  "password" => "!!",
}

puts @out.to_yaml
exit(0)
```

This ENC script performs the following actions:

- Loads the YAML ruby library providing the to_yaml method

- Defines a hash named @out with two keys: classes and parameters

- Adds the account_resources parameter to the parameter hash

- Adds the account information for Bob and Alice to the account_resources hash

- Puts the @out output hash as a YAML string to standard output

- Exits with a status code of 0 indicating to Puppet that node classification is successful

Accounts Ruby DSL Module

With the account information defined by the ENC in a parameter named account_resources, the developer then writes the accounts_ruby class. This class declares user resources for all of the accounts. Once the developer writes the class new accounts only need to be added to node classification for Puppet to manage them. The Puppet module and manifests themselves need not be modified as people join the organization. This implementation cleanly separates code and data. The implementation also allows the developer the freedom to improve the ENC script without modifying Puppet. Information may be retrieved from data sources like the Human Resources directory, LDAP, or an SQL database. The complete Ruby DSL accounts_ruby class the developer has written is shown in Listing 8-28.

Listing 8-28. The accounts_ruby class

```
$ cat <modulepath>/accounts_ruby/manifests/init.rb
# Define a new accounts_ruby class. This is equivalent to:
# class accounts_ruby { ... }
hostclass :accounts_ruby do

  # Bring the accounts resources defined in the ENC into a local
  # Ruby variable.
  accounts = scope.lookupvar("account_resources")

  # Perform a sanity check on the data provided by the ENC.
  raise Puppet::Error,
    "account_resources must be a Hash" unless accounts.kind_of?(Hash)

  # First declare groups required by the accounts. These groups may be
  # referenced in /etc/sudoers to grant sudo access and access without
  # a password entry.
  group([:sudo, :sudo_nopw], :ensure => "present")

  # Iterate over each account
  # The Hash key will be stored in the local title variable
  # The value of the hash entry will be stored in parameters
  # The parameters are the resource parameters for each user account.
  accounts.each do |title, parameters|

    # Some more sanity checking on the data passed in from the ENC.
    raise Puppet::Error,
      "account_resources[#{title}] must be a Hash" unless parameters.kind_of?(Hash)

    # Manage the home directory of this account with a file resource.
    file(parameters["home"],
        :ensure => "directory",
        :owner  => title,
```

```
                :group  => title,
                :mode   => 0700)

        # Each account should have a group of the same name.
        group(title,
              :ensure => "present",
              :gid    => parameters["gid"])

        # Declare the user resource with the parameters for this account.
        user(title,
            :ensure     => "present",
            :uid        => parameters["uid"],
            :gid        => parameters["gid"],
            :comment    => parameters["comment"],
            :groups     => parameters["groups"],
            :shell      => parameters["shell"],
            :password   => parameters["password"],
            :home       => parameters["home"],
            :managehome => false)

    end

end
```

The accounts_ruby module class in Listing 8-28 carries out a number of actions when declared in the Puppet catalog. These actions are:

- Defines a new Puppet class named accounts_ruby using the hostclass method.

- Sets a local accounts Ruby variable containing the information set by the ENC in the account_resources parameter.

- Validates the data from the ENC is stored in something like a Hash

- Declares two Group resources, sudo and sudo_nopw.

- Iterates over every account entry and:

- Declares a file, group and user resource for the account.

The Ruby code composing the accounts_ruby module may be a little much to absorb at first. Like Puppet, Ruby code is often quite readable; so let's see how the developer solves the accounts problem. First, he defines a new class named accounts_ruby using the hostclass method. He passes a Ruby Block to the hostclass method. This block will be evaluated when the class is declared in the catalog. Recall from Listing 8-26 that the ENC script is declaring this class in the classes list.

With the new class defined in the init.rb file of the module manifests directory, the developer proceeds to bring the data defined in the ENC into the local scope. This is again accomplished with the scope.lookupvar method. In addition, the data is validated using the kind_of? method. This method returns true or false if the receiving object is a kind of the specified class. In this case the developer is checking to see if a Hash was actually passed into Puppet by the ENC or not. In the Puppet DSL, the fail() function may be used to abort catalog compilation if this check does not pass. In the Ruby DSL, an exception class named Puppet::Error is one way to abort catalog compilation if invalid data has been passed in.

With the data validated, the sudo and sudo_pw groups are declared, just like they would be in a manifest written in Puppet syntax. With the basic requirements established, the developer then uses the Ruby idiom of calling the each method on the accounts Hash to iterate over each entry supplied by the ENC. This method also takes a block and executes this block of code once for each entry in the Hash. Inside the block, the hash key and value are stored in the local variables title and parameters, indicating these variables represent the resource title and contain parameters about the resource.

Finally, inside the block the developer declares three resources. First, a file resource manages the home directory of the user account. Next, a new group with the same name as the account is declared. Finally, the user account itself is declared. The parameters for all of these resources are retrieved from the information passed in the ENC script.

Testing the Ruby DSL Accounts Module

Let's see, in Listing 8-29, how the accounts_ruby module looks when Puppet runs.

Listing 8-29. Running Puppet with the accounts_ruby module

```
# puppet apply --verbose --noop /etc/puppet/manifests/site.pp
info: Applying configuration version '1298536173'
notice: /Stage[main]/Accounts_ruby/Group[alice]/ensure: is absent, should be present (noop)
notice: /Stage[main]/Accounts_ruby/User[alice]/ensure: is absent, should be present (noop)
notice: /Stage[main]/Accounts_ruby/File[/home/alice]/ensure: is absent, should be directory↵
 (noop)
notice: /Stage[main]/Accounts_ruby/Group[bob]/ensure: is absent, should be present (noop)
notice: /Stage[main]/Accounts_ruby/User[bob]/ensure: is absent, should be present (noop)
notice: /Stage[main]/Accounts_ruby/File[/home/bob]/ensure: is absent, should be directory
(noop)
```

As we can see, Puppet is being run in no-operation mode, and would have created six resources: three for Bob and three for Alice, each person having a user, group and home directory managed for them. The developer has not explicitly declared any relationships among these resources, Puppet is managing them using the implicit relationships between file owners and groups and a user resources relationship to its group members. The relationship graph looks like that shown in Figure 8-1.

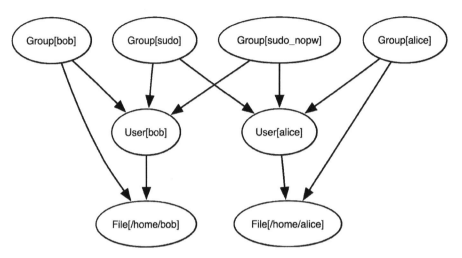

Figure 8-1. *Relationship graph for accounts_ruby*

Adding new accounts managed by Puppet is now simply a matter of setting them in the ENC. No code in Puppet needs to be changed. Let's see how the developer adds a new account in Listing 8-30. The ENC script is modified to produce a third entry in the account_resources parameter for a local administrator account.

Listing 8-30. *Extending the Ruby DSL ENC to have a third account resource*

```
# /etc/puppet/resources_enc.rb
---
parameters:
  enc_location: Florida
  account_resources:
    alice:
      groups:
      - sudo
      - sudo_nopw
      - devel
      comment: Alice
      gid: 601
      uid: 601
      shell: /bin/bash
      password: "!!"
      home: /home/alice
    localadmin:
      groups:
      - sudo
      - sudo_nopw
      - ops
      comment: Local Administrator
      gid: 600
```

```
            uid: 600
            shell: /bin/bash
            password: "!!"
            home: /home/localadmin
        bob:
            groups:
            - sudo
            - sudo_nopw
            - ops
            comment: Bob
            gid: 602
            uid: 602
            shell: /bin/zsh
            password: "!!"
            home: /home/bob
classes:
- motd_location
- accounts_ruby
```

Notice there is now a third entry in the output of the external node classifier script. This information contains only the data related to the Local Administrator account. The modification to the script is simply a matter of adding the hash entry to the account_resources object, as you can see in the diff shown in Listing 8-31.

Listing 8-31. Adding a third account resource to the ENC script

```
# git diff
diff --git a/resources_enc.rb b/resources_enc.rb
index d7a94d9..bd0e46e 100755
--- a/resources_enc.rb
+++ b/resources_enc.rb
@@ -25,6 +25,16 @@ require 'yaml'
 # parameter. These values could come from LDAP, SQL, etc...
 @out["parameters"]['account_resources'] = Hash.new

+@out["parameters"]['account_resources']["localadmin"] = {
+    "comment"  => "Local Administrator",
+    "home"     => "/home/localadmin",
+    "uid"      => 600,
+    "gid"      => 600,
+    "groups"   => [ "sudo", "sudo_nopw", "ops" ],
+    "shell"    => "/bin/bash",
+    "password" => "!!",
+}
+
 @out["parameters"]['account_resources']["alice"] = {
    "comment"  => "Alice",
    "home"     => "/home/alice",
```

The developer is directly declaring Hash resources in the script, but this information could just as easily come from YAML data files stored on disk, LDAP or an SQL database. Finally, the developer runs

Puppet as shown in Listing 8-32. Puppet manages additional resources based on the new data coming through the ENC API.

Listing 8-32. Puppet adding additional resources from the ENC information

```
$ puppet apply --verbose --noop /etc/puppet/manifests/site.pp
notice: /Stage[main]/Accounts_ruby/Group[alice]/ensure: is absent, should be present (noop)
notice: /Stage[main]/Accounts_ruby/Group[localadmin]/ensure: is absent, should be present↵
(noop)
notice: /Stage[main]/Accounts_ruby/User[alice]/ensure: is absent, should be present (noop)
notice: /Stage[main]/Accounts_ruby/File[/home/alice]/ensure: is absent, should be directory↵
(noop)
notice: /Stage[main]/Accounts_ruby/User[localadmin]/ensure: is absent, should be present↵
(noop)
notice: /Stage[main]/Accounts_ruby/File[/home/localadmin]/ensure: is absent, should be↵
directory (noop)
notice: /Stage[main]/Accounts_ruby/Group[bob]/ensure: is absent, should be present (noop)
notice: /Stage[main]/Accounts_ruby/User[bob]/ensure: is absent, should be present (noop)
notice: /Stage[main]/Accounts_ruby/File[/home/bob]/ensure: is absent, should be directory
(noop)
```

This shows that Puppet is now managing nine resources instead of the six in the previous run. Puppet is managing the Local Administrator account simply by adding additional data to the external node classifier. This implementation would have been very difficult to carry out using only the Puppet language, since there is no easy way to iterate over a Hash. By using the each method in Ruby, the developer is able to declare an arbitrary and dynamically changing number of resources based on external data.

In the next section, we switch gears and examine another valuable tool in the Puppet ecosystem. Cucumber Puppet allows you to easily and clearly test your Puppet infrastructure.

Cucumber Puppet

A common problem with Puppet and configuration management in general is testing. After working with Puppet for some time, the Example.com operator has the nagging question, "How can I test changes I make to my systems with Puppet?" A frequently-used solution to this problem is to maintain an entirely separate network identically configured to the production network. Changes to Puppet are then deployed to the testing network prior to deploying them to production. While effective, this strategy incurs the overhead of maintaining a separate network. Additional hardware and time must be invested in the testing network.

Automated testing tools like Cucumber Puppet do not fully replace a rigorous testing network identically configured to production. However, in situations where a testing network is not available or feasible, Cucumber Puppet solves many of the problems related to testing and change control.

Cucumber Puppet is a tool that allows you to specify the desired behavior of a Puppet configuration catalog. Once specified, the tool also allows you to verify changes to the Puppet modules and manifests, resulting in a configuration catalog with the same specified behavior. This functionality allows you to make changes with confidence, knowing unintended side effects will not be introduced.

If you're already familiar with Cucumber, the specifications used by Cucumber Puppet will be familiar. Cucumber Puppet is inspired by the natural language descriptions of application behavior used in Cucumber. More information about Cucumber is available at http://cukes.info/. Let's see how the

Example.com operator installs and uses Cucumber Puppet to test and validate changes to his Puppet configuration.

Installing Cucumber Puppet

Similar to the puppet-module tool discussed in this chapter, The Cucumber Puppet tool, cucumber-puppet, is not available as a native package on most operating systems. However, the software is easily installed using the RubyGems gem command (see Listing 8-33).

Listing 8-33. Installing cucumber-puppet with RubyGems

```
# gem install cucumber-puppet
Building native extensions. This could take a while...

(::) (::) (::) (::) (::) (::) (::) (::) (::) (::) (::) (::) (::) (::) (::)

Thank you for installing cucumber-0.10.0.
Please be sure to read http://wiki.github.com/aslakhellesoy/cucumber/upgrading
for important information about this release. Happy cuking!

(::) (::) (::) (::) (::) (::) (::) (::) (::) (::) (::) (::) (::) (::) (::)

Successfully installed json-1.4.6
Successfully installed gherkin-2.3.3
Successfully installed term-ansicolor-1.0.5
Successfully installed builder-3.0.0
Successfully installed diff-lcs-1.1.2
Successfully installed cucumber-0.10.0
Successfully installed gem-man-0.2.0
Successfully installed highline-1.6.1
Successfully installed extlib-0.9.15
Successfully installed templater-1.0.0
Successfully installed cucumber-puppet-0.1.1
11 gems installed
```

If you're installing on a Debian-based system, the gem command may be configured to install executable scripts in a location not in the PATH environment variable. On a Debian system, this location is /var/lib/gems/1.8/bin. If you encounter the "command not found" message shown in Listing 8-34, which the operator experiences on a Debian 6.0 system, you may use the gem environment command shown in Listing 8-35 to find where the executable scripts are installed.

Listing 8-34. Testing if the cucumber-puppet executable is in the PATH variable

```
# which cucumber-puppet
cucumber-puppet not found
```

Listing 8-35. Using the gem environment to locate the executable directory

```
# gem environment
RubyGems Environment:
  - RUBYGEMS VERSION: 1.3.7
```

```
- RUBY VERSION: 1.8.7 (2010-08-16 patchlevel 302) [i486-linux]
- INSTALLATION DIRECTORY: /var/lib/gems/1.8
- RUBY EXECUTABLE: /usr/bin/ruby1.8
- EXECUTABLE DIRECTORY: /var/lib/gems/1.8/bin
- RUBYGEMS PLATFORMS:
  - ruby
  - x86-linux
- GEM PATHS:
  - /var/lib/gems/1.8
  - /root/.gem/ruby/1.8
- GEM CONFIGURATION:
  - :update_sources => true
  - :verbose => true
  - :benchmark => false
  - :backtrace => false
  - :bulk_threshold => 1000
- REMOTE SOURCES:
  - http://rubygems.org/
```

In this example, the gem command installs executables to /var/lib/gems/1.8/gems. The operator adds this file system location to the PATH variable, as shown in Listing 8-36, to complete the installation of cucumber-puppet.

Listing 8-36. *Adding the gem executable directory to the PATH*

```
# export PATH="/var/lib/gems/1.8/bin:$PATH"
# which cucumber-puppet
/var/lib/gems/1.8/bin/cucumber-puppet
```

Once the cucumber-puppet command is available, we may proceed with writing a story describing the desired Puppet catalog behavior.

Writing a Story

The behavior of Puppet is described in Cucumber "stories." Before writing a story describing the catalog behavior and features, the cucumber-puppet testing directory needs to be created. On a testing system, basic example step definitions should be installed using the cucumber-puppet-gen command (see Listing 8-37).

Listing 8-37. *Installing basic step defintions with cucumber-puppet-gen*

```
# cd /etc/puppet
#  cucumber-puppet-gen world
Generating with world generator:
    [ADDED]  features/support/world.rb
    [ADDED]  features/steps
    [ADDED]  features/support/hooks.rb
```

Once the basic steps have been installed, the Example.com operator configures cucumber-puppet by modifying the hooks.rb file. Before doing so, he adds and commits the new files to the Git repository as shown in Listing 8-38.

Listing 8-38. Adding cucumber-puppet steps to Git

```
# cd /etc/puppet
# git add features
# git commit -m 'Add cucumber-puppet generated steps'
```

Once added to Git, the operator modifies the hooks.rb file to configure cucumber-puppet, as shown in Listing 8-39.

Listing 8-39. Changes to hooks.rb to configure cucumber-puppet

```
# git diff
diff --git a/features/support/hooks.rb b/features/support/hooks.rb
index 77db992..3588300 100644
--- a/features/support/hooks.rb
+++ b/features/support/hooks.rb
@@ -1,7 +1,9 @@
 Before do
   # local configuration
   # @confdir = File.join(File.dirname(__FILE__), '..', '..')
+  @confdir = "/etc/puppet"
   # @manifest = File.join(@confdir, 'manifests', 'site.pp')
+  @manifest = "/etc/puppet/manifests/site.pp"
   # adjust facts like this
   @facts['architecture'] = "i386"
 End
```

As you can see, the operator added two lines to the hooks.rb file. First, the configuration directory for Puppet is set to /etc/puppet. This corresponds to the confdir configuration setting. Next, the main site.pp file is configured using the @manifest variable. This setting should point to the full path of the site.pp file, /etc/puppet/manifests/site.pp by default.

Once cucumber-puppet is configured, the catalog policy in Listing 8-40 is used to test and verify the behavior of the catalog. The Example.com operator uses the cucumber-puppet-gen command to generate a template catalog policy file.

Listing 8-40. The initial web server cucumber-puppet policy.feature file

```
# cd /etc/puppet/
# cucumber-puppet-gen policy
Generating with policy generator:
     [ADDED]  features/catalog

# git add features/catalog/

# git commit -m 'Add initial catalog policy template'
[master a0c6c3c] Add initial catalog policy template
 1 files changed, 14 insertions(+), 0 deletions(-)
 create mode 100644 features/catalog/policy.feature
```

With these three commands, the operator generates a new template for the catalog policy, adds the policy to the Git index, and then commits the new file to the repository. The cucumber-puppet policies closely resemble the natural language stories of Cucumber, as shown in Listing 8-41.

Listing 8-41. *A template cucumber-puppet policy*

```
# cat /etc/puppet/features/catalog/policy.feature
Feature: General policy for all catalogs
  In order to ensure applicability of a host's catalog
  As a manifest developer
  I want all catalogs to obey some general rules

  Scenario Outline: Compile and verify catalog
    Given a node specified by "features/yaml/<hostname>.example.com.yaml"
    When I compile its catalog
    Then compilation should succeed
    And all resource dependencies should resolve

  Examples:
    | hostname  |
    | localhost |
```

There are a few key sections of the policy file. First, the Scenario section is tested for every node listed in the Examples section. Cucumber-puppet substitutes the name listed underneath the hostname header into the filename listed in the Given a node specified by section. This node cache contains a list of top-level parameters set by site.pp, the ENC, and Facter. Using the cached node information stored on the Puppet master allows cucumber-puppet to effectively simulate a catalog request from each Puppet agent.

In order to populate these node definition files, the Example.com operator copies the cached node files from the Puppet Master as shown in Listing 8-42. These node files are located in $yamldir /node/, where $yamldir is a configuration setting on the Master system. Let's see how the operator provides this information to cucumber-puppet.

Listing 8-42. *Copying node YAML files from the Puppet Master into cucumber-puppet*

```
# cd /etc/puppet
# mkdir /etc/puppet/features/yaml

# puppet master --configprint yamldir
/var/lib/puppet/yaml

# cp /var/lib/puppet/yaml/node/{www,mail}.example.com.yaml \
  /etc/puppet/features/yaml/
```

First, the operator changes to the Puppet configuration directory, then creates the /etc/puppet/features/yaml directory. He then determines where the Puppet Master caches nodes compiled by the Puppet Master using the --configprint yamldir option. With this information, he copies the cached node information for the mail and web server into the cucumber-puppet directory structure.

With the node information in place, he modifies the catalog policy slightly to test catalog compilation for the mail and web server, replacing the localhost entry in the template. This modification is shown in Listing 8-43.

Listing 8-43. Add www and mail to the cucumber-puppet catalog policy

```
# git diff
diff --git a/features/catalog/policy.feature b/features/catalog/policy.feature
index c742189..1ea545e 100644
--- a/features/catalog/policy.feature
+++ b/features/catalog/policy.feature
@@ -11,4 +11,5 @@ Feature: General policy for all catalogs

     Examples:
       | hostname  |
-      | localhost |
+      | www |
+      | mail |
```

We can see that the operator replaces the localhost entry with two additional entries for www and mail. These names will be substituted into the file path when cucumber-puppet loads the node information. They also match the two YAML node files copied from the Puppet master yaml directory.

With this information in place, the operator commits the changes using the commands in Listing 8-44 and is ready to start testing changes to the Puppet manifests.

Listing 8-44. Committing node information and catalog policy to the git repository

```
$ git status
#On branch master
# Changes to be committed:
#   (use "git reset HEAD <file>..." to unstage)
#
#       new file:   features/yaml/mail.example.com.yaml
#       new file:   features/yaml/www.example.com.yaml
#
# Changed but not updated:
#   (use "git add <file>..." to update what will be committed)
#   (use "git checkout -- <file>..." to discard changes in working directory)
#
#       modified:   features/catalog/policy.feature
#

# git commit -m 'Add mail and web node YAML, update catalog policy'
[master c71e527] Add mail and web node YAML, update catalog policy
 3 files changed, 141 insertions(+), 1 deletions(-)
 create mode 100644 features/yaml/mail.example.com.yaml
 create mode 100644 features/yaml/www.example.com.yaml
```

Testing the Basic Catalog Policy

With the YAML node caches copied into place and the catalog policy updated, the operator simply executes cucumber-puppet as shown in Listing 8-45, testing his current manifests.

Listing 8-45. Testing manifests with cucumber-puppet

```
$ cucumber-puppet features/catalog/policy.feature
Feature: General policy for all catalogs
  In order to ensure applicability of a host's catalog
  As a manifest developer
  I want all catalogs to obey some general rules

  Scenario Outline: Compile and verify catalog
    Given a node specified by "features/yaml/<hostname>.example.com.yaml"
    When I compile its catalog
    Then compilation should succeed
    And all resource dependencies should resolve

    Examples:
      | hostname |
      | www      |
      | mail     |

2 scenarios (2 passed)
8 steps (8 passed)
0m0.104s
```

While in the /etc/puppet directory, the operator executes cucumber-puppet with the path to the catalog policy file. Cucumber-puppet then tests both the mail and web server and validates that the catalog compilation succeeds. The operator expects as much, but a basic site.pp file is being used with an empty node declaration of node default { }.

Testing the failure case

To verify that cucumber-puppet will properly report catalog failures, he modifies the site.pp in Listing 8-46 to contain the following node definitions:

Listing 8-46. /etc/puppet/manifests/site.pp test failure with cucumber-puppet

```
# /etc/puppet/manifests/site.pp
node default {
  notify { "unclassified":
    message => "This node is not classified",
  }
}

node www {
  notify { "web":
    message => "This node is the web server.",
  }
```

```
}
node mail {
  notify { "mail":
    message => "This node is the mail server.",
  }
  fail("This is a deliberate catalog compilation failure")
}
```

The operator has reconfigured the site.pp to deliberately fail a catalog compilation when compiling the catalog for the mail server. The web server, however, should still produce a valid catalog. He then verifies these expectations in Listing 8-47 by re-running the cucumber-puppet command.

Listing 8-47. Verifying that catalog failures are caught by cucumber-puppet

```
# cucumber-puppet features/catalog/policy.feature
Feature: General policy for all catalogs
  In order to ensure applicability of a host's catalog
  As a manifest developer
  I want all catalogs to obey some general rules

  Scenario Outline: Compile and verify catalog
    Given a node specified by "features/yaml/<hostname>.example.com.yaml"
    When I compile its catalog
    Then compilation should succeed
    And all resource dependencies should resolve

    Examples:
      | hostname |
      | www      |
      |This is a deliberate catalog compilation failure at /etc/puppet/manifests/site.pp:17↵
 on node mail.example.com
 mail     |
      exit (SystemExit)
      features/catalog/policy.feature:8:in `When I compile its catalog'

Failing Scenarios:
cucumber features/catalog/policy.feature:6 # Scenario: Compile and verify catalog

2 scenarios (1 failed, 1 passed)
8 steps (1 failed, 2 skipped, 5 passed)
0m0.132s
```

The operator uses the fail function to deliberately fail the catalog compilation for the mail server. As expected, cucumber-puppet reports one failed and one successful scenario. The specific error message and line number is returned in the output of cucumber-puppet, allowing the operator to quickly correct the problem.

So far, you've learned how the operator configures cucumber-puppet to test and validate catalog compilation. Next, you'll see how to validate that specific critical resources remain part of the configuration catalog when changes are made to the Puppet modules and manifests.

Validating Specific Resources

In the previous section, you learned how to validate catalog compilation successfully after making changes to the Puppet manifests. In this section, you'll see how the operator adds additional scenarios to ensure specific resources remain defined in the configuration catalog.

Catalog compilation errors will be obvious when they occur; the affected nodes will no longer receive a valid catalog. A resource omitted from the catalog is much more difficult to identify, however, because the affected node will still receive and apply the rest of the Puppet catalog. Cucumber-puppet allows the operator to make changes to conditional logic and verify that key resources are not excluded by the change. Let's see how this works.

First, the operator adds another step to the catalog policy. This step expresses his requirement that every Puppet catalog manages a `localadmin` account. This ensures that he'll always be able to log in to the systems Puppet manages. The local administrator account will grant access even if the central LDAP server is down. With the `accounts_ruby` module introduced in this chapter, accounts may no longer be directly managed in the Puppet manifests. Instead, external data supplied through the ENC script determines the accounts that are and are not managed by Puppet. This configuration introduces the possibility of the external data changing and therefore the `localadmin` account being omitted from the configuration catalog.

Adding a Check Step to the Policy

Adding a step to the cucumber-puppet policy is straightforward and readable. Let's see what the change and resulting policy check look like in Listing 8-48.

Listing 8-48. Adding a step to the catalog policy

```
# git diff /etc/puppet/features/catalog/policy.feature
diff --git a/features/catalog/policy.feature b/features/catalog/policy.feature
index ea81ae0..51f374e 100644
--- a/features/catalog/policy.feature
+++ b/features/catalog/policy.feature
@@ -8,6 +8,7 @@ Feature: General policy for all catalogs
     When I compile its catalog
     Then compilation should succeed
     And all resource dependencies should resolve
+    And it should have a localadmin account

    Examples:
        | hostname |
```

The operator adds a single line to the policy file describing the step cucumber-puppet should validate. He hasn't yet implemented this check or step, but cucumber-puppet provides useful information to guide the process. In Listing 8-49 the operator runs cucumber-puppet to see what happens when an unimplemented step is encountered.

Listing 8-49. Cucumber-puppet with missing steps

```
# cucumber-puppet features/catalog/policy.feature
Feature: General policy for all catalogs
  In order to ensure applicability of a host's catalog
```

```
  As a manifest developer
  I want all catalogs to obey some general rules

  Scenario Outline: Compile and verify catalog
    Given a node specified by "features/yaml/<hostname>.example.com.yaml"
    When I compile its catalog
    Then compilation should succeed
    And all resource dependencies should resolve
    And it should have a localadmin account

    Examples:
      | hostname |
      | login    |
      Undefined step: "it should have a localadmin account" (Cucumber::Undefined)
      features/catalog/policy.feature:11:in `And it should have a localadmin account'

1 scenario (1 undefined)
5 steps (1 undefined, 4 passed)
0m0.421s

You can implement step definitions for undefined steps with these snippets:

Then /^it should have a localadmin account$/ do
  pending # express the regexp above with the code you wish you had
end
```

Cucumber-puppet provides helpful output about how to add the step definition using a template snippet. Let's see how the operator uses this information to validate the administrator account. First, he copies and pastes the snippet into the file /etc/puppet/features/steps/user.rb. Then, he runs cucumber puppet in Listing 8-50 to verify that the step is being matched by the regular expression.

Listing 8-50. *Adding a pending step to cucumber-puppet*

```
# cucumber-puppet features/catalog/policy.feature
Feature: General policy for all catalogs
  In order to ensure applicability of a host's catalog
  As a manifest developer
  I want all catalogs to obey some general rules

  Scenario Outline: Compile and verify catalog                       #↵
 features/catalog/policy.feature:6
    Given a node specified by "features/yaml/<hostname>.example.com.yaml"
    When I compile its catalog
    Then compilation should succeed
    And all resource dependencies should resolve
    And it should have a localadmin account

    Examples:
      | hostname |
      | login    |
      TODO (Cucumber::Pending)
      ./features/steps/user.rb:18:in `/^it should have a localadmin account$/'
```

225

```
        features/catalog/policy.feature:11:in `And it should have a localadmin account'

1 scenario (1 pending)
5 steps (1 pending, 4 passed)
0m0.516s
```

Implementing the Cucumber Check

After adding the step snippet to the user.rb file, running cucumber-puppet indicates the step is pending. This validates that the regular expression is matching the line added to the policy. Next, the operator modifies the regular expression for the step. In addition, he adds the bit of Ruby code shown in Listing 8-51 to ensure that the account resource is declared.

Listing 8-51. Implementing validation of the localadmin user resource

```
# git diff
diff --git a/features/steps/user.rb b/features/steps/user.rb
index 92e0170..1644d28 100644
--- a/features/steps/user.rb
+++ b/features/steps/user.rb
@@ -14,6 +14,8 @@ Then /^the user should be in groups "([^\"]*)"$/ do |groups|
   fail unless g_s == groups
 end

-Then /^it should have a localadmin account$/ do
-   pending # express the regexp above with the code you wish you had
+Then /^it should have a (\w+) account$/ do |user|
+  steps %Q{
+    Then there should be a resource "User[#{user}]"
+  }
 End
```

The operator adjusts the regular expression to match any user account, not just the specific localadmin account. The \w+ (word character) portion of the regular expression performs this match. In addition, the surrounding parentheses cause the word within to be placed in the user variable. Finally, an additional step is added, substituting the name of the user account inside the resource title.

Running cucumber-puppet in Listing 8-52 indicates that all steps are passing successfully.

Listing 8-52. Cucumber-puppet validating the localadmin account

```
# cucumber-puppet features/catalog/policy.feature
Feature: General policy for all catalogs
  In order to ensure applicability of a host's catalog
  As a manifest developer
  I want all catalogs to obey some general rules

  Scenario Outline: Compile and verify catalog    Given a node specified by↵
  "features/yaml/<hostname>.example.com.yaml"
    When I compile its catalog
    Then compilation should succeed
```

```
        And all resource dependencies should resolve
        And it should have a localadmin account

        Examples:
          | hostname |
          | login    |

1 scenario (1 passed)
5 steps (5 passed)
0m0.391s
```

Catching Changes in the ENC Data

The operator isn't convinced yet. He wants to make sure that cucumber-puppet will catch the situation where the administrator account is not set by the ENC. To test this situation, he modifies the ENC script shown in Listing 8-32 and removes the administrator account. This updated script is shown in Listing 8-53.

Listing 8-53. Removing the administrator account from the ENC

```
# git diff /etc/puppet/resoruces_enc.rb
diff --git a/resources_enc.rb b/resources_enc.rb
index bd0e46e..d7a10c5 100755
--- a/resources_enc.rb
+++ b/resources_enc.rb
@@ -25,15 +25,15 @@ require 'yaml'
 # parameter. These values could come from LDAP, SQL, etc...
 @out["parameters"]['account_resources'] = Hash.new

-@out["parameters"]['account_resources']["localadmin"] = {
-  "comment"  => "Local Administrator",
-  "home"     => "/home/localadmin",
-  "uid"      => 600,
-  "gid"      => 600,
-  "groups"   => [ "sudo", "sudo_nopw", "ops" ],
-  "shell"    => "/bin/bash",
-  "password" => "!!",
-}
+# @out["parameters"]['account_resources']["localadmin"] = {
+#   "comment"  => "Local Administrator",
+#   "home"     => "/home/localadmin",
+#   "uid"      => 600,
+#   "gid"      => 600,
+#   "groups"   => [ "sudo", "sudo_nopw", "ops" ],
+#   "shell"    => "/bin/bash",
+#   "password" => "!!",
+# }

 @out["parameters"]['account_resources']["alice"] = {
   "comment"  => "Alice",
```

The operator simply commented out the administrator account from the external node classifier script. The cucumber-puppet node cache must be updated for the new test to be valid. To update the cache, the operator runs Puppet Agent as shown in Listing 8-54 and then copies the YAML node file into the features directory.

Listing 8-54. *Updating the cucumber-puppet node cache*

```
# cp /var/lib/puppet/yaml/node/login.example.com.yaml \
    /etc/puppet/features/yaml/
```

After updating the node definition, the operator validates that cucumber-puppet catches the missing administrator account (see Listing 8-55).

Listing 8-55. *Cucumber-puppet identifies the missing administrator account*

```
# cucumber-puppet features/catalog/policy.feature
Feature: General policy for all catalogs
  In order to ensure applicability of a host's catalog
  As a manifest developer
  I want all catalogs to obey some general rules

  Scenario Outline: Compile and verify catalog
    Given a node specified by "features/yaml/<hostname>.example.com.yaml"
    When I compile its catalog
    Then compilation should succeed
    And all resource dependencies should resolve
    And it should have a localadmin account

    Examples:
      | hostname |
      | login    |
        (RuntimeError)
        ./features/steps/puppet.rb:69:in `/^there should be a resource "([^\"]*)"$/'
        features/catalog/policy.feature:11:in `And it should have a localadmin account'

Failing Scenarios:
cucumber features/catalog/policy.feature:6 # Scenario: Compile and verify catalog

1 scenario (1 failed)
5 steps (1 failed, 4 passed)
0m0.369s
```

As expected, cucumber-puppet catches the missing user resource. The operator is confident now that the additional step is properly catching the missing account resource.

As you've just seen, cucumber-puppet provides a convenient and easy to use method for testing Puppet Catalogs. By defining policy steps for resources that should by managed, the operator remains confident while making changes. If the Local Administrator account information is no longer set by the ENC script, the problem will be quickly caught. In addition, changes to the puppet manifests and modules can be made with confidence so long as critical resources are being tested and verified with cucumber-puppet.

Summary

In this chapter, you've seen a number of tools related to, and part of, Puppet 2.6. First, the Puppet Module tool provides a command line interface to working with Puppet modules. The operator is able to use puppet-module to generate module skeleton templates. Once the configuration code is filled into the template, the operator is able to package and publish the module to forge.puppetlabs.com. Even if you don't plan to publish modules to the Forge, puppet-module provides the means to track module versions and install them into your own Puppet configuration. In addition to generating skeleton templates for modules, puppet-module allows you to search, download and install publically-available modules. You learned how the operator easily installed and made use of a module managing the host-based iptables firewall. Downloading and using public modules greatly reduces time and effort.

In addition to the module tool, you learned about the new Ruby DSL in Puppet 2.6. Using the Ruby language allowed the developer to declare an arbitrary number of account resources in Puppet. Without the ability to iterate in Ruby, the developer would have had a difficult time managing a growing number of accounts with Puppet. Puppet version 2.6 allows both Ruby and Puppet manifests to be intermixed in the same catalog run, and even within the same module.

Finally, you learned about a unique and novel approach to testing Puppet catalogs with the cucumber-puppet tool. Inspired by Cucumber, the framework encourages a natural language specification of requirements. In addition, cucumber-puppet provides a very helpful and intuitive interface. Once a specification is written, helpful boilerplate code is given back if cucumber-puppet does not yet understand how to validate the specification. Using this boilerplate allows tests to be quickly implemented and written without a deep understanding of Ruby.

Puppet is a fast-moving project with a very active community. Tools designed to work with Puppet will continue to be written as time moves on.

Resources

The following resources are a great place to keep track of the tools and work being done by members of the Puppet Community.

- https://github.com/search?q=puppet
- Puppet Users Mailing List - mailto:puppet-users+subscribe@googlegroups.com
- Puppet Developer Mailing List - mailto:puppet-dev+subscribe@googlegroups.com
- http://blog.puppetlabs.com/

For more information about the Ruby DSL, please see the following resources:

- https://github.com/bobsh/puppet-rubydsl-examples
- http://www.puppetlabs.com/blog/ruby-dsl/
- http://projects.puppetlabs.com/projects/1/wiki/Ruby_Dsl

Further information about cucumber-puppet and Cucumber is available online at:

- `http://www.slideshare.net/nistude/cucumberpuppet`
- `http://projects.puppetlabs.com/projects/cucumber-puppet/wiki/`
- `https://github.com/nistude/cucumber-puppet`
- `https://github.com/aslakhellesoy/cucumber/wiki`

CHAPTER 9

■ ■ ■

Reporting with Puppet

One of the most important aspects of any configuration management system is reporting. Reporting is critical for providing information on accuracy, performance, and compliance to policy and standards, and it can provide graphical representations of the overall state of your configuration. Indeed, we've already seen some examples of how to display Puppet reports (i.e., via a management console) in Chapter 7, when we looked at Puppet Dashboard and Foreman.

Puppet's reporting engine has undergone a lot of development in recent releases, especially with the new and more detailed reporting format first introduced in version 2.6.0. In this chapter, we explain what command-line and data-based reports are available, how to configure reporting and reports, and how to work with them, then we look at graphing our reporting data and discuss how to build custom reports.

Getting Started

Puppet agents can be configured to return data at the end of each configuration run. Puppet calls this data a "transaction report." The transaction reports are sent to the master server where a number of report processors exist that can utilize this data and present it in a variety of forms. You can also develop your own report processors to customize the reporting output.

The default transaction report comes in the form of a YAML file. As mentioned in earlier chapters, YAML is a recursive acronym for "YAML Ain't Markup Language." YAML is a human-readable data serialization format that draws heavily from concepts in XML and the Python and C programming languages.

The transaction reports contain all events and log messages generated by the transaction and some additional metrics. The metrics fall into three general types: time, resource and change metrics. Within each of these metrics there are one or more values. They include the time taken for the transaction, the number of resources and changes in the transaction and the success or failure of those resources.

In Listing 9-1 you can see an example of a portion of a YAML Puppet transaction report.

Listing 9-1. A partial Puppet transaction report

```
--- !ruby/object:Puppet::Transaction::Report
  external_times:
    !ruby/sym config_retrieval: 0.280263900756836
  host: mail.example.com
  logs:
    - !ruby/object:Puppet::Util::Log
      level: !ruby/sym info
      message: Caching catalog for mail.example.com
      source: //mail.example.com/Puppet
      tags:
```

```
      - info
    time: 2010-12-18 08:41:19.252599 -08:00
    version: &id001 2.6.4
 - !ruby/object:Puppet::Util::Log
    level: !ruby/sym info
    message: Applying configuration version '1292690479'
    source: //mail.example.com/Puppet
    tags:
      - info
    time: 2010-12-18 08:41:19.330582 -08:00
    version: *id001
 - !ruby/object:Puppet::Util::Log
    level: !ruby/sym info
    message: "FileBucket adding /etc/sudoers as {md5}49085c571a7ec7ff54270c7a53a79146"
    source: //mail.example.com/Puppet
    tags:
      - info
    time: 2010-12-18 08:41:19.429069 -08:00
    version: *id001
...
  resources: !ruby/object:Puppet::Util::Metric
    label: Resources
    name: resources
    values:
      - - !ruby/sym out_of_sync
        - Out of sync
        - 1
      - - !ruby/sym changed
        - Changed
        - 1
      - - !ruby/sym total
        - Total
        - 8
  changes: !ruby/object:Puppet::Util::Metric
    label: Changes
    name: changes
    values:
      - - !ruby/sym total
        - Total
        - 2
  events: !ruby/object:Puppet::Util::Metric
    label: Events
    name: events
    values:
      - - success
        - Success
        - 2
      - - !ruby/sym total
        - Total
        - 2
  time: 2010-12-18 08:41:15.515624 -08:00
```

Here you can see that the YAML file is divided into sections. The first section contains any log messages. The log messages are any events generated during the Puppet run, for example, the messages that would typically go to standard out or syslog. The second section contains events related to resources, and it tracks each resource managed by Puppet and the changes made to that resource during the Puppet run. The remaining sections detail the value of each metric that Puppet collects. Each metric has a label, a name and values that make it easy to parse the data, if you wish to use it for reporting or manipulation. Metrics include the number of changes Puppet made, the number of resources managed, and the number and type of events during the run.

The YAML format of the reporting output is very well supported by Ruby, and can be easily consumed in Ruby and other languages to make use of Puppet reporting data.

Configuring Reporting

In order to get Puppet to output the reports we want, we need to configure it correctly. As of version 2.6.0, each agent is configured by default to not report back to the master; reporting needs to be enabled. The first step to doing this is to ensure that the Puppet agent on the host is started with the `--report` option, like so:

```
$ sudo puppet agent --report
```

This will cause the Puppet agent to start creating and sending reports to the master. You could also set the report option in the puppet.conf configuration file:

```
[agent]
report = true
```

▓ **Tip** By default, once enabled, the agent will send the reports back to the Puppet master configuring it. You can set up a separate Puppet master for reports only, if you like. Direct all reports to this server by using the `report_server` option on the agent (see http://docs.puppetlabs.com/references/latest/configuration.html#reportserver).

By default, the reports generated by the agent will be sent to the master and stored as YAML-formatted files in the report directory. These files are the output of the default report processor, `store`. Reports are written into sub-directories under the report directory and a directory created for each agent that is reporting. Report file names are the date stamp when the report was generated and are suffixed with `.yaml`, for example: `201010130604.yaml`.

The report directory is `$vardir/reports` (usually `/var/lib/puppet/reports` on most distributions), but you can override this by configuring the `reportdir` option on the Puppet master `puppet.conf` configuration file, like so:

```
[master]
reportdir = /etc/puppet/reports
```

Here, we've set the new report directory to `/etc/puppet/reports`. You can specify whichever directory suits your environment.

▓ **Tip** In future releases, from 2.7.0 onwards, reporting will be enabled by default and you won't need to configure the `report` option on the agent or the master.

Report Processors

There are a number of different report processors available. Report processors are stored on the Puppet master. We've already seen one in Chapter 7 when we used the `http` report processor to send reports from the master to the Puppet Dashboard.

The default report, `store`, simply stores the report file on the disk. There is also the `log` processor that sends logs to the local log destination, to syslog for example. Also available is the `tagmail` report processor that sends email messages based on particular tags in transaction reports. Next, the `rrdgraph` report processor that converts transaction reports into RRD-based graphs. Lastly, we've already seen the `http` report processor in Chapter 8.

Selecting which report processors will run is done using the `reports` configuration option in the `puppet.conf` configuration file.

```
[master]
reports = store,log,tagmail,rrdgraph
```

Each report processor you want to enable should be listed in the `reports` option with multiple processors separated by commas. By default, only `store` is enabled. You can also enable report processors on the command line.

```
$ sudo puppet master --reports log,tagmail
```

Now let's look at each individual report processor, starting with the `log` processor.

log

The `log` report processor sends the log entries from transaction reports to syslog. It is the simplest of the report processors. The syslog destination facility is controlled by the `syslogfacility` configuration option, which defaults to the `daemon` facility.

```
[master]
syslogfacility = user
```

On the previous line, we've directed all syslog output to the `user` facility.

▓ **Note** The log report processor only logs entries if the Puppet master is running in daemon-mode. If you keep it running in the foreground, then no syslog messages will be generated.

---

tagmail

The `tagmail` report sends log messages via email based on the tags that are present in each log message. Tags allow you to set context for your resources, for example you can tag all resources that belong to a particular operating system, location or any other characteristic. Tags can also be specified in your `puppet.conf` configuration file to tell your agents to only apply configuration tagged with the specified tags.

▦ **Tip** You can learn more about tags and tagging at

`http://projects.puppetlabs.com/projects/puppet/wiki/Using_Tags`.

The `tagmail` report uses these same tags to generate email reports. The tags assigned to your resources are added to the log results and then Puppet generates emails based on matching particular tags with particular email addresses. This matching occurs in a configuration file called `tagmail.conf`. By default, the `tagmail.conf` file is located in `$confdir` directory, usually `/etc/puppet`. This is controlled by the `tagmap` configuration option in the `puppet.conf` file.

```
[master]
tagmap = $confdir/tagmail.conf
```

The `tagmail.conf` file contains a list of tags and email addresses separated by colons. Multiple tags and email addresses can be specified by separating them with commas. You can see an example of this file in Listing 9-2.

Listing 9-2. A sample tagmail.conf file

```
all:    configuration@example.com
mail, www:     operations@example.com
db, !mail:     dba@example.com,apps@example.com
```

The first tag in Listing 10-2, `all`, is a special tag that tells Puppet to send all reports to the specified email address.

▦ **Tip** There is a special tag called `err`. Specifying this tag will make the report return all error messages generated during a configuration run.

The second set of tags specifies that Puppet should send all reports tagged with the tags `mail` and `www` to the email address operations@example.com. The last tags tell Puppet to send reports for all log entries with the `db` tag but not the `mail` tag to both the dba@example.com and apps@example.com email addresses. You can see that the `mail` tag has been negated using the `!` symbol.

rrdgraph

One of the more useful built-in report processors is the rrdgraph type, which takes advantage of Tobias Oetiker's RRD graphing libraries. The rrdgraph report processor generates RRD files, graphs and some HTML files to display those graphs. It is a very quick and easy way of implementing graphs of your Puppet configuration activities.

In order to make use of this report processor we'll first need to install the RRDTools and the Ruby bindings for RRD. We can install RRDTools via package on most platforms and distributions. The Ruby bindings, unfortunately, are less well-supported on a lot of platforms. They can be installed from source, or some distributions do have packages available. There are also suitable rrdtool-ruby RPMs that should work on most RPM-based distributions like Red Hat, CentOS, and Mandriva versions available at Dag Wieer's repository at http://dag.wieers.com/rpm/packages/rrdtool/. There is also a development package for Gentoo called ruby-rrd that provides the required bindings that you should be able to install via emerge.

You can see a list of the required package for Debian/Ubuntu, Fedora, and Red Hat platforms in Table 9-1.

Table 9-1. Package names for rrdtools

OS	Packages		
Debian/Ubuntu	rrdtool	librrd2	librrd2-dev
Fedora	rrdtool	rrdtool-ruby	
Red Hat	rrdtool	rrdtool-ruby	

▪ **Note** Your package manager may prompt you to install additional packages when installing RRDTool.

You can also install the RRD Ruby bindings via one of two gems, RubyRRDtool or librrd:

```
$ sudo gem install RubyRRDtool
```

```
$ sudo gem install librrd
```

Both gems should work to produce the appropriate RRD graphs.

Lastly, if there is no Ruby bindings package for your platform, you can install the bindings via source. Download the latest bindings package from Rubyforge, unpack it and change into the resulting directory. At the time of writing, the latest version was 0.6.0:

```
$ wget http://rubyforge.org/frs/download.php/13992/RubyRRDtool-0.6.0.tgz
$ tar -zxf RubyRRDtool-0.6.0.tgz
$ cd RubyRRDtool-0.6.0
$ ruby extconf.rb
$ make
$ sudo make install
```

To customize RRD support, you can also change some configuration options in the puppet.conf configuration file:

```
[master]
rrddir = $vardir/rrd
rrdinternval = $runinterval
```

The rrddir directory specifies the default location for the generated RRD files. It defaults to $vardir/rrd, which is usually /var/lib/puppet/rrd. The rrdinterval specifies how often RRD should expect to receive data. This defaults to $runinterval, so as to match how often agents report back to the master.

Underneath the $vardir/rrd directory, Puppet will create a directory for each agent that reports to the master. Graphs (and the associated HTML files to display them) will be generated in that directory. A graph will be generated for each metric that Puppet collects. You can then serve this directory out using your web server and display the graphs.

http

The http report processor sends Puppet reports to a HTTP URL and port. The Puppet reports are sent as a YAML dump in the form of a HTTP Post. You can control the destination with the reporturl configuration option in the puppet.conf configuration file on the master:

```
[master]
reporturl = http://localhost:3000/reports
```

Here the report destination is set to its default, which assumes that you are sending reports to Puppet Dashboard.

Custom Reporting

You are not limited to the provided report processors. Puppet also allows you to create your own report processors. There are two methods for doing this. The first method is to use the existing store reports, which are YAML files, and write an external report processor to make use of this information, for example graphing it or storing it in an external database. This is also how the report importation process works within Puppet Dashboard. These external report processors can easily be written in Ruby to take advantage of Ruby's ability to de-serialize the YAML files and make use of the resulting objects. You can use any tool that supports the importation of third-party YAML data.

The second method involves writing your own report processor and adding it to Puppet. Unlike plug-ins for facts, functions, types and providers, Puppet doesn't have an automatic way to distribute custom reports.

▪ **Note** We show how to distribute other forms of custom code, like facts, in Chapter 10.

Instead the report processors are stored in the lib/puppet/reports directory. For example, on an Ubuntu Puppet master we'd add our custom report processor to the

/usr/local/lib/site_ruby/1.8/puppet/reports directory with the existing report processors. We would then specify the new report in the reports configuration option.

The existing report processors make excellent templates for new processors. In Listing 10-3 you can see the Ruby code for the http report processor.

Listing 9-3.   *The http report processor*

```
require 'puppet'
require 'net/http'
require 'uri'

Puppet::Reports.register_report(:http) do

    desc <<-DESC
    Send report information via HTTP to the `reporturl`. Each host sends
    its report as a YAML dump and this sends this YAML to a client via HTTP POST.
    The YAML is the `report` parameter of the request."
    DESC

    def process
        url = URI.parse(Puppet[:reporturl])
        req = Net::HTTP::Post.new(url.path)
        req.body = self.to_yaml
        req.content_type = "application/x-yaml"
        Net::HTTP.new(url.host, url.port).start {|http|
            http.request(req)
        }
    end
end
```

As you can see from this example, it is very easy to create your own report processor.

▨ **Tip** Other ideas for Puppet report processors include RSS feeds for new reports, IRC, XMPP or instant messaging, or SMS notifications of new reports. You could also parse particular events in reports or collate metrics for use in other kinds of performance management systems.

First, you need to require Puppet itself: require 'puppet'. Then you simply specify the Puppet::Reports.register_report method and the name of the new report processor you are creating. You can see a simple example of a report processor in Listing 9-4.

Listing 9-4. *A custom summary report*

```
require 'puppet'

Puppet::Reports.register_report(:summary) do
```

```
    desc <<-DESC
    Send summary report information to the report directory."
    DESC

    def process
      client = self.host
      summary = self.summary
      dir = File.join(Puppet[:reportdir], client)
      client = self.host
      file = "summary.txt"
      destination = File.join(dir, file)
      File.open(destination,"w") do |f|
        f.write(summary)
      end
    end
  end
end
```

In this report processor, we've defined a method called process to hold our report's core logic. We've extracted some information from our report: the host, using the self.host method, and a summary of the changes, using the summary method. You also have access to the report's logs and metrics using the self.logs and self.metrics methods.

We also wrote our summary report out to a directory named after the Puppet agent host located underneath the reports directory, which we specified using the value of the reportdir configuration option.

We would then add our report name to Puppet in the puppet.conf configuration file:

```
reports=store,log,summary
```

After we restarted the Puppet master and performed a Puppet run, the new report would be generated. In our case, the final report is contained in a file called summary.txt and looks something like this:

```
Changes:
            Total: 1
Events:
          Success: 1
            Total: 1
Resources:
          Changed: 1
      Out of sync: 1
            Total: 8
Time:
   Config retrieval: 0.19
             File: 0.05
        Filebucket: 0.00
          Schedule: 0.00
```

▓ **Tip** You can see other examples of how to use and extract reporting data from the code of the existing reports, at https://github.com/puppetlabs/puppet/tree/master/lib/puppet/reports.

Summary

In this chapter, we've demonstrated the basics of Puppet reporting, including how to configure reporting and some details on each report type and its configuration.

We've also shown you how to create custom reports of your own, making use of the report data in its YAML form or via processing with a custom report processor.

Resources

- Report Reference: http://docs.puppetlabs.com/references/latest/report.html

- Reports and Reporting:
  http://projects.puppetlabs.com/projects/puppet/wiki/Reports_And_Reporting

- Existing reports:
  https://github.com/puppetlabs/puppet/tree/master/lib/puppet/reports

CHAPTER 10

■ ■ ■

Extending Facter and Puppet

Among the most powerful features of Puppet are its flexibility and extensibility. In addition to the existing facts, resource types, providers, and functions, you can quickly and easily add custom code specific to your environment or to meet a particular need.

In the first part of this chapter we're going to examine how to add your own custom facts. Adding custom facts is highly useful for gathering and making use of information specific to your environment. Indeed, we've used Facter extensively in this book to provide information about our hosts, applications and services, and you've seen the array of facts available across many platforms. You may have noted, though, that Facter isn't comprehensive; many facts about your hosts and environments are not available as Facter facts.

In the second part of the chapter, we're going to examine how to add your own custom types, providers and functions to Puppet and how to have Puppet distribute these, and we'll discuss how to make use of them. These are among Puppet's most powerful features, and are at the heart of its flexibility and extensibility. Being able to add your own enhancements in addition to the existing resources types, providers and functions, you can quickly and easily add custom code specific to your environment or to meet a particular need.

Writing and Distributing Custom Facts

Creating your own custom facts to Puppet is a very simple process. Indeed, it only requires a basic understanding of Ruby. Luckily for you, Ruby is incredibly easy to pick up and there are lots of resources available to help (refer to the "Resources" section at the end of the chapter for some helpful links).

In the following sections, you'll see how to successfully extend Facter. We first configure Puppet so we can write custom facts, then we test our new facts to confirm they are working properly.

■ **Note** If the idea of learning any Ruby is at all daunting, a fast alternative way to add a fact without writing any Ruby code is via Facter's support of environmental variables. Any environmental variables set by the user Facter is running as (usually the `root` user) that are prefixed with `FACTER_` will be added to Facter as facts. So, if you were to set an environmental variable of `FACTER_datacenter` with a value of `Chicago`, then this would become a fact called `datacenter` with the value of `Chicago`.

Configuring Puppet for Custom Facts

The best way to distribute custom facts is to include them in modules, using a Puppet concept called "plug-ins in modules." This concept allows you to place your custom code inside an existing or new

Puppet module and then use that module in your Puppet environment. Custom facts, custom types, providers, and functions are then distributed to any host that includes a particular module.

Modules that distribute facts are no different from other modules, and there are two popular approaches to doing so. Some people distribute facts related to a particular function in the module that they use to configure that function. For example, a fact with some Bind data in it might be distributed with the module you use to configure Bind. This clusters facts specific to a function together and allows a greater portability. Other sites include all custom facts (and other items) in a single, central module, such as a module called facts or plugins. This centralizes facts in one location for ease of management and maintenance.

Each approach has pros and cons and you should select one that suits your organization and its workflow. We personally prefer the former approach because it limits custom facts and other items to only those clients that require them, rather than all hosts. For some environments, this may be a neater approach. We're going to use this approach in this section when demonstrating managing custom facts.

So where in our modules do facts go? Let's create a simple module called bind as an example:

```
bind/
bind/manifests
bind/manifests/init.pp
bind/files
bind/templates
bind/lib/facter
```

Here we've created our standard module directory structure, but we've added another directory, lib. The lib directory contains any "plug-ins" or additional facts, types or functions we want to add to Puppet. We're going to focus on adding facts; these are stored in the lib/facter directory.

In addition to adding the lib/facter directory to modules that will distribute facts, you need to enable "plug-ins in modules" in your Puppet configuration. To do this, enable options in the [main] section of the Puppet master's puppet.conf configuration file, as you can see on the next line:

```
[main]
pluginsync = true
```

When set to true, the pluginsync setting turns on the "plug-ins in modules" capability. Now, when clients connect to the master, each client will check its modules for facts and other custom items. Puppet will take these facts and other custom items and sync them to the relevant clients, so they can then be used on these clients.

▧ **Caution** The sync of facts and other items occurs during the Puppet run. In some cases, the custom items synchronized may not be available in that initial Puppet run. For example, if you sync a fact during a Puppet run and rely on the value of that fact in configuration you are using in the SAME run, then that configuration may fail. This is because Puppet has yet to re-run Facter and assign a value for the new custom fact you've provided. On subsequent runs, the new fact's value will be populated and available to Puppet.

Writing Custom Facts

After configuring Puppet to deliver our custom facts, you should actually create some new facts! Each fact is a snippet of Ruby code wrapped in a Facter method to add the result of our Ruby code as a fact. Let's look at a simple example in Listing 10-1.

Listing 10-1. *Our first custom fact*

```
Facter.add("home") do
      setcode do
          ENV['HOME']
      end
end
```

In this example, our custom fact returns the value of the HOME environmental value as a fact called home, which in turn would be available in our manifests as the variable $home.

The Facter.add method allows us to specify the name of our new fact. We then use the setcode block to specify the contents of our new fact, in our case using Ruby's built-in ENV variable to access an environmental variable. Facter will set the value of our new fact using the result of the code executed inside this block.

In Listing 10-2, you can see a custom fact that reads a file to return the value of the fact.

Listing 10-2. *Another custom fact*

```
Facter.add("timezone") do
      confine :operatingsystem => :debian
      setcode do
          File.readlines("/etc/timezone").to_a.last
      end
end
```

Here, we're returning the timezone of a Debian host. We've also done two interesting things. First, we've specified a confine statement. This statement restricts the execution of the fact if a particular criteria is not met. This restriction is commonly implemented by taking advantage of the values of other facts. In this case, we've specified that the value of the operatingsystem fact should be Debian for the fact to be executed. We can also use the values of other facts, for example:

```
confine :kernel => :linux
```

The previous confine is commonly used to limit the use of a particular fact to nodes with Linux-based kernels.

Second, we've used the readlines File method to read in the contents of the /etc/timezone file. The contents are returned as the fact timezone, which in turn would be available as the variable $timezone.

```
timezone => Australia/Melbourne
```

We've established how to confine the execution of a fact but we can also use other fact values to influence our fact determination, for example:

```
Facter.add("timezone") do
      setcode do
        if Facter.value(:operatingsystem) =~ /Debian|Ubuntu/
```

```
            File.readlines("/etc/timezone").to_a.last
        else
            tz = Time.new.zone
        end
    end
end
```

Here, if the operating system is Debian or Ubuntu, it will return a time zone value by returning the value from the /etc/timezone file. Otherwise, the fact will use Ruby's in-built time handling to return a time zone.

You could also use a case statement to select different fact values, for example as used in the operatingsystemrelease fact shown in Listing 10-3.

Listing 10-3. *Using a case statement to select fact values*

```
Facter.add(:operatingsystemrelease) do
    confine :operatingsystem => %w{CentOS Fedora oel ovs RedHat MeeGo}
    setcode do
        case Facter.value(:operatingsystem)
        when "CentOS", "RedHat"
            releasefile = "/etc/redhat-release"
        when "Fedora"
            releasefile = "/etc/fedora-release"
        when "MeeGo"
            releasefile = "/etc/meego-release"
        when "OEL", "oel"
            releasefile = "/etc/enterprise-release"
        when "OVS", "ovs"
            releasefile = "/etc/ovs-release"
        end
        File::open(releasefile, "r") do |f|
            line = f.readline.chomp
            if line =~ /\(Rawhide\)$/
                "Rawhide"
            elsif line =~ /release (\d[\d.]*)/
                $1
            end
        end
    end
end
```

You can use other fact values for any purpose you like, not just for determining how to retrieve a fact. Some facts return another fact value if they cannot find a way to determine the correct value. For example, the operatingsystem fact returns the current kernel, Facter.value(:kernel), as the value of operatingsystem if Facter cannot determine the operating system it is being run on.

You can create more complex facts and even return more than one fact in your Ruby snippets, as you can see in Listing 10-4.

Listing 10-4. A more complex fact

```
    netname = nil
     netaddr = nil
     test = {}
     File.open("/etc/networks").each do |line|
         netname = $1 and netaddr = $2 if line ↵
=~ /^(\w+.?\w+)\s+([0-9]+\.[0-9]+\.[0-9]+\.[0-9]+)/
         if netname != nil && netaddr != nil
             test["network_" + netname] = netaddr
             netname = nil
             netaddr = nil
             end
    end
       test.each{|name,fact|
             Facter.add(name) do
                 setcode do
                     fact
                     end
                 end
    }
```

This fact actually creates a series of facts, each fact taken from information collected from the /etc/networks file. This file associates network names with networks. Our snippet parses this file and adds a series of facts, one per each network in the file. So, if our file looked like:

```
default     0.0.0.0
loopback    127.0.0.0
link-local    169.254.0.0
```

Then three facts would be returned:

```
network_default => 0.0.0.0
network_loopback => 127.0.0.0
network_link-local => 169.254.0.0
```

You can take a similar approach to commands, or files, or a variety of other sources.

Testing the Facts

There is a simple process for testing your facts: Import them into Facter and use it to test them before using them in Puppet. To do this, you need to set up a testing environment. Create a directory structure to hold our test facts—we'll call ours lib/ruby/facter. Situate this structure beneath the root user's home directory. Then create an environmental variable, $RUBYLIB, that references this directory and will allow Facter to find our test facts:

```
# mkdir -p ~/lib/ruby/facter
# export RUBYLIB=~/lib/ruby
```

Then copy your fact snippets into this new directory:

```
# cp /var/puppet/facts/home.rb $RUBYLIB/facter
```

After this, you can call Facter with the name of the fact you've just created. If the required output appears, your fact is working correctly. On the following lines, we've tested our home fact and discovered it has returned the correct value:

```
# facter home
/root
```

If your fact is not working correctly, an error message you can debug will be generated.

Facts just scratch the surface of Puppet's extensibility, and adding to types, providers, and functions adds even more capability. We're going to demonstrate that in the next section.

Developing Custom Types, Providers and Functions

When developing custom types, providers and functions it is important to remember that Puppet and Facter are open-source tools developed by both Puppet Labs and a wide community of contributors. Sharing custom facts and resource types helps everyone in the community, and it means you can also get input from the community on your work. Extending Puppet or Facter is also an excellent way to give back to that community. You can share your custom code via the Puppet mailing list or on the Puppet Wiki, by logging a Redmine ticket, or by setting up your own source repository for Puppet code on the Puppet forge (http://forge.puppetlabs.com).

Lastly, don't underestimate the usefulness of code people before you have already developed that you can use and adapt for your environment. Explore existing Puppet modules, plug-ins, facts and other code via Google and on resources like GitHub. Like all systems administrators, we know that imitation is the ultimate form of flattery.

In the following sections, we demonstrate how to configure Puppet to distribute your own custom code. You'll also see how to write a variety of custom types and providers, and finally how to write your own Puppet functions.

Configuring Puppet for Types, Providers and Functions

The best way to distribute custom types, providers and functions is to include them in modules, using "plug-ins in modules," the same concept we introduced earlier this chapter to distribute custom facts. Just like custom facts, you again place your custom code into a Puppet module and use that module in your configuration. Puppet will take care of distributing your code to your Puppet masters and agents.

Again, just like custom facts, you can take two approaches to managing custom code: placing it in function-specific modules or centralizing it into a single module. We're going to demonstrate adding custom code in a single, function-specific module.

So, where in our modules does custom code go? Let's create a simple module called apache as an example:

```
apache/
apache/manifests
apache/manifests/init.pp
apache/files
apache/templates
apache/lib/facter
```

```
apache/lib/puppet/type
apache/lib/puppet/provider
apache/lib/puppet/parser/functions
```

Here we've created our standard module directory structure, but we've added another directory, `lib`. We saw the `lib` directory earlier in the chapter when we placed custom facts into its Facter subdirectory. The lib directory also contains other "plug-ins" like types, providers and functions, which we want to add to Puppet. The `lib/puppet/type` and `lib/puppet/provider` directories hold custom types and providers respectively. The last directory, `lib/puppet/parser/functions`, holds custom functions.

Like we did when we configured Puppet for custom facts, you need to enable "plug-ins in modules" in your Puppet configuration. To do this, enable the `pluginsync` option in the [`main`] section of the Puppet master's `puppet.conf` configuration file, as follows:

```
[main]
pluginsync = true
```

The `pluginsync` setting, when set to true, turns on the "plug-ins in modules" capability. Now, when agents connect to the master, each agent will check its modules for custom code. Puppet will take this custom code and sync it to the relevant agents. It can then be used on these agents. The only exception to this is custom functions. Functions run on the Puppet master rather than the Puppet agents, so they won't be synched down to an agent. They will only be synched if the Puppet agent is run on the Puppet master, i.e., if you are managing Puppet with Puppet.

▓ **Note** In earlier releases of Puppet, "plug-ins in modules" required some additional configuration. You can read about that configuration on the Puppet Labs Documentation site at http://docs.puppetlabs.com/guides/plugins_in_modules.html.

Writing a Puppet Type and Provider

Puppet types are used to manage individual configuration items. Puppet has a package type, a service type, a user type, and all the other types available. Each type has one or more providers. Each provider handles the management of that configuration on a different platform or tool: for example, the package type has aptitude, yum, RPM, and DMG providers (among 22 others).

We're going to show you a simple example of how to create an additional type and provider, one that manages version control systems (VCS), which we're going to call repo. In this case we're going to create the type and two providers, one for Git and one for SVN. Our type is going to allow you to create, manage and delete VCS repositories.

A Puppet type contains the characteristics of the configuration item we're describing, for example in the case of VCS management type:

- The name of the repository being managed

- The source of the repository

Correspondingly, the Puppet providers specify the actions required to manage the state of the configuration item. Obviously, each provider has a set of similar actions that tell it how to:

- Create the resource

- Delete the resource

- Check for the resource's existence or state

- Make changes to the resource's content

Creating Our Type

Let's start by creating our type. We're going to create a module called custom to store it in:

```
custom/
custom/manifests/init.pp
custom/lib/puppet/type
custom/lib/puppet/provider
```

Inside the lib/puppet/type directory, we're going to create a file called repo.rb to store our type definition:

```
custom/lib/puppet/type/repo.rb
```

You can see that file in Listing 10-5.

Listing 10-5. The repo type

```
Puppet::Type.newtype(:repo) do
    @doc = "Manage repos"
    ensurable

    newparam(:source) do
        desc "The repo source"

        validate do |value|
            if value =~ /^git/
                resource[:provider] = :git
            else
                resource[:provider] = :svn
            end
        end

        isnamevar
    end

    newparam(:path) do
        desc "Destination path"

        validate do |value|
            unless value =~ /^\/[a-z0-9]+/
                raise ArgumentError , "%s is not a valid file path" % value
            end
```

```
        end
      end
end
```

In this example, we start our type with the `Puppet::Type.newtype` block and specify the name of type to be created, repo. We can also see a `@doc` string which is where we specify the documentation for your type. We recommend you provide clear documentation including examples of how to use the type, for a good example have a look at the documentation provided for the Cron type at https://github.com/puppetlabs/puppet/blob/master/lib/puppet/type/cron.rb.

The next statement is ensurable. The ensurable statement is a useful shortcut that tells Puppet to create an ensure property for this type. The ensure property determines the state of the configuration item, for example:

```
service { "sshd":
  ensure => present,
}
```

The ensurable statement tells Puppet to expect three methods: `create`, `destroy` and `exists?` in our provider (You'll see the code for this in Listing 10-6). These methods are, respectively:

- A command to create the resource

- A command to delete the resource

- A command to check for the existence of the resource

All we then need to do is specify these methods and their contents and Puppet creates the supporting infrastructure around them. Types have two kinds of values - properties and parameters. Properties "do things." They tell us how the provider works. We've only defined one property, ensure, by using the ensurable statement. Puppet expects that properties will generally have corresponding methods in the provider that we'll see later in this chapter. Parameters are variables and contain information relevant to configuring the resource the type manages, rather than "doing things."

Next, we've defined a parameter, called source:

```
newparam(:source) do
  desc "The repo source"

  validate do |value|
    if value =~ /^git/
      resource[:provider] = :git
    else
      resource[:provider] = :svn
  end
 end
   isnamevar
end
```

The source parameter will tell the repo type where to go to retrieve, clone, or check out our source repository.

In the source parameter we're also using a hook called validate. It's normally used to check the parameter value for appropriateness; here, we're using it to take a guess at what provider to use.

▪ **Note** In addition to the `validate` hook, Puppet also has the `munge` hook. You can use the `munge` hook to adjust the value of the parameter rather than validating it before passing it to the provider.

Our `validate` code specifies that if the source parameter starts with `git`, then use the Git provider; if not, then default to the Subversion provider. This is fairly crude as a default, and you can override this by defining the `provider` attribute in your resource, like so:

```
repo { "puppet":
  source => "git://github.com/puppetlabs/puppet.git",
  path => "/home/puppet",
  provider => git,
  ensure => present,
}
```

We've also used another piece of Puppet auto-magic, the `isnamevar` method, to make this parameter the "name" variable for this type so that the value of this parameter is used as the name of the resource. Finally, we've defined another parameter, `path`:

```
newparam(:path) do
  desc "Destination path"

  validate do |value|
    unless value =~ /^\/[a-z0-9]+/
      raise ArgumentError, "%s is not a valid file path" % value
    end
  end
end
```

This is a parameter value that specifies where the repo type should put the cloned/checked-out repository. In this parameter we've again used the `validate` hook to create a block that checks the value for appropriateness. In this case we're just checking, very crudely, to make sure it looks like the destination path is a valid, fully-qualified file path. We could also use this validation for the source parameter to confirm that a valid source URL/location is being provided.

Creating the Subversion Provider

Next, we need to create a Subversion provider for our type. We create the provider and put it into:

`custom/lib/puppet/provider/repo/svn.rb`

You can see the Subversion provider in Listing 10-6.

Listing 10-6. The Subversion provider

```
require 'fileutils'
```

```
Puppet::Type.type(:repo).provide(:svn) do
  desc "Provides Subversion support for the repo type"

  commands :svncmd => "svn"
  commands :svnadmin => "svnadmin"

  def create
    svncmd "checkout", resource[:name], resource[:path]
  end

  def destroy
    FileUtils.rm_rf resource[:path]
  end

  def exists?
    File.directory? resource[:path]
  end
end
```

In the provider code, we first required the fileutils library, which we're going to use some methods from. Next, we defined the provider block itself:

```
Puppet::Type.type(:repo).provide(:svn) do
```

We specified that the provider is called svn and is a provider for the type called repo.

Then we used the desc method, which allows us to add some documentation to our provider.

Next, we defined the commands that this provider will use, the svn and svnadmin binaries, to manipulate our resource's configuration:

```
commands :svncmd => "svn"
commands :svnadmin => "svnadmin"
```

Puppet uses these commands to determine if the provider is appropriate to use on an agent. If Puppet can't find these commands in the local path, then it will disable the provider. Any resources that use this provider will fail and Puppet will report an error.

Next, we defined three methods - create, destroy and exists?. These are the methods that the ensurable statement expects to find in the provider.

The create method ensures our resource is created. It uses the svn command to check out a repository specified by resource[:name]. This references the value of the name parameter of the type. In our case, the source parameter in our type is also the name variable of the type, so we could also specify resource[:source]. We also specified the destination for the checkout using the resource[:path] hash.

The delete method ensures the deletion of the resource. In this case, it deletes the directory and files specified by the resource[:path] parameter.

Lastly, the exists? method checks to see if the resource exists. Its operation is pretty simple and closely linked with the value of the ensure attribute in the resource:

- If exists? is false and ensure is set to present, then the create method will be called.

- If exists? is true and ensure is set to absent, then the destroy method will be called.

In the case of our method, the exists? method works by checking if there is already a directory at the location specified in the resource[:path] parameter.

We can also add another provider, this one for Git, in:

```
custom/lib/puppet/provider/repo/git.rb
```

We can see this provider in Listing 10-7.

Listing 10-7. *The Git provider*

```
require 'fileutils'
Puppet::Type.type(:repo).provide(:git) do

  desc "Provides Git support for the repo provider"

  commands :gitcmd => "git"

  def create
    gitcmd "clone", resource[:name], resource[:path]
  end

  def destroy
    FileUtils.rm_rf resource[:path]
  end

  def exists?
    File.directory? resource[:path]
  end

end
```

You can see that this provider is nearly identical to the Subversion provider we saw in Listing 10-3. We used the git command and its clone function rather than the Subversion equivalents, but you can see that the destroy and exists? methods are identical.

Using Your New Type

Once you've got your type and providers in place, you can run Puppet and distribute them to the agents you wish to use the repo type in and create resources that use this type, for example:

```
repo { "wordpress":
  source => "http://core.svn.wordpress.org/trunk/",
  path => "/var/www/wp",
  provider => svn,
  ensure => present,
}
```

■ **Note** You can find a far more sophisticated version of the `repo` type, and with additional providers, at
https://github.com/puppetlabs/puppet-vcsrepo.

Writing a Parsed File Type and Provider

You've just seen a very simple type and provider that uses commands to create, delete and check for the status of a resource. In addition to these kinds of types and providers, Puppet also comes with a helper that allows you to parse and edit simple configuration files. This helper is called ParsedFile.

Unfortunately, you can only manage simple files with ParsedFile, generally files with single lines of configuration like the /etc/hosts file or the example we're going to examine. This is a type that manages the /etc/shells file rather than multi-line configuration files.

To use a ParsedFile type and provider, we need to include its capabilities. Let's start with our /etc/shells management type which we're going to call shells. This file will be located in:

custom/lib/puppet/type/shells.rb.

The Shells Type

Let's start with our type in Listing 10-8.

Listing 10-8. The shells type

```
Puppet::Type.newtype(:shells) do
    @doc = "Manage the contents of /etc/shells
    shells { "/bin/newshell":
                ensure => present,
    }"

ensurable

newparam(:shell) do
  desc "The shell to manage"
  isnamevar
end

newproperty(:target) do
  desc "Location of the shells file"
  defaultto {
    if @resource.class.defaultprovider.ancestors.include? (Puppet::Provider::ParsedFile)
      @resource.class.defaultprovider.default_target
    else
      nil
  end
  }
 end
end
```

In our type, we've created a block, Puppet::Type.newtype(:shells), that creates a new type, which we've called shells. Inside the block we've got a @doc string. As we've already seen, this should contain the documentation for the type; in this case, we've included an example of the shells resource in action.

We've also used the ensurable statement to create the basic create, delete and exists ensure structure we saw in our previous type.

We then defined a new parameter, called shell, that will contain the name of the shell we want to manage:

```
newparam(:shell) do
  desc "The shell to manage"
  isnamevar
end
```

We also used another piece of Puppet automagic that we saw earlier, isnamevar, to make this parameter the name variable for this type.

Lastly, in our type we specified an optional parameter, target, that allows us to override the default location of the shells file, usually /etc/shells.

The target parameter is optional and would only be specified if the shells file wasn't located in the /etc/ directory. It uses the defaultto structure to specify that the default value for the parameter is the value of default_target variable, which we will set in the provider.

The Shells Provider

Let's look at the shells provider now, in Listing 10-9.

Listing 10-9. The shells provider

```
require 'puppet/provider/parsedfile'

shells = "/etc/shells"

Puppet::Type.type(:shells).provide(:parsed, :parent => Puppet::Provider::ParsedFile,
:default_target => shells, :filetype => :flat) do

  desc "The shells provider that uses the ParsedFile class"

  text_line :comment, :match => /^#/;
  text_line :blank, :match => /^\s*$/;

  record_line :parsed, :fields => %w{name}
end
```

Unlike other providers, ParsedFile providers are stored in a file called parsed.rb located in the provider's directory, here:

```
custom/lib/puppet/provider/shells/parsed.rb
```

The file needs to be named parsed.rb to allow Puppet to load the appropriate ParsedFile support (unlike other providers, which need to be named for the provider itself).

In our provider, we first need to include the ParsedFile provider code at the top of our provider using a Ruby require statement:

```
require 'puppet/provider/parsedfile'
```

We then set a variable called shells to the location of the /etc/shells file. We're going to use this variable shortly.

Then we tell Puppet that this is a provider called shells. We specify a :parent value that tells Puppet that this provider should inherit the ParsedFile provider and make its functions available. We then specify the :default_target variable to the shells variable we just created. This tells the provider, that unless it is overridden by the target attribute in a resource, that the file to act upon is /etc/shells.

We then use a desc method that allows us to add some documentation to our provider.

The next lines in the provider are the core of a ParsedFile provider. They tell the Puppet how to manipulate the target file to add or remove the required shell. The first two lines, both called text_line, tell Puppet how to match comments and blank lines, respectively, in the configuration file. You should specify these for any file that might have blank lines or comments:

```
text_line :comment, :match => /^#/;
text_line :blank, :match => /^\s*$/;
```

We specify these to let Puppet know to ignore these lines as unimportant. The text_line lines are constructed by specifying the type of line to match, a comment or a blank, then specifying a regular expression that specifies the actual content to be matched.

The next line performs the actual parsing of the relevant line of configuration in the /etc/shells file:

```
record_line :parsed, :fields => %w{name}
```

The record_line parses each line and divides it into fields. In our case, we only have one field, name. The name in this case is the shell we want to manage. So if we specify:

```
shells { "/bin/anothershell":
    ensure => present,
}
```

Puppet would then use the provider to add the /bin/anothershell by parsing each line of the /etc/shells file and checking if the /bin/anothershell shell is present. If it is, then Puppet will do nothing. If not, then Puppet will add anothershell to the file.

If we changed the ensure attribute to absent, then Puppet would go through the file and remove the anothershell shell if it is present.

This is quite a simple example of a ParsedFile provider. There are a number of others that ship with Puppet, for example the cron type, that can demonstrate the sophisticated things you can do with the ParsedFile provider helper.

A More Complex Type and Provider

In this section we're going to show you a slightly more complex type and provider used to manage HTTP authentication password files. It's a similarly ensureable type and provider, but with some more sophisticated components.

The httpauth Type

Let's start by looking at the httpauth type shown in Listing 10-10.

Listing 10-10. The httpauth type

```
Puppet::Type.newtype(:httpauth) do
    @doc = "Manage HTTP Basic or Digest password files." +
           "    httpauth { 'user':                      " +
           "      file => '/path/to/password/file',     " +
           "      password => 'password',               " +
           "      mechanism => basic,                   " +
           "      ensure => present,                    " +
           "    }                                       "

    ensurable do
      newvalue(:present) do
          provider.create
      end

      newvalue(:absent) do
          provider.destroy
      end

      defaultto :present
    end

    newparam(:name) do
      desc "The name of the user to be managed."

      isnamevar
    end

    newparam(:file) do
      desc "The HTTP password file to be managed. If it doesn't exist it is created."
    end

    newparam(:password) do
      desc "The password in plaintext."

    end

    newparam(:realm) do
      desc "The realm - defaults to nil and mainly used for Digest authentication."

      defaultto "nil"
    end

    newparam(:mechanism) do
      desc "The authentication mechanism to use - either basic or digest. Default to basic."
```

```
    newvalues(:basic, :digest)

    defaultto :basic
end

# Ensure a password is always specified
validate do
    raise Puppet::Error, "You must specify a password for the user." unless
@parameters.include?(:password)
    end

end
```

In the httpauth type we're managing a number of attributes, principally the user, password and password file. We also provide some associated information, like the realm (A HTTP Digest Authentication value) and the mechanism we're going to use, Basic or Digest Authentication.

First, notice that we've added some code to our ensurable method. In this case, we're telling Puppet some specifics about the operation of our ensure attribute. We're specifying that for each state, present and absent, exactly which method in the provider should be called, here create and destroy, respectively. We're also specifying the default behavior of the ensure attribute. This means that if we omit the ensure attribute that the httpauth resource will assume present as the value. The resource will then check for the presence of the user we want to manage, and if it doesn't exist, then it will create that user.

We've also used some other useful methods. The first is the defaultto method that specifies a default value for a parameter or property. If the resource does not specify this attribute, then Puppet will use to this default value to populate it. The other is the newvalues method that allows you to specify the values that the parameter or property will accept. In Listing 10-10, you can see the mechanism parameter that the newvalues method specifies will take the values of basic or digest.

Lastly, you can see that we used the validate method to return an error if the httpauth resource is specified without the password attribute.

The httpauth Provider

Now let's look at the provider for the httpauth type, shown in Listing 10-11.

Listing 10-11. The httpauth provider

```
begin
    require 'webrick'
rescue
    Puppet.warning "You need WEBrick installed to manage HTTP Authentication files."
end

Puppet::Type.type(:httpauth).provide(:httpauth) do
    desc "Manage HTTP Basic and Digest authentication files"

    def create
        # Create a user in the file we opened in the mech method
        @htauth.set_passwd(resource[:realm], resource[:name], resource[:password])
        @htauth.flush
```

```
    end

    def destroy
        # Delete a user in the file we opened in the mech method
        @htauth.delete_passwd(resource[:realm], resource[:name])
        @htauth.flush
    end

    def exists?
        # Check if the file exists at all
        if File.exists?(resource[:file])
            # If it does exist open the file
            mech(resource[:file])

            # Check if the user exists in the file
            cp = @htauth.get_passwd(resource[:realm], resource[:name], false)

            # Check if the current password matches the proposed password
            return check_passwd(resource[:realm], resource[:name], resource[:password], cp)
        else
            # If the file doesn't exist then create it
            File.new(resource[:file], "w")
            mech(resource[:file])
            return false
        end
    end

    # Open the password file
    def mech(file)
        if resource[:mechanism] == :digest
            @htauth = WEBrick::HTTPAuth::Htdigest.new(file)
        elsif resource[:mechanism] == :basic
            @htauth = WEBrick::HTTPAuth::Htpasswd.new(file)
        end
    end

    # Check password matches
    def check_passwd(realm, user, password, cp)
        if resource[:mechanism] == :digest
            WEBrick::HTTPAuth::DigestAuth.make_passwd(realm, user, password) == cp
        elsif resource[:mechanism] == :basic
            # Can't ask webbrick as it uses a random seed
            password.crypt(cp[0,2]) == cp
        end
    end
end
```

This provider is more complex than what we've seen before. We've still got the methods that handle Puppet's ensurable capabilities: create, destroy and exists?. In addition, though, we've got additional methods that manipulate our password files.

Our provider first checks for the existence of the Webrick library, which it needs in order to manipulate HTTP password files. The provider will fail to run if this library is not present. Fortunately, Webrick is commonly present in most Ruby distributions (and indeed, is used by Puppet as its basic server framework, as we learned in 2).

▨ **Tip** As an alternative to requiring the Webrick library, we could use Puppet's feature capability. You can see some examples of this in

`https://github.com/puppetlabs/puppet/blob/master/lib/puppet/feature/base.rb`. This capability allows you to enabled or disable features based on whether certain capabilities are present or not. The obvious limitation is that this approach requires adding a new feature to Puppet's core, rather than simply adding a new type or provider.

Our provider then has the three ensurable methods. The `create` and `destroy` methods are relatively simple. They use methods from the Webrick library to either set or delete a password specified in the HTTP password file managed by the resource. The file being referred to here using the `resource[:file]` value which is controlled by setting the `file` attribute in the `httpauth` resource, for example:

```
httpauth { "bob":
  file => "/etc/apache2/htpasswd.basic",
  password => "password",
  mechanism => basic,
}
```

Lastly, you'll also see in the `create` and `destroy` methods that we call the `flush` method. This flushes the buffer and writes out our changes.

The `exists?` method is more complex and calls several helper methods to check whether the user and password already exist, and if they do, whether the current and proposed passwords match.

Testing Types and Providers

Like facts, you can test your types and providers. The best way to do this is add them to a module in your development or testing environment and enable pluginsync to test them there before using them in your production environment, for example let's add our HTTPAuth type to a module called httpauth, first adding the required directories:

```
$ mkdir -p /etc/puppet/modules/httpauth/(manifests,files,templates,lib}
$ mkdir -p /etc/puppet/modules/httpauth/lib/{type,provider}
$ mkdir -p /etc/puppet/modules/httpauth/lib/provider/httpauth
```

Then copying in the type and provider to the requisite directories.

```
# cp type/httpauth.rb /etc/puppet/modules/lib/type/httpauth.rb
# cp provider/httpauth.rb /etc/puppet/modules/lib/provider/httpauth/httpauth.rb
```

When Puppet is run (and pluginsync enabled) it will find your types and providers in these directories, deploy them and make them available to be used in your Puppet manifests.

Writing Custom Functions

The last type of custom Puppet code we're going to look at is the function. You've seen a number of functions in this book already, for example: `include`, `notice` and `template` are all functions we've used. But you can extend the scope of the available functions by writing your own.

There are two types of functions: statements and rvalues. Statements perform some action, for example the `fail` function, and rvalues return a value, for example if you pass in a value, the function will process it and return a value. The `split` function is an example of an rvalue function.

▓ **Note** Remember that functions are executed on the Puppet master. They only have access to resources and data that are contained on the master.

We're going to write a simple function and distribute it to our agents. Like plug-ins, we can use plug-in sync to distribute functions to agents; they are stored in:

```
custom/lib/puppet/parser/functions
```

The file containing the function must be named after the function it contains; for example, the `template` function should be contained in the `template.rb` file.

Let's take a look at a simple function in Listing 10-12.

Listing 10-12. The SHA512 function

```
Puppet::Parser::Functions::newfunction(:sha512, :type => :rvalue, :doc => "Returns a SHA1
hash value from a provided string.") do |args|

  require 'sha1'

  Digest::SHA512.hexdigest(args[0])

end
```

Puppet contains an existing function called sha1 that generates a SHA1 hash value from a provided string. In Listing 10-12, we've updated that function to support SHA512 instead. Let's break that function down. To create the function we call the `Puppet::Parser::Functions::newfunction` method and pass it some values. First, we name the function, in our case sha512. We then specify the type of function it is, here rvalue, for a function that returns a value. If we don't specify the type at all then Puppet assumes the function is a statement. Lastly, we specify a `:doc` string to document the function.

The `newfunction` block takes the incoming argument and we process it, first adding in support for working with SHA hashes by requiring the sha1 library, and then passing the argument to the hexdigest method. As this is an rvalue function, it will return the created hash as the result of the function.

▓ **Note** The last value returned by the `newfunction` block will be returned to Puppet as the rvalue.

We mentioned earlier that functions run on the Puppet master. This means we only have access to the resources and data available on the master, but this does include some quite useful information, most importantly fact data. You can look up and use the value of facts in your functions using the lookupvar function, like so:

```
lookupvar('fqdn')
```

Replace fqdn with the name of the fact whose value you wish to look up.

You can see how easy it is to create some very powerful functions in only a few lines of code. We recommend having a look at the existing functions (most of which are very succinct) as a way to get started on your first functions. Some of the common functions include tools to manipulate paths, regular expressions and substitutions, and functions to retrieve data from external sources. There are numerous examples (many on Github or searchable via Google) of functions that you can copy or adapt for your environment.

After you've created your function you should test that it works correctly. There are a couple of ways you can do this. Some basic testing of the function can be performed by executing the function file with Ruby, like so:

```
$ ruby -rpuppet sha512.rb
```

This loads the Puppet library (Puppet must be installed on the host) and then runs the file containing the function we created in Listing 10-12. This will allow us to determine whether the file parses without error. It does not tell us if the function performed correctly.

■ **Tip** You can raise an error in your function using raise Puppet::ParseError, "raise this error". Replace "raise this error" with the error text you'd like to raise.

We can also use the Ruby IRB (Interactive Ruby Shell) to confirm our function is properly defined, like so:

```
$ irb
irb> require 'puppet'
=> true
irb> require '/tmp/sha512.rb'
=> true
irb> Puppet::Parser::Functions.function(:sha512)
=> "function_sha512"
```

Here we've launched irb and then required Puppet and our new function. We then confirm that Puppet can see the new function and that it parses as a correct function.

The best way to test a function is to use it in a manifest, and the easiest way to do that is to add your functions to Puppet's libdir and run a stand-alone manifest. Assuming Puppet is installed, first find your libdir:

```
$ sudo puppet -configprint | grep 'libdir'
/var/lib/puppet/lib
```

Then create a directory to hold our functions:

```
$ sudo mkdir -p /var/lib/puppet/lib/puppet/parser/functions
```

Then copy in our function:

```
$ sudo cp sha512.rb /var/lib/puppet/lib/puppet/parser/functions
```

Then a manifest to execute our new function:

```
$ cat /tmp/sha.pp
$hash = sha512("test")
notify { $hash: }
```

And finally run the function:

```
$ puppet /tmp/sha.pp
notice:
ee26b0dd4af7e749aa1a8ee3c10ae9923f618980772e473f8819a5d4940e0db27ac185f8a0e1d5f84f88bc887fd67b
143732c304cc5fa9ad8e6f57f50028a8ff
notice:
/Stage[main]//Notify[ee26b0dd4af7e749aa1a8ee3c10ae9923f618980772e473f8819a5d4940e0db27ac185f
8a0e1d5f84f88bc887fd67b143732c304cc5fa9ad8e6f57f50028a8ff]/message: defined 'message' as
'ee26b0dd4af7e749aa1a8ee3c10ae9923f618980772e473f8819a5d4940e0db27ac185f8a0e1d5f84f88bc887fd
67b143732c304cc5fa9ad8e6f57f50028a8ff'
```

We can see that our notify resource returned a 512-bit hash generated by our sha512 function.

▓ **Note** You can call a function from another function by prefixing the function to be called with function_, for
example function_notice.

Summary

In this chapter, you learned how to extend Puppet and Facter with your own custom types, providers, functions and facts. We demonstrated how to:

- Configure Puppet to distribute your custom facts in your modules
- Write your own custom facts
- Test your new custom facts
- Utilize two ensure-style types and providers
- Use a ParsedFile type and provider to edit simple configuration files

- Write Puppet functions

- Test Puppet functions

There are also a lot of examples of extensions and additions to Puppet that are available for you to add to your Puppet installation, or which can serve as examples of how to develop particular extensions. A good place to start looking for these is on GitHub (http://www.github.com).

Resources

- Adding custom facts http://puppetlabs.com/trac/puppet/wiki/AddingFacts

- Try Ruby (http://tryruby.org/) online tutorial

- Learn to Program tutorial (http://pine.fm/LearnToProgram/)

- Programming Ruby (http://ruby-doc.org/docs/ProgrammingRuby/)

- Beginning Ruby (http://beginningruby.org/).

- Documentation on how to create custom types:
  http://docs.puppetlabs.com/guides/custom_types.html

- A complete example of resource type creation:
  http://projects.puppetlabs.com/projects/puppet/wiki/Development_Complete_R esource_Example

- Documentation on detailed provider development:
  http://projects.puppetlabs.com/projects/puppet/wiki/Development_Provider_D evelopment

- Practical set of documentation covering type development:
  http://projects.puppetlabs.com/projects/puppet/wiki/Development_Practical_T ypes

- Writing your own functions:
  http://projects.puppetlabs.com/projects/1/wiki/Writing_Your_Own_Functions

- Writing tests for Puppet:
  http://projects.puppetlabs.com/projects/puppet/wiki/Development_Writing_Te sts

- Try Ruby (http://tryruby.org/) online tutorial

- Learn to Program tutorial (http://pine.fm/LearnToProgram/)

- Programming Ruby (http://ruby-doc.org/docs/ProgrammingRuby/)

- Beginning Ruby (http://beginningruby.org/).

CHAPTER 11

■ ■ ■

Marionette Collective

In Chapter 10, you learned about the puppet-module and cucumber-puppet tools. Both of these tools help automate the process of developing and testing Puppet modules. Similarly, Marionette Collective (MCollective) is an orchestration framework closely related to Puppet. Puppet excels at managing the state of your systems; however, the default 30-minute run interval of the Puppet agent makes it unsuitable for real-time command and control. MCollective addresses the need to execute commands in real-time on a large number of systems in a novel and unique manner. With MCollective, nodes are easily divided into collections based on information about the node itself rather than hostnames. The use of metadata means you don't need to maintain long lists of hostnames or IP addresses. All systems in the collection can report information about themselves in real-time on demand. Armed with this information, the overall population of machines can be divided into collectives. Procedures are carried out remotely against a collective rather than against a single machine.

MCollective was created to provide an API for the orchestration tasks that systems engineers and developers frequently need to perform. Command and control tools are numerous and effectively provide the same functionality of the Unix shell. Though powerful, the shell interface is not an ideal application-programming interface. In addition, commands dispatched to systems in this manner are difficult to manage using the same tools and processes that you manage code with. With a robust API, orchestration actions may be implemented as small agent plugins and treated like other pieces of code in a software development lifecycle. MCollective agents are testable, version-controlled, and consistently repeatable.

There are a number of problems and use cases that MCollective is particularly well-suited to address. Through the use of real-time messaging and metadata addressing, a number of tasks previously carried out with SSH or other deployment tools are more efficiently solved with MCollective. In particular, the following actions and questions are addressed extremely well with MCollective:

- How many systems have 32 GB of memory?

- What systems are online *right now*?

- Deploy version 1.2.3 of my application to all systems.

- Deploy version 1.2.4 of my application to the quality assurance systems.

- Deploy version 1.2.5rc2 of my application to the development systems.

- Run Puppet on all systems, ensuring that at most 10 runs are happening at once.

- Restart the Apache service on all systems in North America.

In addition to the actions MCollective already handles, it is quite straightforward to write custom agents in Ruby to carry out your own actions on all of your systems. The MCollective RPC framework alleviates much of the effort you would otherwise have to spend writing code to connect to your machines, issue commands to them, and handle logging and exceptions. If you need to take action on all of your systems, MCollective agents distributed through Puppet are an excellent way to quickly tackle the problem.

MCollective takes advantage of modern technologies to handle communication between the nodes in a collective. In this chapter, you'll learn how to install the RabbitMQ message bus and connect MCollective servers to a message queue. Once that's installed, you'll also learn how integrate MCollective with Facter to provide a large amount of metadata that's useful to divide the population into collectives and then command them. In addition, you'll learn how Puppet works well with MCollective to orchestrate and reconfigure your nodes on demand and in a controlled manner. Plugins for MCollective provide these integrations with Puppet, specifically the Puppet Agent plugin and Puppet Commander plugin. Let's get started with the installation of the RabbitMQ messaging bus.

Installing and Configuring RabbitMQ

MCollective makes use of publish and subscription messaging techniques. These publications and subscriptions are often implemented using asynchronous messaging software such as ActiveMQ and RabbitMQ. The broad category of messaging software is often referred to as messaging middleware. MCollective is developed and tested with the Apache ActiveMQ middleware, however the requirement of Java and XML configuration files have driven increased attention and interest in the RabbitMQ middleware service.

MCollective sends and receives messages using the Stomp protocol. Any messaging middleware implementing a robust Stomp listener should work with MCollective. However, ActiveMQ and RabbitMQ are the two most widely deployed and tested middleware services used with MCollective. It is important to keep in mind that only one messaging service on one system is required to get started with MCollective. A single RabbitMQ server will easily support hundreds of connected MCollective server processes. Advanced configurations with multiple security zones and tens of thousands of nodes may consider deploying multiple, federated messaging services to scale with demand. In a multi-datacenter configuration, ActiveMQ is an excellent choice. ActiveMQ and MCollective have been deployed together across multiple data centers and geographic continents in redundant and reliable configurations.

It is worth noting that MCollective and RabbitMQ are not bundled with the distribution of Enterprise Linux or Debian and Ubuntu systems as of the writing of this book. However, both RabbitMQ and MCollective will be included in the Natty Narwhal release of Ubuntu, scheduled to be version 11.04 of the operating system. If you are running a Natty or a more recent version of Ubuntu, the easiest installation route will be to simply install the packages from the distribution repositories using aptitude.

MCOLLECTIVE MESSAGING ARCHITECTURE

MCollective employs asynchronous messaging middleware services to broadcast messages and collect responses from nodes. An overview of this messaging architecture is available online at:
http://docs.puppetlabs.com/mcollective/reference/basic/messageflow.html

If you have multiple security zones or data centers, you may be interested in running multiple middleware servers to federate and distribute messaging requests. Information on this configuration with ActiveMQ is available online at:
http://docs.puppetlabs.com/mcollective/reference/integration/activemq_clusters.html

In addition, general information about publish/subscribe middleware is available online at:
http://en.wikipedia.org/wiki/Publish/subscribe

RabbitMQ is a message queue service implementing the Advanced Message Queuing Protocol, or AMQP. RabbitMQ is built using the OTP (Open Telecom Platform) and implemented in the Erlang language and runtime environment. To get started with RabbitMQ, first see how the Example.com operator installs and configures the Erlang runtime on each platform, then install and configure RabbitMQ and plugins required for MCollective. The information in this chapter is specific to RabbitMQ for ease of configuration and installation on both Debian and Enterprise Linux systems. While ActiveMQ is equally suitable to the task, many people find the XML configuration file more complex than the direct command line interface of RabbitMQ.

■ **Note** Puppet modules to deploy and manage RabbitMQ are available online at `http://forge.puppetlabs.com/` and `http://github.com/puppetlabs/puppetlabs-rabbitmq`. This Puppet module will help you bring a RabbitMQ server online quickly and easily using Puppet.

Installing RabbitMQ on Debian

Debian and Ubuntu systems provide the Erlang runtime as precompiled binary packages. The operator installs Erlang before RabbitMQ using the aptitude install command as shown in Listing 11-1.

Listing 11-1. Installing Erlang on Debian

```
$ sudo aptitude install erlang
Setting up openjdk-6-jre-lib (6b18-1.8.3-2+squeeze1) ...
Setting up odbcinst1debian2 (2.2.14p2-1) ...
Setting up unixodbc (2.2.14p2-1) ...
Setting up erlang-odbc (1:14.a-dfsg-3) ...
Setting up erlang (1:14.a-dfsg-3) ...
Setting up erlang-jinterface (1:14.a-dfsg-3) ...
Setting up erlang-ic-java (1:14.a-dfsg-3) ...
Setting up icedtea-6-jre-cacao (6b18-1.8.3-2+squeeze1) ...
Setting up default-jre-headless (1:1.6-40) ...
Setting up ca-certificates-java (20100412) ...
creating /etc/ssl/certs/java/cacerts...
done.
```

On Debian-based systems, installation of the Erlang runtime is straightforward. The operator simply uses aptitude to install the erlang package. Next, in Listing 11-2, the operator installs the RabbitMQ server package. This package is not available in the main Debian repositories, so the best way to install RabbitMQ is by adding the RabbitMQ repositories to the apt packaging system.

Listing 11-2. Adding the RabbitMQ apt repository to Debian

```
$ sudo puppet resource file /etc/apt/sources.list.d/rabbitmq.list \
    content="deb http://www.rabbitmq.com/debian/ testing main"
$ cd /tmp
$ wget http://www.rabbitmq.com/rabbitmq-signing-key-public.asc
$ sudo apt-key add rabbitmq-signing-key-public.asc
OK
```

```
$ sudo apt-get update
Get:1 http://www.rabbitmq.com testing Release.gpg [197 B]
Ign http://www.rabbitmq.com/debian/ testing/main Translation-en
Ign http://www.rabbitmq.com/debian/ testing/main Translation-en_US
Get:2 http://www.rabbitmq.com testing Release [8,033 B]
Hit http://debian.osuosl.org squeeze Release.gpg
Ign http://www.rabbitmq.com testing/main i386 Packages
Ign http://debian.osuosl.org/debian/ squeeze/main Translation-en
Hit http://www.rabbitmq.com testing/main i386 Packages
Ign http://debian.osuosl.org/debian/ squeeze/main Translation-en_US
Hit http://security.debian.org squeeze/updates Release.gpg
Hit http://debian.osuosl.org squeeze-updates Release.gpg
Ign http://debian.osuosl.org/debian/ squeeze-updates/main Translation-en
Ign http://security.debian.org/ squeeze/updates/main Translation-en
Ign http://debian.osuosl.org/debian/ squeeze-updates/main Translation-en_US
Ign http://security.debian.org/ squeeze/updates/main Translation-en_US
Hit http://debian.osuosl.org squeeze Release
Hit http://debian.osuosl.org squeeze-updates Release
Hit http://security.debian.org squeeze/updates Release
Hit http://debian.osuosl.org squeeze/main Sources
Hit http://debian.osuosl.org squeeze/main i386 Packages
Hit http://security.debian.org squeeze/updates/main Sources
Hit http://debian.osuosl.org squeeze-updates/main Sources
Hit http://security.debian.org squeeze/updates/main i386 Packages
Hit http://debian.osuosl.org squeeze-updates/main i386 Packages
Fetched 198 B in 0s (238 B/s)
Reading package lists... Done
```

In order to enable the RabbitMQ repository, the operator uses the puppet resource command to set the contents of the rabbitmq apt source file. If the version of Debian you are running does not have an /etc/apt/sources.list.d directory, you'll need to append the line listed in the content attribute to the /etc/apt.sources.list file instead of creating a new file.

Next, the operator downloads the RabbitMQ public key to verify the package signatures and adds this key to the apt package management system. Finally, the apt-get update command should not return any errors about verifying the authenticity of the package repository. If you receive any such errors, please make sure the RabbitMQ public key has been added successfully.

With the apt repository configured and updated, the RabbitMQ server software may be installed, as shown in Listing 11-3 using a straightforward aptitude install command.

Listing 11-3. Installing RabbitMQ on Debian

```
$ sudo aptitude install rabbitmq-server
The following NEW packages will be installed:
  rabbitmq-server
0 packages upgraded, 1 newly installed, 0 to remove and 3 not upgraded.
Need to get 0 B/949 kB of archives. After unpacking 1,749 kB will be used.
Selecting previously deselected package rabbitmq-server.
(Reading database ... 40745 files and directories currently installed.)
Unpacking rabbitmq-server (from .../rabbitmq-server_2.3.1-1_all.deb) ...
Processing triggers for man-db ...
Setting up rabbitmq-server (2.3.1-1) ...
```

```
Starting rabbitmq-server: SUCCESS
rabbitmq-server.
```

The RabbitMQ server software alone is not sufficient to provide messaging services for MCollective. Two additional plugins for RabbitMQ need to be installed to provide Stomp protocol support and AMQP protocol support. These plugins are specific to the version of RabbitMQ installed and are available online at: http://www.rabbitmq.com/plugins.html. Listing 11-4 references RabbitMQ version 2.3.1. If there is a new version of RabbitMQ available at the time of writing, please update the environment variable to reflect your version.

Listing 11-4. Installing the RabbitMQ AMQP and Stomp plugins on Debian

```
$ rabbitmq_version=2.3.1
$ cd /usr/lib/rabbitmq/lib/rabbitmq_server-${rabbitmq_version}/plugins/
$ sudo wget -q http://www.rabbitmq.com/releases/plugins/v${rabbitmq_version}↵
/amqp_client-${rabbitmq_version}.ez
$ sudo wget -q http://www.rabbitmq.com/releases/plugins/v${rabbitmq_version}↵
/rabbit_stomp-${rabbitmq_version}.ez
$ sudo /sbin/service rabbitmq-server restart
Restarting rabbitmq-server: SUCCESS
rabbitmq-server.
```

The operator changes directories to the plugin directory for RabbitMQ. This directory is specific to the version of RabbitMQ installed and may need to be adjusted slightly if you have not installed version 2.3.1 of RabbitMQ on your system. Once in the plugin directory, the operator downloads the amqp_client and rabbit_stomp Erlang modules. Finally, to activate the plugins, the operator restarts the rabbitmq-server service. Once the RabbitMQ software and plugins have been installed, please proceed to the RabbitMQ Configuration section.

Installing RabbitMQ on RHEL / CentOS

Similar to installation on Debian-based systems, RabbitMQ on Enterprise Linux systems requires the Erlang runtime to be installed first. RabbitMQ packages are also available for Enterprise Linux, and the operator uses these packages to install the RabbitMQ software. Finally, the plugins to enable Stomp in RabbitMQ need to be installed. Listing 11-5 illustrates how the operator performs these tasks on an Enterprise Linux system. Please remember only one system needs to run the RabbitMQ service, and all MCollective clients and servers will connect to this system to exchange messages.

Listing 11-5. Install RabbitMQ on Enterprise Linux

```
$ sudo yum -y install erlang
…
$ sudo rpm -Uvh http://www.rabbitmq.com/releases/rabbitmq-server/v2.3.1↵
/rabbitmq-server-2.3.1-1.noarch.rpm
Retrieving http://www.rabbitmq.com/releases/rabbitmq-server/v2.3.1↵
/rabbitmq-server-2.3.1-1.noarch.rpm
Preparing...              ########################################### [100%]
   1:rabbitmq-server       ########################################### [100%]
```

The operator first installs the Erlang runtime from the Enterprise Linux package repository. Erlang is included in the Enterprise Linux distribution, so no third party packages are required. Unfortunately,

RabbitMQ is not included in the distribution. The operator uses the rpm command to directly install the RabbitMQ server software from the upstream vendor. Please check http://www.rabbitmq.com to find out if more recent releases are available for Enterprise Linux systems.

Once the server software is installed, the Stomp connector plugins need to be installed. These plugins should be placed into /usr/lib/rabbitmq/lib/rabbitmq_server-2.3.1/plugins on Enterprise Linux systems. The installation of the plugins is shown in Listing 11-6.

Listing 11-6. *Installing RabbitMQ Stomp plugins*

```
$ cd /usr/lib/rabbitmq/lib/rabbitmq_server-2.3.1/plugins
$ sudo wget -q http://www.rabbitmq.com/releases/plugins/v2.3.1/amqp_client-2.3.1.ez
$ sudo wget -q http://www.rabbitmq.com/releases/plugins/v2.3.1/rabbit_stomp-2.3.1.ez
$ sudo chmod 644 *.ez
$ sudo /sbin/rabbitmq-server restart
Restarting rabbitmq-server: No nodes running
SUCCESS
rabbitmq-server.
```

Similar to the Debian installation, the operator downloads the AMQP and Stomp connector libraries into the RabbitMQ plugins directory and then restarts the rabbitmq-server service. Once the service has been restarted, the operator proceeds to configure RabbitMQ to enable the Stomp protocol and listen on TCP port 6163.

RabbitMQ Configuration

Once the RabbitMQ packages and plugins have been installed, some configuration is required. The configuration of RabbitMQ for use with MCollective is identical for both Debian-based and Enterprise Linux-based systems. As mentioned in the installation sections, MCollective communicates using the Stomp protocol. The use of the Stop protocol required the installation of the AMQP and Stop plugins for RabbitMQ in the previous section.

The Example.com operator reconfigures RabbitMQ to enable the Stomp listener on TCP Port 6163. The configuration file for RabbitMQ is located at /etc/rabbitmq/rabbitmq.config and needs to contain only a single line to change the Stomp port. In Listing 11-7, see how the operator uses Puppet to make sure this line is present in the configuration file.

Listing 11-7. *Configuring the the RabbitMQ Stomp listener*

```
$ sudo puppet resource file /etc/rabbitmq/rabbitmq.config \
 content='[ {rabbit_stomp, [{tcp_listeners, [6163]} ]} ].'
file { '/etc/rabbitmq/rabbitmq.config':
    ensure => 'file',    content => '{md5}8e195d71567368ea5446930bce473952
}
```

Using the puppet resource command, the operator manages the contents of the rabbitmq.config configuration file. Finally, the RabbitMQ server should be restarted to configure the Stomp listener (see Listing 11-8).

Listing 11-8. Restarting RabbitMQ and verifying Stomp TCP port

```
$ sudo /sbin/service rabbitmq-server restart
Restarting rabbitmq-server: SUCCESS
rabbitmq-server.

$ sudo netstat -nlp | grep 6163
tcp6       0      0 :::6163                    :::*                    LISTEN      3424/beam
```

The operator first restarts the `rabbitmq-server` service, then uses the `netstat` command to verify that Port 6163 is bound and listening. The beam process is the main RabbitMQ process and is correctly bound to port 6163 in Listing 11-8. If you do not see the beam process bound to port 6163, please verify the `rabbimq.conf` configuration file syntax.

Listing 11-9 shows the last step of configuring RabbitMQ for use with MCollective. This step creates a user account in RabbitMQ for MCollective to use. The MCollective client and server processes will use this information to make Stomp connections to RabbitMQ.

Listing 11-9. Configuring the RabbitMQ MCollective account

```
$ sudo rabbitmqctl add_user mcollective iwillchangethispassword
Creating user "mcollective" ...
...done.

$ sudo rabbitmqctl set_permissions -p / mcollective "^amq.gen-.*" ".*" ".*"
Setting permissions for user "mcollective" in vhost "/" ...
...done.
```

The operator uses the `rabbitmqctl` command to add the `mcollective` account with a password. Once added, permissions are granted to allow MCollective client and server processes to exchange messages. More information about RabbitMQ accounts and permissions is available online at http://www.rabbitmq.com/admin-guide.html.

Finally, RabbitMQ configures a default guest account with full access to the message queues. For security purposes the guest account should be deleted using the delete_user action shown in Listing 11-10.

Listing 11-10. Removing the RabbitMQ guest account

```
$ sudo rabbitmqctl delete_user guest
Deleting user "guest" ...
...done.
```

Once the guest account has been deleted, RabbitMQ is ready for use with MCollective. Let's move on to installing the MCollective software and configuring the client and server to communicate through the new RabbitMQ message service.

Installing MCollective on Debian and Ubuntu

In the previous sections, the RabbitMQ middleware service had been installed and configured on a central server system. The operator will now install and configure the MCollective software to connect with the messaging middleware. Each managed node will run the MCollective server process to receive messages and act upon them. The MCollective client program provides the command line interface to communicate with the MCollective servers.

On Debian-based systems, installation of MCollective is straight–forward, using the packages provided at http://puppetlabs.com/downloads/. On a node being managed, the operator downloads two packages: the common package and the server package. See how he does this in Listing 11-11.

Listing 11-11. Installing MCollective packages on Debian-based systems

```
$ mkdir /var/tmp/mcollective
$ cd /var/tmp/mcollective
$ wget http://www.puppetlabs.com/downloads/mcollective/mcollective-common_1.0.1-1_all.deb
$ wget http://www.puppetlabs.com/downloads/mcollective/mcollective_1.0.1-1_all.deb
$ sudo dpkg -i mcollective*.deb
Selecting previously deselected package mcollective.
(Reading database ... 40800 files and directories currently installed.)
Unpacking mcollective (from mcollective_1.0.1-1_all.deb) ...
Selecting previously deselected package mcollective-common.
Unpacking mcollective-common (from mcollective-common_1.0.1-1_all.deb) ...
Setting up mcollective-common (1.0.1-1) ...
Setting up mcollective (1.0.1-1) ...
```

Only these two packages need to be installed on nodes MCollective is going to be managing. On nodes where MCollective commands will be executed, the MCollective client package also needs to be installed, as shown in Listing 11-12. The MCollective servers will execute actions through the use of agent plugins. These agents will be invoked using a remote procedure call command, mc-rpc, contained in the mcollective-client package.

Listing 11-12. Installing the MCollective client on Debian-based systems

```
$ mkdir /var/tmp/mcollective-client
$ cd /var/tmp/mcollective-client
$ wget http://www.puppetlabs.com/downloads/mcollective/mcollective-common_1.0.1-1_all.deb
$ wget http://www.puppetlabs.com/downloads/mcollective/mcollective-client_1.0.1-1_all.deb
$ sudo dpkg -i mcollective*.deb
Selecting previously deselected package mcollective-client.
(Reading database ... 40794 files and directories currently installed.)
Unpacking mcollective-client (from mcollective-client_1.0.1-1_all.deb) ...
Selecting previously deselected package mcollective-common.
Unpacking mcollective-common (from mcollective-common_1.0.1-1_all.deb) ...
Setting up mcollective-common (1.0.1-1) ...
Setting up mcollective-client (1.0.1-1) ...
```

In addition to the MCollective packages, the STOMP protocol Ruby library needs to be installed. This Ruby library is available in the standard package repositories. If your platform does not have the libstomp-ruby package, please install the library using the gem install stomp command. The packages provided by Ubuntu are shown in Listing 11-13.

Listing 11-13. Installing the Ruby Stomp library on Debian

```
$ sudo aptitude install libstomp-ruby
The following NEW packages will be installed:
```

```
  libstomp-ruby libstomp-ruby1.8{a}
0 packages upgraded, 2 newly installed, 0 to remove and 82 not upgraded.
Need to get 7,204B of archives. After unpacking 94.2kB will be used.
Do you want to continue? [Y/n/?]  Y
Get:1 http://us.archive.ubuntu.com/ubuntu/ maverick/universe libstomp-ruby1.8 all↵
 1.0.4-2 [5,548B]
Get:2 http://us.archive.ubuntu.com/ubuntu/ maverick/universe libstomp-ruby all↵
 1.0.4-2 [1,656B]
Fetched 7,204B in 0s (9,951B/s)
Selecting previously deselected package libstomp-ruby1.8.
(Reading database ... 48472 files and directories currently installed.)
Unpacking libstomp-ruby1.8 (from .../libstomp-ruby1.8_1.0.4-2_all.deb) ...
Selecting previously deselected package libstomp-ruby.
Unpacking libstomp-ruby (from .../libstomp-ruby_1.0.4-2_all.deb) ...
Setting up libstomp-ruby1.8 (1.0.4-2) ...
Setting up libstomp-ruby (1.0.4-2) ...
```

Once the MCollective server and client software packages are installed, the operator proceeds to configure both packages to communicate with each other. Remember that the client and server do not need to be on the same system; often the client will be installed on an administrative terminal in the data center. Each managed node only needs the MCollective server software installed.

Installing MCollective on Enterprise Linux

MCollective is also distributed via packages on Enterprise Linux-based systems. The packages are split into a common package, and a client and server package. On nodes to be managed by MCollective, the mcollective-server and mcollective-common packages need to be installed, as shown in Listing 11-14.

Listing 11-14. Installing MCollective server on Enterprise Linux

```
$ mkdir /var/tmp/mcollective
$  cd /var/tmp/mcollective
$ wget http://www.puppetlabs.com/downloads/mcollective/mcollective-common↵
-1.0.1-1.el5.noarch.rpm
$ wget http://www.puppetlabs.com/downloads/mcollective/mcollective-1.0.1-1.el5.noarch.rpm
$ sudo rpm -Uvh mcollective*.rpm
Preparing...                ########################################### [100%]
   1:mcollective-common     ########################################### [ 50%]
   2:mcollective            ########################################### [100%]
```

Here, the operator downloads and installs the RPM packages for the MCollective server software. These packages should be installed on all systems where actions will be carried out. In addition, the MCollective client packages need to be installed on at least one system. The operator installs these packages as shown in Listing 11-15. RPC commands will be sent from the client system to the collection of MCollective servers.

Listing 11-15. Installing the MCollective client on Enterprise Linux

```
$ mkdir /var/tmp/mcollective-client
$ cd /var/tmp/mcollective-client
$ wget http://www.puppetlabs.com/downloads/mcollective/mcollective-common↵
```

```
-1.0.1-1.el5.noarch.rpm
$ wget http://www.puppetlabs.com/downloads/mcollective/mcollective-client↵
-1.0.1-1.el5.noarch.rpm
$ sudo rpm -Uvh *.rpm
Preparing...              ######################################### [100%]
   1:mcollective-common   ######################################### [ 50%]
   2:mcollective-client   ######################################### [100%]
```

Once the MCollective client and server packages are installed, the Ruby STOMP protocol library also needs to be installed. MCollective communicates with the messaging middleware using the STOMP protocol. The Stomp gem provides the API to this protocol. On Enterprise Linux systems, the most effective way to install the Stomp gem is to use the gem command, as shown in Listing 11-16.

Listing 11-16. Installing the Stomp gem on Enterprise Linux systems

```
$ sudo gem install stomp
Successfully installed stomp-1.1.8
1 gem installed
Installing ri documentation for stomp-1.1.8...
Installing RDoc documentation for stomp-1.1.8...
```

Similar to the MCollective server software, only the client and common packages need to be installed on an administrative console. Once the software has been installed, the operator must configure the MCollective client and server systems to connect to the RabbitMQ service. In the next section, you'll see how MCollective is configured on all platforms.

MCollective Server Configuration

The MCollective server needs to be configured to connect to the RabbitMQ server. The MCollective process connects to the service using a standard TCP connection to port 6313. Let's see how the operator configures the MCollective server in Listing 11-17.

Listing 11-17. Configuring the MCollective server

```
$ cat /etc/mcollective/server.cfg
topicprefix = /topic/mcollective
libdir = /usr/share/mcollective/plugins
logfile = /var/log/mcollective.log
loglevel = info
daemonize = 1
# Plugins
securityprovider = psk
plugin.psk = klot2oj2ked2tayn3hu5on7l
connector = stomp
plugin.stomp.host = stomp.example.com
plugin.stomp.port = 6163
plugin.stomp.user = mcollective
plugin.stomp.password = iwillchangethispassword
# Facts
factsource = yaml
plugin.yaml = /etc/mcollective/facts.yaml
```

There are three key settings to change when installing and configuring MCollective. These settings are:

- plugin.psk: The pre-shared key MCollective uses to verify message authenticity

- plugin.stomp.host: The hostname or IP address of a Stomp message queue service

- plugin.stop.password: The password MCollective uses to authenticate the connection to the Stomp server. This password should match the password used in Listing 11-9, "Configuring the RabbitMQ MCollective account."

The operator first configures the hostname of the Stomp protocol server. The Stomp server is provided by the RabbitMQ service. Next, the operator configures MCollective to log in to the Stomp service using the username mcollective and a password. These credentials correspond to the rabbitctl add_user commands he used to create these accounts in Listing 11-9. Finally, the operator configures a pre-shared key to sign messages as they travel across the message bus. This pre-shared key should be a long, randomly generated string. The same string should be used on all MCollective systems, both client and server. Other MCollective processes will also be configured with this key to authenticate messages among each other.

Once the MCollective server is configured, in Listing 11-18 the operator restarts the service to connect MCollective to the message bus.

Listing 11-18. Restarting the MCollective server after configuration

```
$ sudo /sbin/service mcollective restart
service mcollective restart
Shutting down mcollective: [  OK  ]
Starting mcollective: [  OK  ]
```

At this point, the MCollective server will initiate a connection to the RabbitMQ server and begin listening for messages. This process is commonly referred to as subscribing to a message queue. The operator then configures the MCollective client to send the first message to the collective. The MCollective client is often installed on a different system from all of the MCollective servers. The configuration the operator is using for the MCollective client is shown in Listing 11-19. Notice that the plugin.psk (Pre Shared Key) setting identically matches the setting in the server configuration.

Listing 11-19. Configuring the MCollective client

```
$ sudo cat /etc/mcollective/client.cfg
topicprefix = /topic/mcollective
libdir = /usr/share/mcollective/plugins
logfile = /dev/null
loglevel = info
# Plugins
securityprovider = psk
plugin.psk = klot2oj2ked2tayn3hu5on7l
connector = stomp
plugin.stomp.host = stomp.example.com
plugin.stomp.port = 6163
plugin.stomp.user = mcollective
plugin.stomp.password = iwillchangethispassword
# Facts
```

```
factsource = yaml
plugin.yaml = /etc/mcollective/facts.yaml
```

Similar to the server configuration file, the operator configures the pre-shared key that MCollective uses to authenticate messages. In addition, the Stomp server the client will connect to is configured as stomp.example.com, with the username mcollective and the password iwillchangethispassword.

With the client configured, the operator uses the mc-ping command, as shown in Listing 11-20, to test communication with the MCollective server processes. The operator has also configured the MCollective server on the example.com web and mail servers.

Listing 11-20. Using the mc-ping command

```
$ mc-ping
webserver        time=43.11 ms
mailserver       time=46.81 ms
---- ping statistics ----
2 replies max: 46.81 min: 43.11 avg: 44.96 Agents
```

The mc-ping command informs the operator that the MCollective server is running and responding to messages on both the web server and the mail server. This command verifies that the configuration settings in the RabbitMQ middleware and the MCollective server and client configuration files are working.

TROUBLESHOOTING MCOLLECTIVE

If the mc-ping command does not return results for the MCollective servers running on your network, the following things may be the source of the problem:

The pre-shared key in the client and server configuration files does not match.

The Stomp user name or password are not correct in the client or server configuration.

RabbitMQ is not listening on TCP port 6163.

Debugging information for RabbitMQ is located in /var/log/rabbitmq, and may contain information about invalid logins if the Stomp username and password are not correct. In addition, the MCollective log file is located at /var/log/mcollective.log and may contain useful troubleshooting information.

With the MCollective server and client processes configured, the operator is in a position to execute Puppet runs on an ad-hoc basis using MCollective. Let's see how he accomplishes this now.

MCollective Plugins

MCollective is extensible in a number of ways. The most common way to extend MCollective is to re-use already written agent plugins. These small Ruby libraries enable MCollective to execute custom commands on the entire collective.

An agent plugin usually contains a Ruby library that must be distributed to all of the nodes running the MCollective agent. In addition, a data definition file provides a description of the input parameters the plugin accepts. This DDL file should be installed on the MCollective client systems. Finally, a script to execute MCollective using the specified agent plugin should also be installed on all of the MCollective client systems.

In this section, you'll learn about a number of MCollective agent plugins. Additional plugins are also available at https://github.com/puppetlabs/mcollective-plugins. These plugins provide a good example of how to write your own agent plugins for MCollective to execute additional commands specific to the tasks you need to manage.

Puppet Agent MCollective Plugins

MCollective does not contain an agent for Puppet out of the box. An agent plugin is provided, however, in the plugin repository located at http://projects.puppetlabs.com/projects/mcollective-plugins/wiki.

In this section, you'll learn how the Example.com operator downloads and installs the MCollective Puppet agent plugin (puppetd.rb). This plugin allows the operator to execute Puppet agent runs on-demand. He does not need to wait for the run interval of the Puppet agent, or kick off jobs using other tools.

Downloading the Plugins

First, the mcollective-plugins repository should be downloaded to gain access to the Puppet agent plugins. This download is easily accomplished with the git clone command, as shown in Listing 11-21.

Listing 11-21. Cloning the mcollective-plugins repository

```
$ git clone git://github.com/puppetlabs/mcollective-plugins.git
Initialized empty Git repository in /Users/jeff/plabs/mcollective/mcollective-plugins/.git/
remote: Counting objects: 1233, done.
remote: Compressing objects: 100% (817/817), done.
remote: Total 1233 (delta 463), reused 864 (delta 287)
Receiving objects: 100% (1233/1233), 162.19 KiB, done.
Resolving deltas: 100% (463/463), done.
```

Alternatively, if Git is not available, the GitHub site provides a downloadable tar archive of the repository. Simply download the tar archive and unpack into the current working directory to obtain the Puppet agent MCollective plugin.

Installing an MCollective Agent Plugin

Next, the operator distributes the Puppet agent Ruby library and data definition, puppetd.rb and puppetd.ddl, to all of the MCollective agent systems. MCollective plugins should be placed in the directory specified by the libdir setting in the server.cfg configuration file. Puppet is an excellent way to distribute these plugins. On the Debian test system, the operator puts the plugin into place using the commands shown in Listing 11-22.

Listing 11-22. Determining the plugin directory

```
$ sudo grep libdir /etc/mcollective/server.cfg
libdir = /usr/share/mcollective/plugins
```

Once the plugin directory has been located, the operator copies into place the puppetd agent files from the mcollective-plugins repository (see Listing 11-23). The operator has cloned the mcollective-plugins repository into his home directory.

Listing 11-23. Installing the Puppet agent plugin on an MCollective agent

```
$ cd /usr/share/mcollective/plugins/mcollective
$  cp ~/mcollective-plugins/agent/puppetd/puppetd.rb ./agent/
$  cp ~/mcollective-plugins/agent/puppetd/puppetd.ddl ./agent/
$ ls /usr/share/mcollective/plugins/agent/
discovery.rb
puppetd.ddl
puppetd.rb
rpcutil.ddl
rpcutil.rb
```

We see the operator has copied the puppet.rb plugin library and the data definition into the agent subdirectory. This directory is a subdirectory of the library path specified in the MCollective server.cfg configuration file.

Loading the Agent Plugin

With the plugin installed, the MCollective daemon needs to reload all of the agent configuration files. The operator uses the mc-controller command in Listing 11-24 on a MCollective client to tell all servers to reload their agent plugins.

Listing 11-24. Commanding MCollective daemons to reload agents

```
$ mc-controller reload_agents
Determining the amount of hosts matching filter for 2 seconds .... 1

                    www> reloaded all agents

---- mcollectived controller summary ----
           Nodes: 1 / 1
      Start Time: Sun Mar 13 20:43:43 -0400 2011
  Discovery Time: 2002.84ms
      Agent Time: 46.47ms
      Total Time: 2049.32ms
```

Verifying the Agent Plugin is Loaded

Once the MCollective servers finish reloading their agent plugins, the next step is to verify that the new plugin is available. In order to verify the list of available agent plugins, the operator uses the mc-rpc command as shown in Listing 11-25 to obtain an inventory of available agents. In this example, the operator calls the agent_inventory action on the rpcutil agent.

Listing 11-25. Using the mc-rpc rpcutil agent_inventory command

```
$ mc-rpc rpcutil agent_inventory

www
   Agents:
      [{:license=>"Apache License, Version 2",
        :agent=>"discovery",
        :author=>"R.I.Pienaar <rip@devco.net>"},
      {:license=>"Apache License 2.0",
        :timeout=>20,
        :description=>"Agent to manage the puppet daemon",
        :agent=>"puppetd",
        :version=>"1.3",
        :author=>"R.I.Pienaar",
        :name=>"SimpleRPC Puppet Agent",
        :url=>"http://mcollective-plugins.googlecode.com/"},
      {:license=>"Apache License, Version 2.0",
        :timeout=>10,
        :description=>
         "General helpful actions that expose stats and internals to SimpleRPC clients",
        :agent=>"rpcutil",
        :version=>"1.0",
        :author=>"R.I.Pienaar <rip@devco.net>",
        :name=>"Utilities and Helpers for SimpleRPC Agents",
        :url=>"http://marionette-collective.org/"}]

Finished processing hosts in 44.89 ms
```

Notice the :agent => "puppet" line in the output report of the available agents on the system named Debian. The output of the agent inventory RPC command indicates that the MCollective server running on the Debian system has properly loaded the newly-installed Puppet agent plugin.

Running Puppet from MCollective

With the Puppet agent installed on a MCollective server, the operator decides to kick off a Puppet agent run using MCollective. To do so, he executes the mc-puppetd script on a MCollective client system. The mc-puppetd script is a convenience wrapper around the remote procedure call agent and associated actions. The mc-puppetd command may be copied from the plugin directory into the /usr/sbin/ directory on the MCollective client systems. Alternatively, the mc-rpc command that comes with the MCollective packages may be used to call agent actions, as shown in Listing 11-26.

Listing 11-26. Executing mc-puppetd to start Puppet agent runs

```
$ mc-puppetd -v runonce
Determining the amount of hosts matching filter for 2 seconds .... 1
www                                  : OK
    {:output=>""}

---- rpc stats ----
           Nodes: 1 / 1
      Pass / Fail: 1 / 0
       Start Time: Sun Mar 13 20:55:53 -0400 2011
  Discovery Time: 2002.94ms
      Agent Time: 1926.36ms
      Total Time: 3929.30ms
```

Here the operator used the mc-puppetd command, turned on verbose output using the -v flag, and commanded all of the MCollective servers to run the Puppet agent once. This is equivalent to executing puppetd --runonce on all of the systems in the collection.

MULTIPLE INSTANCES OF PUPPET AGENT

When running Puppet from MCollective, the Puppet agent daemon on all managed nodes may be disabled. MCollective will spawn a new Puppet process each time the puppetd agent is invoked using the mc-puppetd command. This process will be in addition to any already running Puppet agent daemon, duplicating functionality.

If the Puppet agent daemon is disabled, periodic catalog runs will no longer take place, so please make sure to trigger periodic runs using mc-puppetd or configure the agent to run periodically through cron. In any case, if multiple Puppet processes run simultaneously, only one will perform a catalog run at once. Multiple simultaneous catalog runs are prevented by the use of a lock file at /var/lib/puppet/state/puppetdlock. This file may be in a different location on your system and may be found using the command: puppet agent --configprint puppetdlockfile.

When Puppet is run with the --runonce option, the agent will fork to the background. The actual Puppet agent run may not have succeeded, even though MCollective successfully launches Puppet. The Puppet reports should be inspected for the overall status results of each Puppet agent run. The OK result from MCollective indicates only that the MCollective server was able to successfully start the puppetd process and did not receive any output.

Listing All Loaded Agent Plugins

The mc-puppetd command is useful to work with the Puppet agent directly. However, as additional agents are installed, it may become cumbersome to keep track of a large number of different commands on the MCollective client systems. As an alternative to the mc-puppetd command, most agents are callable through the mc-rpc command. The mc-rpc command has the added benefit of reading the DDL file for each agent when the client is invoked. Let's see how mc-rpc is able to provide information about the input and output parameters of an MCollective agent by reading the DDL file for the agent, shown in Listing 11-27.

Listing 11-27. *Using mc-rpc to obtain actions from an agent*

```
# mc-rpc --agent-help puppetd
SimpleRPC Puppet Agent
======================

Agent to manage the puppet daemon

      Author: R.I.Pienaar
     Version: 1.3
     License: Apache License 2.0
     Timeout: 20
   Home Page: http://mcollective-plugins.googlecode.com/

ACTIONS:
========
   disable, enable, runonce, status

   disable action:
   ---------------
      Disables the Puppetd

      INPUT:

      OUTPUT:
          output:
              Description: String indicating status
               Display As: Status

   enable action:
   --------------
      Enables the Puppetd

      INPUT:

      OUTPUT:
          output:
              Description: String indicating status
               Display As: Status

   runonce action:
   ---------------
      Initiates a single Puppet run

      INPUT:

      OUTPUT:
          output:
              Description: Output from puppetd
```

```
        Display As: Output

status action:
--------------
    Status of the Puppet daemon

    INPUT:

    OUTPUT:
        enabled:
            Description: Is the agent enabled
            Display As: Enabled

        lastrun:
            Description: When last did the agent run
            Display As: Last Run

        output:
            Description: String displaying agent status
            Display As: Status

        running:
            Description: Is the agent running
            Display As: Running
```

The output shown in Listing 11-27 comes from information stored in the DDL file accompanying each MCollective agent. When installing agent plugins, the DDL file should b installed on the system where the mc-rpc command is invoked to provide documentation on the command line.

So far we've seen how MCollective is useful for starting Puppet agent runs on demand on all hosts in the collective. What if the operator wants to perform actions on only a subset of the collection? MCollective allows systems to be addressed by any value returned from Facter. Let's see how the operator configures MCollective to work with Facter to obtain this information.

The Facter Plugin for MCollective

MCollective allows systems to be addressed by metadata about the each system in addition to the system host name. This provides much more flexibility because any relevant information about each node can be used to group systems into collectives. MCollective integrates with the Facter library to collect this metadata on each server and on demand. By default, the metadata MCollective uses is statically defined in the file /etc/mcollective/facts.yaml. In most situations, a library like Facter should be used to dynamically generate metadata for each system.

Let's see how the Example.com operator reconfigures MCollective in Listing 11-28 to obtain metadata about each system from Facter.

Listing 11-28. Installing the MCollecitve Facter plugin on Debian

```
$ sudo cp ~/mcollective-plugins/facts/facter/facter.rb \
  /usr/share/mcollective/plugins/mcollective/facts/
```

On Enterprise Linux-based systems, the MCollective plugin directory is located in /usr/libexec/mcollective rather than /usr/share/mcollective/plugins on Debian. The operator installs the Facter plugin on Enterprise Linux using the command shown in Listing 11-29.

Listing 11-29. Installing the MCollective Facter plugin on Enterprise Linux

```
$ sudo cp ~/mcollective-plugins/facts/facter/facter.rb \
  /usr/libexec/mcollective/mcollective/facts
```

Once the Facter plugin is installed, configuration is simply a matter of adding a few lines to the server.cfg file and restarting the MCollective servers on all of the nodes. The output shown in Listing 11-30 are the lines the operator uses to configure MCollective for use with Facter in /etc/mcollective/server.cfg.

Listing 11-30. Configuring the MCollective Facter plugin in server.cfg

```
$ grep facter /etc/mcollective/server.cfg
factsource = facter
```

We can see the operator has changed the default configuration of factsource = yaml to use Facter instead. Finally, the operator restarts the MCollective server daemon in Listing 11-31 to activate the change.

Listing 11-31. Restarting the MCollective server daemon to activate Facter

```
sudo /sbin/service mcollective restart
Shutting down mcollective:                              [  OK  ]
Starting mcollective:                                   [  OK  ]
```

The operator is ready to test if MCollective is properly obtaining information about each system from Facter. This is easily accomplished with the mc-facts command. This command accepts a Facter variable and returns a count of the number of systems with each value set. Let's see what this looks like in Listing 11-32.

Listing 11-32. Counting operatingsystem types with mc-facts

```
$ mc-facts operatingsystem
Report for fact: operatingsystem

        CentOS                          found 1 times
        Debian                          found 1 times

Finished processing 2 hosts in 45.32 ms
```

We can see from the output of the mc-facts command that two systems are in the collection, one of them a CentOS system and one of them a Debian-based system. In the next section we'll show how to make more advanced use of the rich metadata Facter provides. Specifically, this information about each node may be used to divide the nodes into collections and only execute commands on systems matching specific criteria.

Additional Plugins

The mcollective-plugins project mentioned in this chapter contains a number of useful agent plugins for MCollective. However, you may find the need to write your own agents and actions to carry out deployment or administrative tasks on your systems. Please visit the latest MCollective documentation at http://docs.puppetlabs.com/ to learn more about writing agents for MCollective.

We also recommend you fork the mcollective-plugins project on GitHub and use some of the small agent plugins as a reference to writing your own. The filemgr.rb plugin is a great starting point to get started with MCollective. If you do write a new agent, please don't hesitate to submit a pull request to share your work with the rest of the MCollective community.

Addressing Hosts with Metadata

In the previous section, you learned how the Example.com operator uses MCollective with Facter to obtain metadata about each system. This dynamic information provides a unique way to execute commands on a large number of systems. Specific systems matching exact criteria may also be selected to execute MCollective commands on. The operator no longer needs to maintain cumbersome spreadsheets with all of the hostnames for his systems. If a command needs to be executed, MCollective provides a simple and straightforward way to do so rather than connecting to each machine in succession over SSH.

When working with Puppet and MCollective, hosts may be addressed by any Facter value or any class the host has been assigned from Puppet. These classes are read from /var/lib/puppet/state/classes.txt. This file may be in a different location on your system and can be found using the command puppet agent --configprint classfile.

To address all systems that are Debian or CentOS, the operator uses the --with-fact option of MCollective client commands. Let's see how the operator finds the amount of free memory without knowing the hostname of the systems (Listing 11-33).

Listing 11-33. The MCollecive client --with-fact option

```
# mc-facts -v --with-fact operatingsystem='/CentOS|Debian/' memoryfree
Determining the amount of hosts matching filter for 2 seconds .... 2
Report for fact: memoryfree
        342.03 MB                            found 1 times
            www.example.com
        438.38 MB                            found 1 times
            mail.example.com

---- rpc stats ----
           Nodes: 2 / 2
      Pass / Fail: 0 / 0
       Start Time: Sat Mar 26 09:36:25 -0700 2011
   Discovery Time: 2003.41ms
       Agent Time: 52.65ms
       Total Time: 2056.06ms
```

The operator uses a regular expression to execute the facts agent on systems where Facter reports the operatingsystem to be CentOS or Debian. By using this regular expression, the operator is easily able to exclude systems and obtain information only from the systems he's interested in.

Host filters work nearly everywhere in MCollective. The pervasiveness of filters is a key differentiator between MCollective and other command and control tools. Notice in Listing 11-34 how the `mc-rpc` command is able to execute agent plugins using host filtering.

Listing 11-34. Using host filters with mc-rpc

```
# mc-rpc --with-fact operatingsystem=/Debian/ puppetd status

www.example.com
     Status: Enabled, not running, last run 2116078 seconds ago
     Enabled: 1
     Running: 0
    Last Run: 1299043683

Finished processing 1/1 hosts in 45.93 ms
```

The operator uses the `--with-fact` option to send the status action to the puppetd agent to the collection of Debian systems. In addition to specifying one filter, the operator is able to narrow down the selection of nodes for the collective using multiple filters. Let's see how this works in Listing 11-35.

Listing 11-35. Using multiple host filters with mc-rpc

```
# mc-rpc --np -F operatingsystem=/CentOS/ -F fqdn=/mail/ puppetd status
Determining the amount of hosts matching filter for 2 seconds .... 1

mail.example.com
     Status: Enabled, not running, last run 1697383 seconds ago
     Enabled: 1
     Running: 0
    Last Run: 1299465342

Finished processing 1 / 1 hosts in 45.96 ms
```

The Example.com operator uses the short version of the `--with-fact` option to filter against both the operatingsystem and fqdn facts. With this command, any CentOS system with the word "mail" in the fully qualified hostname will match the filter. This regular expression matching, in real-time, allows the operator to write scripts that will take into account additional systems. Perhaps mail01 and mail02 will come online in the future in addition to the single mail system. With the ability to filter on any Facter value and combine multiple filters, actions may be carried out that take into account the number of systems automatically. Scripts no longer need to be updated as hosts are added to the network.

Summary

In this chapter, you learned how MCollective provides real-time, metadata-driven command and control of Puppet-managed systems. MCollective takes an innovative and unique approach to the problem of orchestrating a large number of systems. Instead of using hostnames to uniquely identify and access systems, MCollective integrates with Facter, allowing the operator to filter out machines he does not want to carry out actions on.

In addition to the unique approach of addressing machines through metadata, MCollective uses the STOMP messaging protocol to communicate. The MCollective client (most commonly accessed through the `mc-rpc` command) and the MCollective server take advantage of the proven scalability and performance of asynchronous messaging services.

You also learned how to configure the RabbitMQ messaging service for use with MCollective as well. While RabbitMQ is relatively easy to configure and get running, there may be performance and scalability considerations that make ActiveMQ a better choice for your deployment. In addition, MCollective is most heavily developed and tested with ActiveMQ. RabbitMQ support was recently added and the STOMP connector for RabbitMQ works well with MCollective as of version 2.3.

MCollective gives you the ability to obtain information from your systems in real-time, without the tedium of scripting SSH connections to each and every hostname on the network. Systems may be added and removed from the network quickly without the need to update scripts or other programs communicating with these systems. In addition, MCollective works extremely well with Facter and Puppet, enabling control of the Puppet agent and filtering of hosts through Facter with ease.

Resources

- `http://devco.net/`

  The blog of R.I. Pienaar, the author of MCollective.

- `http://docs.puppetlabs.com/`

  MCollective Documentation is located on the Puppet Labs curated documentation site.

- `http://docs.puppetlabs.com/mcollective/reference/basic/messageflow.html`

  An architectural overview of how messages travel from client to server processes in MCollective.

- `http://docs.puppetlabs.com/mcollective/reference/integration/activemq_clusters.html`

  Information about setting up multiple ActiveMQ middleware services for use with MCollective. This information may be useful for deployments among multiple data centers or geographic locations.

- `http://en.wikipedia.org/wiki/Publish/subscribe`

  Overview of the publish and subscribe methodology used by MCollective.

- `http://forge.puppetlabs.com/`

  The RabbitMQ Puppet module is available for installation using the puppet-module tool from the Puppet Forge.

- `http://github.com/puppetlabs/puppetlabs-rabbitmq`

  The source code for the RabbitMQ Puppet module is published on GitHub.

- `http://www.rabbitmq.com/plugins.html`

  RabbitMQ Stomp protocol plugins are available as a separate download from the main RabbitMQ website. Please download the version of the AMQP and Stomp plugins from this location.

- `http://www.rabbitmq.com`

  The main website for the RabbitMQ messaging middleware service.

- `http://www.rabbitmq.com/admin-guide.html`

  Additional information about user accounts and access control in RabbitMQ is located in the administrative guide.

- `http://puppetlabs.com/downloads/`

  MCollective packages and source may be downloaded from the Puppet Labs website.

- `https://github.com/puppetlabs/mcollective-plugins`

  Many agent plugins for MCollective are located in the mcollective-plugins Git repository on GitHub.

APPENDIX A

■ ■ ■

Working with Puppet

It is very important to remember that Puppet is an ever-developing tool with an ever-widening community. Not only is the Puppet community growing quickly but many new ideas, developments, patches, and recipes appear every day. This is important for two major reasons:

- More often than not, someone has already solved the issue, problem or challenge you are trying to address

- New features, functions, and fixes are available in every release

It is a good idea to check out the various resources we talk about in the Resources section below, such as the mailing list archives and the Wiki, when you have an issue. These forums are also where announcements are made about new releases of Puppet and related tools.

Getting Support and Training

Puppet is an open-source tool and there are a lot of sources of information and support available for it (including this book!). In addition, Puppet's parent company, Puppet Labs, offers the Puppet Enterprise product (the pre-packaged commercial edition of Puppet), support contracts, and custom development, consulting and training programs worldwide. You can find details of these offerings at http://www.puppetlabs.com/.

■ **Note** Full disclosure: Both authors work for Puppet Labs and have a financial stake in its success.

There are also a number of members of the Puppet community who offer services, implementation support and consulting services. Many local systems implementers and consultants also have Puppet, skills should you require assistance. Posting a message on the Puppet mailing list, or your Linux User Group or Open Source Business Association forums seeking help will usually result in offers of assistance.

Resources

There are a number of useful resources available to get you started with Puppet. We'll refer to these and other references throughout this book. We also strongly recommend subscribing to the Puppet mailing lists (see below) as a lot of useful information, tips and tricks, and trouble-shooting assistance is presented there. Currently the mailing list has over 3000 subscribers and is an active and helpful community.

The Puppet IRC channel, #puppet on the Freenode network, is also a useful place to visit and ask for help. There are 500 people regularly on the channel and while they are all generally busy system administrators, they can usually spare some time to help people new to Puppet.

▓ **Note** Many of the Puppet developers also hang out in #puppet-dev on the Freenode network. If you have development-related questions, this is a good place to start.

Like all requests for help, when asking on email or IRC, you should try to ask a good question. Include your Puppet version, your platform and the exact error you are receiving. The more information you provide, the easier it is for people to help you.

Another good resource for information on asking good questions on the Internet is http://catb.org/esr/faqs/smart-questions.html.

You can also find a searchable log of IRC conversations available at http://pelin.lovedthanlost.net/puppet/.

Web

- Puppet Bug Tracker:
- http://projects.puppetlabs.com
- Puppet Source Code:
- https://github.com/puppetlabs/puppet
- Facter Source Code:
- https://github.com/puppetlabs/facter
- MCollective Source Code:
- https://github.com/puppetlabs/marionette-collective
- Puppet Documentation:
- http://docs.puppetlabs.com/
- http://docs.puppetlabs.com/learning/
- http://docs.puppetlabs.com/references/
- Puppet Documentation in PDF:
- http://www.puppetlabs.com/resources/downloads/
- Puppet Wiki:
- http://projects.puppetlabs.com/projects/puppet/wiki
- Puppet FAQ:

- http://docs.puppetlabs.com/guides/faq.html
- Puppet Style Guide:
- http://docs.puppetlabs.com/guides/style_guide.html
- Puppet Labs:
- http://www.puppetlabs.com

Mailing Lists

- Puppet User Group:
- http://groups.google.com/group/puppet-users/
- Puppet Developer Group:
- http://groups.google.com/group/puppet-dev/

Puppet Module Forge

- http://forge.puppetlabs.com

Puppet Enterprise

- http://www.puppetlabs.com/puppet/puppet-enterprise/

Support (commercial)

- http://puppetlabs.com/services/

Training

- http://puppetlabs.com/training/

IRC

- Puppet IRC Channel:
- irc://irc.freenode.net/puppet
- Puppet Developers IRC Channel:
- irc://irc.freenode.net/puppet-dev

Index

■ N

■ W

■ X

■ Y

■ Z

11264303R0019